Twentieth-Century Sephardic Authors from the Former Yugoslavia

A Judeo-Spanish Tradition

LEGENDA

LEGENDA is the Modern Humanities Research Association's book imprint for new research in the Humanities. Founded in 1995 by Malcolm Bowie and others within the University of Oxford, Legenda has always been a collaborative publishing enterprise, directly governed by scholars. The Modern Humanities Research Association (MHRA) joined this collaboration in 1998, became half-owner in 2004, in partnership with Maney Publishing and then Routledge, and has since 2016 been sole owner. Titles range from medieval texts to contemporary cinema and form a widely comparative view of the modern humanities, including works on Arabic, Catalan, English, French, German, Greek, Italian, Portuguese, Russian, Spanish, and Yiddish literature. Editorial boards and committees of more than 60 leading academic specialists work in collaboration with bodies such as the Society for French Studies, the British Comparative Literature Association and the Association of Hispanists of Great Britain & Ireland.

The MHRA encourages and promotes advanced study and research in the field of the modern humanities, especially modern European languages and literature, including English, and also cinema. It aims to break down the barriers between scholars working in different disciplines and to maintain the unity of humanistic scholarship. The Association fulfils this purpose through the publication of journals, bibliographies, monographs, critical editions, and the MHRA Style Guide, and by making grants in support of research. Membership is open to all who work in the Humanities, whether independent or in a University post, and the participation of younger colleagues entering the field is especially welcomed.

ALSO PUBLISHED BY THE ASSOCIATION

Critical Texts
Tudor and Stuart Translations • *New Translations* • *European Translations*
MHRA Library of Medieval Welsh Literature

MHRA Bibliographies
Publications of the Modern Humanities Research Association

The Annual Bibliography of English Language & Literature
Austrian Studies
Modern Language Review
Portuguese Studies
The Slavonic and East European Review
Working Papers in the Humanities
The Yearbook of English Studies

www.mhra.org.uk
www.legendabooks.com

STUDIES IN HISPANIC AND LUSOPHONE CULTURES

Studies in Hispanic and Lusophone Cultures are selected and edited by the Association of Hispanists of Great Britain & Ireland. The series seeks to publish the best new research in all areas of the literature, thought, history, culture, film, and languages of Spain, Spanish America, and the Portuguese-speaking world.

The Association of Hispanists of Great Britain & Ireland is a professional association which represents a very diverse discipline, in terms of both geographical coverage and objects of study. Its website showcases new work by members, and publicises jobs, conferences and grants in the field.

STUDIES IN HISPANIC AND LUSOPHONE CULTURES

Twentieth-Century Sephardic Authors from the Former Yugoslavia

A Judeo-Spanish Tradition

Željko Jovanović

LEGENDA

Studies in Hispanic and Lusophone Cultures 41
Modern Humanities Research Association
2020

Published by Legenda
an imprint of the Modern Humanities Research Association
Salisbury House, Station Road, Cambridge CB1 2LA

ISBN 978-1-78188-851-3

First published 2020

Copy-Editor: Dr Ellen Jones

CONTENTS

ACKNOWLEDGEMENTS

This book was written as a part of the research project, FFI2017–88021-P, 'El Romancero: nuevas perspectivas en su documentación, edición y estudio' of the Spanish Ministry of Science, Innovation and Universities, National Programme for Fostering Excellence in Scientific and Technical Research, Subprograma estatal de Generación de conocimiento, confinanced with FEDER funds.

The book derives from the PhD dissertation that I defended in 2015 at the University of Cambridge (UK) and thus my foremost thanks is reserved for Dr Louise Haywood who supervised my work there. I am truly grateful for her guidance, help and support, both during my PhD and afterwards. I would like to extend this gratitude to Dr Elizabeth Drayson (Murray Edwards College, Cambridge) for the insightful comments and observations that she made at my viva, as well as for her support and encouragement.

I would probably never have turned to Sephardic studies had I not met Prof. Paloma Díaz-Mas (CSIC, Madrid) back in 2009. She has been a constant support ever since, sharing her wisdom and knowledge, and I came to consider her my academic godmother. Moreover, during the revision process, this book benefited tremendously from her perceptive comments and stimulating questions, and for that, and much more, I am eternally in debt to her. Special thanks goes to my publisher, Legenda, for taking a chance on me. Graham Nelson has been from the outset a wonderfully enthusiastic and supportive editor. Thanks to him, Trevor J. Dadson and Ellen Jones, I felt in good hands.

Support from various sources enabled me to bring this project to completion. It is with immense gratitude that I acknowledge the support of the following bodies: the Spanish Agency for International Cooperation (AECID) for funding my Masters studies at the Universidad Complutense (Madrid); Cambridge Trust for having awarded me a full-time scholarship for my PhD studies at the University of Cambridge (UK); my College, Trinity Hall, for its support, as well as the Department of Spanish and Portuguese of the University of Cambridge; and, finally, the Rothschild Foundation Hanadiv Europe for a two-year Postdoctoral Fellowship, which gave me the opportunity to prepare this book while working at the Instituto de Lengua, Literatura y Antropología of the Spanish National Research Council (CSIC) in Madrid.

Likewise, I owe a profound gratitude to the Fundación Ramón Menéndez Pidal in Madrid and its director, Prof. Jesús Antonio Cid Martínez, and to the Jevrejski istorijski muzej (Jewish Historical Museum) in Belgrade, Serbia, for having warmly opened the doors of their archive for me. Lastly, Marie Sklodowska-Curie Individual Fellowship (reference number 792150), which I have been enjoying from

September 2019, allowed me to make the final corrections and changes to my manuscript.

Many individual colleagues helped me complete this project by discussing, reading, commenting and collaborating in a number of ways. My most heartfelt thanks are due to Álvaro Alonso de Miguel, James Montgomery, Anne Cobby, Maribel Fierro, Clara María Thomas de Antonio, Gila Hadar, Eliezer Papo, Tamar Alexander, Ivana Vučina Simović, Salomé Monasterio Morales, Drita Tutunović, Ana Štulić, Susana Weich-Shahak, Karen Gerson Sarhon, Danijela Popović, José Manuel Pedrosa, Lily Khan, Dominic Keown, Pilar Romeu Ferré, François Clément de Blois, Ian Felce, Aurora González Artigao, Nela Kovačević, Barbara Panić, Branka Džidić and Vojislava Radovanović. This book is greatly in debt to their thoughtful, generous and kind help. Special thanks goes to Sarah Weaver for doing a wonderful job proof-reading my manuscript, and Erica Scarpa for providing me assistance with the Indexes.

In 2009, I met a compatriot and follow-scholar, Krinka Vidaković-Petrov, whose work and deeds have had a massive impact on me, both personally and professionally. A year later, at a conference in London, I was fortunate enough to meet another colleague, Julie Scolnik, who, over the course of time, has become one of my closest fellow-scholars and friends. I am still amazed by Julie's kind help and support, and her infinite generosity and patience with me, for which I cannot find words to express my appreciation and love.

I can freely say that I would have been unable to complete this book if it were not for the love and support of my friends and family. One of the greatest personal achievements in my life is undoubtedly my friends: those with whom I grew up, went to school and studied with back in Serbia as well as those I made while living in Spain and England. My most sincere thanks goes to Jana Tufegdžić, Clara Marías, Sara López Martos, Apanchanit Viranuvat, Mirjana Starčević, Tuğba Öztürk, Dragana Ilić, Erica Scarpa, Daniel Gutiérrez Trápaga, Kristina Ganzinger, Christopher Bayer, Wolfgang Schmied, Arielle Boneville-Roussy, Jessica Soltys and Diana Kudaibergenova; your friendship, uplifting spirit and encouragement have helped me endure throughout this difficult endeavour.

Last but not least, the greatest gratitude goes to my family. I am deeply thankful to both of my uncles, Milan and Branko, for their support, and to my recently departed stepfather, Žarko Stupar, for being there for me. I am greatly indebted to my late father, Aleksandar Jovanović, who awakened my passion for reading; my sister, Aleksandra Jovanović, for being my rock in all that I have set my mind to do; and my mother, Vera Stupar (née Katić), to whom I owe everything.

z.j., Madrid, February 2020

NOTES ON THE TRANSLATION, TRANSCRIPTION, AND PROPER NAMES

❖

Unless otherwise stated, all translations in this book from Ladino and Serbian (Serbo-Croatian) into English are mine. I have not provided an English translation for quotations in Spanish or French.

Regarding the quotations in Judeo-Spanish, all of which have already been written and/or published in Latin characters, I have opted to preserve them as they appear in the original source rather then adapting them to a single system of spelling, such as, for example, that of *Aki Yerushalayim*, which today is the most widely used in the Ladino-speaking world. The idea is to convey the early experience of the Sepharadim after transitioning from the old, *aljamiado* system of writing/publishing Judeo-Spanish in Hebrew characters to the new spelling system in Latin script, which, however, differed depending on the author or the region. Likewise, I have not resorted to correcting orthographic and spelling inconsistencies in Judeo-Spanish quotations for two main reasons. First, they are a reflection of the writing tendencies of Judeo-Spanish speakers of the time; and second, they do not hinder the comprehension of the same.

In this book, the term *Sepharadim* is used to refer to the descendants of Spanish Jews expelled from the Iberian Peninsula in 1492. I prefer this term, which is the Sephardic pronunciation of the Hebrew plural, to the anglicised Ashkenazi pronunciation, *Sephardim*. Their language is called Ladino or Judeo-Spanish, an Ibero-Romance language spoken in the eastern Mediterranean and the Balkans, which began to develop in the sixteenth century, was in full use until the middle of the twentieth century and today is considered to be an endangered language. I use both terms interchangeably. Also, I use Serbian and Serbo-Croatian to refer to the different times in history when these terms were used. Before the unification of Yugoslavia, the Sepharadim in Serbia and Bosnia learned Serbian. After Yugoslavia was created (1918), the official language of the country became Serbo-Croatian. Hence, I indicate that Haim Daviĉo, who passed away in 1918, wrote in Serbian, whereas Isak Papo's work, which appeared in the aftermath of World War II, included the use of Serbo-Croatian in addition to Ladino.

I spell the names of Sephardi (and Serbian) literati as they appear in the sources and as they are known in the Sephardic literary and scholarly environment. This will allow prospective readers to easily search and locate works by and about these authors. Some last names are very common in the Ladino-speaking world, as is the case in this book of the surname Papo (Laura Papo, Isak Papo, Eliezer Papo); therefore, to avoid any confusion, I use their first names as well.

In the titles of Ladino and Serbian periodicals and literary works, I capitalise only the first word (*El amigo del puevlo*), as is common in Romance and Slavic languages.

Regarding the titles of works or periodicals which appear on more than one occasion, I provide the full data when first mentioned (*Le Judaïsme Sephardi*) and then indicate in brackets what abbreviated form will be used from then on (*JS*).

LIST OF ABBREVIATIONS

Alliance	Alliance Israélite Universelle
ANL	Autoridad Nasionala de Ladino
ATU	Antti Aarne, Stith Thompson and Hans-Jörg Uther's classification of tale-types
AS	*Avia de ser*
AY	*Aki Yerushalayim*
BNE	Biblioteca Nacional de España
Cuentos	*Cuentos sobre los sefardíes de Sarajevo*
Del bel para abasho	*Kuentos del bel para abasho*
Don Bueso	*Don Bueso y su hermana*
Djohá ke dize?	*Djohá ke dize? Kuentos populares djudeo-espanyoles*
Esterka	*Esterka: ritrato social de nuestros dias en 3 actos*
Folktales of Joha	*Folktales of Joha: Jewish Trickster*
'Il čuflet'	'Il čuflet dil pastor'
JIM	Jevrejski istorijski muzej
JPS	Jewish Publication Society
JS	*Le Judaïsme Sephardi*
King Solomon	*King Solomon and the Golden Fish*
Kuentos	*Kuentos del folklore de la famiya djudeo-espanyola*
La güerta	*La güerta de oro*
'Luna'	'Jalijske zimnje noći: Luna'
MS	Manuscript
'Naumi'	'Naumi: jalijska noveleta'
'Perla'	'Perla: slika iz beogardske jevrejske male'
Proverbs, Sayings and Tales	*Proverbs, Sayings and Tales of the Sephardic Jews of Macedonia*
'Sekretos'	'Sekretos kero diskuvrir'
'Slike'	'Slike iz jevrejskog života na Jaliji beogradskoj'
Vidas	*Vidas Largas*
Women's Tricks	*Women's Tricks—A Spanish Tale by Tija Bohora la Komerčera from Belgrade's Yalia*
WWII	World War II
Ženske šale	*Ženske šale—španjolska priča tije Bohore la Komerčere sa beogradske Jalije*

INTRODUCTION

The Sepharadim of the Former Yugoslavia

This book examines the survival and reuse or imitation of the medieval Iberian heritage (oral literature, traditions, customs and gastronomy) among the Sephardic communities of the former Yugoslavia from the late nineteenth to the very end of the twentieth century. I specifically limit the discussion to the Sepharadim of the former Yugoslavia as the Judeo-Spanish writing of this area has been studied and analysed to a much lesser degree than that of Turkey or Greece. Three parts, covering two periods within this chronology –– before and after World War II (hereafter WWII) –– highlight how, according to changes in the political and historical backdrop against which this material was elaborated, different practices were engaged in or evolved; these include collection, dissemination, re-creation, imitation, adaptation and even misrepresentation of the heritage.

Following the pattern of the first scholarly history of Ladino culture in the former Yugoslavia, Krinka Vidaković-Petrov's 1986 *Kultura španskih Jevreja na jugoslovenskom tlu: XVI–XX vek* (*The Culture of Spanish Jews on Yugoslav Soil: XVI–XX centuries*), this book aims to shed light on the profound changes that affected the Sephardic communities at the turn of the twentieth century and provide an in-depth analysis of how these circumstances affected the Judeo-Spanish language and its oral tradition.[1] I intend to examine the Yugoslav Sephardic authors and collectors of folk material, most of them hitherto unknown (Isak Papo, Gina Camhy, Žak Konfino), and offer a look from within by analysing the efforts of the Sepharadim themselves to detach from or adhere to their mother tongue and their centuries-long tradition. I place the work of these authors not only within the historical framework of their time, but also within the broader social context of other Sephardic communities in the former Ottoman Empire, as well as other Jewish groups around Europe.

Furthermore, most studies thus far have emphasised the role of Sephardic women as keepers of the tradition and the language. This book enhances this point but adds nuance to it by showing the participation and contribution of men, as well. The book encompasses an equal number of male/female authors/collectors, which provides the opportunity to examine the material from a gender perspective (for example, different interpretations of the same folk song/tale) and discuss which kind of folk literature was more reserved for women or men, or equally shared between them.

The Sepharadim is the name given both to the Jews living in Spain before they were expelled in 1492 and their descendants living in the diaspora. A new chapter in the Jewish history of *galut* (exile, diaspora) was opened when the Catholic monarchs Ferdinand and Isabella of Spain laid out as a political goal the religious unification of their kingdoms under the Catholic religion.[2] This policy included the creation of the Inquisition (1478) to monitor and obligate the numerous converts to adhere to the principles of Christianity, the expulsion of the Jews in 1492 (so as not to represent a negative influence on the converts) and, in 1501, the violation of the agreement made with the Muslims of Granada in 1491 promising to respect their religious freedom. Thus the imposition of the Catholic religion on all their non-Christian subjects represented a clear political plan of the Catholic monarchs.[3]

Confronted with this situation, many Iberian Jews chose to leave their homeland, relocating to different places in Western Europe, North Africa and, above all, the rising Ottoman Empire. Their medieval cultural substratum encompassed Judaic, Christian/Hispanic and Arabic components, which they continued to foster upon abandoning the Iberian Peninsula while enriching them with cultural and linguistic elements of their new surroundings. This particularly applies to their language Ladino, or Judeo-Spanish, an Ibero-Romance language spoken by the Sepharadim in the Eastern Mediterranean and the Balkans until the middle of the twentieth century, which today is recognised as an endangered language. It derives from fifteenth-century Castilian with an important number of loans from other Romance languages (Portuguese, Catalan, French, Italian), Hebrew, Turkish, Greek and South Slavic languages.[4] Although different names have been used to designate this language, such as *espanyol* (*espanyolit*), *levantino*, *djidio* and *djudezmo*, here I use interchangeably the terms *ladino* (Ladino), the name preferred by most of its speakers after WWII, and *judeoespañol* (Judeo-Spanish), a term coined by the scholarly environment. It is true that Haïm-Vidal Sephiha (1973) and his followers sustain that Ladino refers to the calque language of the translations of the religious Hebrew texts and therefore was never employed in day-to-day communication. Nonetheless, as Olga Borovaya succinctly puts it:

> Since by the definition of Ladino-calque, no user could produce an utterance in it without having in front of him a text in another language (Hebrew), it [Ladino] cannot be considered a language or even a language variety but only a functional style (or register). (2012: 15)

Tracy Harris's *Death of a Language: The History of Judeo-Spanish* (1994) is just one example of an increasing awareness that Ladino is rapidly disappearing. Harris published the results of her study after having conducted fieldwork on this language in 1978 and 1985 in the USA and Israel. The research consisted of interviews which, as Harris herself emphasises, comprised questions concerning Judeo-Spanish, the speakers' linguistic skills and attitudes toward the language, samples of free conversation and word elicitation (2006: 64 n. 1). Harris's conclusion was rather pessimistic: Ladino has gradually ceased to be used as a daily language of communication and has been rapidly replaced by other languages.

This process of language shift began towards the end of the nineteenth century but rapidly advanced after WWII, and as a result, the UNESCO Red Book Report on Endangered Languages classified Ladino as 'seriously endangered' in

2002. Although Harris (2006: 63) claims that Judeo-Spanish literature, music and other aspects of Sephardic culture are still productive, I believe that her conclusion regarding the language applies in good part to the markers of the culture as a whole, which have also been in decline. The reasons for this are largely to be found in the historical, political, cultural and linguistic changes to which the Sepharadim were exposed during the Ottoman period and in the new Balkan states that were created upon its disintegration. Likewise, after the Holocaust, Sephardic culture continued to decline further and faster. I shall describe the factors that have impelled the Sepharadim to start abandoning their native language and culture in favour of other languages and cultures, using as a case study the situation in Serbia and Bosnia. The case of Macedonia will only be mentioned briefly as it follows the pattern seen in Serbia and Bosnia.

Within the former Yugoslavia, the main Sephardic centres were found in Serbia, Bosnia and Macedonia. The Sepharadim also settled in Croatia. However, as underscored by Vidaković-Petrov (1990: 14–16), no literary material in Judeo-Spanish has been preserved from this country, which is why I have not included this area.

The Sepharadim settled in Serbia (principally Belgrade) at the beginning of the sixteenth century. At that time, Serbia had already become part of the Ottoman Empire (Antić 2013: 96; Bataković and others 2000: 97–99). Under Ottoman rule, the Sepharadim enjoyed several privileges. In addition to religious freedom, they were allowed to maintain their own social infrastructure, which included rabbinical courts and the ability to own real estate and engage fully in commerce (Levy 1992: 14–19 and Díaz-Mas 2006: 69). At the same time, they were permitted to continue using the language they brought from Spain as well as the Hebrew alphabet.

This relationship between the Islamic state, of which the Ottoman Empire was an example, and its non-Muslim subjects (in this case, the Sepharadim) was set into Muslim law by a covenant of protection known as *zimmi* in Turkish, or *dhimma* in Arabic (Levy 1992: 15). It should be noted that these privileges did not come without a price. They were guaranteed only as long as the Sepharadim paid high taxes to the Ottoman rulers, most commonly the poll tax (Turkish *cizye*), and demonstrated at all times their acceptance of the superiority of Islam and of Muslims.[5]

This situation in Serbia was to last until the beginning of the nineteenth century. It was then that the Ottomans, who had ruled this part of the Empire for four centuries, found themselves confronted with two major insurrections led by the Serbs, 1804–13 and 1815. By 1830, Serbia succeeded in gaining an autonomous state, which was officially confirmed in 1878 by the accords signed at the Congress of Berlin, which put an end to the Russo-Turkish War of 1877–78.

The autonomy of Serbia brought about the integration of the Sepharadim into the Serbian political, economic, social and cultural framework that evolved as the state gradually modernised. The Eastern Mediterranean lifestyle that the Sepharadim had observed under the Ottomans now gave way to European ideas and standards (Vidaković-Petrov 2010a: 309). Sephardic children (both boys and girls) started to attend Serbian schools, a fact which undoubtedly played an important role in the process of integration.[6]

FIG. I.I. *El kal viežo* ['The Old Temple'] in Belgrade
Jevrejski istorijski muzej, Belgrade, Serbia

As was the case in Serbia, in the sixteenth century the Sepharadim settled in Bosnia, which was also part of the vast Ottoman Empire. Thanks to the benefits that the Ottoman authorities bestowed on its minority inhabitants, the Sepharadim here, too, were able to foster to a great extent a particular lifestyle characterised by physical, social, cultural and linguistic isolation from their non-Jewish compatriots. This situation undoubtedly contributed to the maintenance of the Judeo-Spanish language but, at the same time, reduced the community to a state of complete passivity, as Juan Octavio Prenz summarises: 'Durante tres siglos los sefardíes vivirán exclusivamente del patrimonio espiritual que trajeron consigo, sin mayor ambición que la de subsistir' (1968: 167).

When in 1878 Bosnia became part of the Austro-Hungarian Empire, however, a period of transition began in which the Ottoman social, political and cultural model transformed into a European one. This had a profound impact on the relationship between the Bosnian Sephardic community and its environment, eroding its isolation and stimulating integration and identity change. One of the changes was in the demographics of Bosnia. The occupation of Bosnia by Austro-Hungary led to a large number of Muslims abandoning the country, while at the same time the number of Jews increased with the arrival of the Ashkenazim from other Austro-Hungarian states. The two Jewish ethnicities differed in accordance

FIG. I.2. *Sefardska porodica* ['A Sephardic family'], Bosnia,
from the private collection of Eliezer Papo

with the regions from which they had come: the Ashkenazim, who had settled
in the central European region, brought with them a language (German and/or
Yiddish) and culture that differed from that of the Sepharadim, whose culture was
that of the Ottoman Orient (Vidaković-Petrov 2008: 287).[7]

Like Serbia and Bosnia, Macedonia was also part of the Ottoman Empire; it
continued as such until 1913, when it became part of Serbia, and later, after World
War I, part of the Kingdom of Serbs, Croatians and Slovenes. Once it became part
of the new country, the Macedonian Sepharadim began to go through the process
of assimilation seen in Serbia and Bosnia.[8]

These changes led to the gradual disappearance of the Spanish element in the
heritage of Sephardic culture, which was precisely what had made this Jewish
group unique. In Serbia, for instance, rather than recognising themselves as being
Sepharadim, i.e., descendants of Spanish Jews, they started calling themselves Serbs
of the faith of Moses (N. Jovanović 1992: 137). This shows clearly that it was not
the Judaic element that was affected by the ongoing changes. What was gradually
forsaken was the Hispanic heritage reflected principally in the language and some
aspects of tradition and customs that encompassed genres of folk literature (ballads,
poems, tales and proverbs).[9]

FIG. I.3. Synagogue Kahal Kados Aragon, Bitola (former Monastir), Macedonia.
Jevrejski istorijski muzej, Belgrade, Serbia

Perhaps the most important change within the Sephardic community occurred with gender roles. Owing to the role they had played within traditional Sephardic society, women had transmitted traditional values and the Judeo-Spanish language to their children for centuries, assuring the maintenance of the language within the family and the Sephardic quarter (Romeu Ferré 2000: 9). This was due to the fact that, during the Ottoman period, Sephardic women had no access to social power or any option of establishing social relations with members of other communities. This isolation favoured the maintenance of a specific social order in which social power and control belonged to men, and the influence of women was limited to the home and Sephardic quarter.

Furthermore, until the second half of the nineteenth century — and even later in some Sephardic communities such as those from Skopje (Macedonia) or Sarajevo (Bosnia), for instance — girls had no access whatsoever to any formal education. Whilst Sephardic boys would attend schools called *meldares* or *Talmud Torá*, where they received an education of a religious nature, girls would stay at home with their mothers, help them with the household chores and prepare for their future roles as wives and mothers (Filipović and Vučina Simović 2010: 262). This was the case for almost all Sephardic girls, regardless of the social status of their families or the particular community to which they belonged (Veselinović 1998: 486–87; Filipović and Vučina Simović 2010: 262).

However, in the second half of the nineteenth century, education gradually began to be accessible to Sephardic girls, although this took place at different times in each community within the Ottoman Empire depending on the differing historical and political circumstances of the region. For instance, in Serbia, the first school for Sephardic girls was opened in 1864 as part of a reformation of Jewish education that sought to include it within the Serbian national school system (Vučina Simović and Filipović 2009: 102). Both this school and the one for boys followed the Serbian syllabus, which was taught by Serbian teachers; the exception was religion, which continued to be delivered by Jewish teachers only.

It is significant that this initiative to unify the Jewish and Serbian educational systems came from the Jewish community itself. This is because traditional Sephardic education had failed to impact the professional prospects of their children inasmuch as it was purely religious as opposed to practical, which is why the community sought to modernise the system of education. In addition, when the Ashkenazim started settling in Belgrade from the 1830s, their more progressive Western-European mentality conflicted with the long-established conservative principles that comprised the Sephardic education offered by the only existing Jewish school (Vučina Simović and Filipović 2009: 101–02). Lastly, language was an issue as the Ashkenazim did not speak Judeo-Spanish, the language of the classroom of the traditional Sephardic school (Vučina Simović and Filipović 2009: 101–02). For these reasons, the Belgrade Sephardic community sent a request to the Ministarstvo prosvete i crkvenih dela (Serbian Ministry of Education and Religion) seeking help to overcome these difficulties. The Serbian Ministry responded positively to the community's request and in 1864 opened a school for boys and the school for girls mentioned above.

In Bosnia, however, a similar reformation of the Sephardic educational system, including the incorporation of Sephardic girls, did not take place until 1894, thirty years later, when Serbian was made the language of the classroom. It is interesting to note that this switch to Serbian was accomplished during the period of Austro-Hungarian rule and not, as one might expect, after World War I when Bosnia officially became part of the Kingdom of Serbs, Croats and Slovenes, later renamed Yugoslavia. As in Serbia, this educational initiative also came from the Jewish community. A major problem was finding money for teachers since the Jewish community was not able to cover their fees. In the end, the Zemaljska vlada (The Country Government) agreed to allocate funds to cover part of this expense (Vučina Simović 2016: 124).

The Sephardic community in Skopje (Macedonia) is another example of Sephardic girls being incorporated late into the educational system. The first school for girls in Skopje was opened in 1902 by the local Sephardic community. In 1905, this school became part of the Alliance Israélite Universelle's chain of schools and followed its syllabus in French (Vučina Simović 2016: 127). Both the communities in Sarajevo and Skopje were more conservatively traditional than the one in Belgrade and thus the reformation and modernisation of the educational system, including the incorporation of girls, inevitably took place later in those places (Vučina Simović 2016: 127–28).[10]

Nonetheless, in spite of the fact that these political and historical circumstances undoubtedly played an important role in prompting these changes in the Sephardic educational system in the former Yugoslavia, the increased interest that Western European countries showed in the Eastern Mediterranean Sepharadim is what fundamentally initiated this transition to a different educational policy: from purely religious to a more secular education, from Judeo-Spanish being the language of the classroom to including other languages, such as French and Italian, and from education being limited only to boys to including girls as well.

This new climate, which became apparent from the mid-nineteenth century, led to various educational centres being opened throughout the Ottoman Empire. For example, the Italian Dante Alighieri Schools were established in several cities of the Eastern Mediterranean alongside English and Scottish Protestant missions whose aim was to attract the Sepharadim to Christianity (Díaz-Mas 2006: 82). Nevertheless, it was the French educational institution, the Alliance Israélite Universelle (hereafter the Alliance), which introduced the Sepharadim to a world which was almost entirely unknown to them, the West:

> Pero la gran labor corrió sin duda a cargo de la Alliance Israélite Universelle, institución francesa orientada a los judíos que había sido fundada en París en 1860. En 1865 abrió en Salónica su primera escuela para los sefardíes de Oriente [...] hasta totalizar en todo el ámbito mediterráneo ciento cincuenta centros, en los que recibían enseñanza en lengua francesa más de cuarenta mil alumnos entre judíos, griegos y armenios. (Díaz-Mas 2006: 82)

The Alliance was founded in Paris by a group of Western Jewish philanthropists with the aim of opening schools for Jews in the East, the East being the term used to designate the Ottoman Empire (Turkey and the Balkans), North Africa and the Middle East (Díaz-Mas and Sánchez-Pérez 2010: 16). In these schools, Jews gained a modern education whose goal was to help them overcome their cultural backwardness and enable them to partake in the progress that the countries in which they lived were enjoying. Crucial to the successful operation of the Alliance was the attitude of the Ottoman authorities. In spite of their strong French orientation, the schools of the Alliance were set up as local community institutions and, unlike other European schools, they did not request the protection of foreign powers. Their curricula stressed modernity and Ottoman patriotism and were, therefore, seen by the Ottoman authorities as complementing the work of the state schools, which Jews had been attending as well (Levy 1992: 113–14).[11]

The existing obstacles to the operation of these schools did not, therefore, derive from the Ottoman authorities but rather from within the Sephardic community itself. At the very beginning, the chain of Alliance's schools caused considerable unrest among certain Sephardic groups which preferred traditional teaching that was religious, male-only and delivered in Judeo-Spanish. The didacticism of the schools of the Alliance was in complete contrast to that which for centuries had been the educational policy of the Sepharadim.

From the outset, the Alliance's schools offered a secular education in French. In addition, some of the centres provided education for girls, as in the case of Laura

Papo, one of the Bosnian authors examined here, who attended one such school in Istanbul. Despite the Sepharadim's reluctance to accept this new style of education, 'poco a poco el nuevo tipo de enseñanza fue imponiéndose entre las clases más acomodadas y las escuelas tradicionales quedaron para los más pobres' (Díaz-Mas 2006: 83). Therefore, assimilation and secular education were undoubtedly the main factors that prompted changes in the Sephardic world and as a consequence endangered the Ladino language and its legacy.

As soon as the assimilation process began in the former Yugoslavia, there emerged individuals who initiated work for the conservation, collection and revitalisation of the Ladino legacy, giving particular attention to oral literature, the material I examine here. This task of conserving the Judeo-Spanish language and its oral literature was performed both by the Sepharadim and non-Sepharadim.[12] Here I focus on the Sephardic authors and collectors from the region of the former Yugoslavia, examining the different ways that they accomplished this task and analysing the various techniques and practices they applied. I shall demonstrate that in keeping with different historical circumstances, these techniques and practices differed over the course of time. For that reason, I focus on two historical moments, before and after WWII, as the use of oral literature by the Sepharadim of the former Yugoslavia from the first half of the twentieth century differs from that of the second half. Consequently, I organise the discussion into three parts, each of which is divided into chapters.

Part I focuses on two leading Sephardic authors at the turn of the twentieth century, Haim S. Davičo (1854–1918) from Serbia and Laura Papo (1891–1942) from Bosnia. Their opposing political and cultural agendas faithfully reflect the community's conflict between modernity and tradition, assimilation and continuity. I place both authors within a wider Sephardic context of that time to show the specificities of Davičo's and Papo's work. Davičo supported the idea of the Sepharadim integrating into wider Serbian society, which meant abandoning their language and traditional way of life. Aware of the consequences this process would have on his native culture, Davičo's aim in writing about the Sepharadim from Serbia was to preserve the memory of their culture. However, he does so in the Serbian language, an act that was meant to endorse his political goals. Laura Papo, by contrast, opted for Judeo-Spanish, as she intended to revitalise the language and secure its continuation. Her works were aimed at members of her community as well as other Sephardic communities in the region rather than the general readership in the area. Although their agendas differ, both authors make ample use of the Sephardic folk tradition as one of the most authentic identity markers of the Judeo-Spanish culture. I examine various techniques they apply, such as collection, re-creation, adaptation or imitation of the lore, showing not only different approaches but also different outcomes.

Part II examines the work of two Bosnian Sephardic authors, Gina Camhy (1909–1990) and Isak Papo (1912–1994), in the aftermath of WWII. As in *Part I*, I examine the works of one male and one female author. It is interesting to note that neither Camhy nor Isak Papo were writers by profession. I argue here that they were motivated by ideological desires to collect, safeguard and, if possible, revitalise their native culture and language. The work of both authors represents an act of memorialisation and is very much in line with the literary production of other post-Holocaust Sephardic authors worldwide.[13] Camhy endeavoured to recover the dying legacy in exile, living in Paris rather than her native Sarajevo, as part of an emerging Sephardic activism there. Relying on her memory, she used oral tradition as a strong political weapon against the devastations of WWII and pessimistic predictions concerning Ladino and its culture. She published her entire work not only in Judeo-Spanish but also in the most influential Sephardic newspaper of the time, *Le Judaïsme Sephardi*. By doing so, she sought to safeguard and disseminate the little that was left of her community. Isak Papo, on the other hand, created his work in his native Bosnia, where he remained after WWII. He also collected evidence of his native heritage (tales and songs) from memory. However, in contrast to Davičo and Laura Papo, the practice of Camhy and Isak Papo was mainly to collect evidence of the existence of oral literature. I argue, moreover, that the topics of their work and the type of oral literature which they recorded were greatly conditioned by their gender. This fact is closely related to the role accorded to women in Jewish/Sephardic culture, which is centred around the house and household chores (preparation of food according to *Kashrut*, the celebration of holy days and so forth).

Finally, *Part III* examines the endurance in the Sephardic world to date of the comic character Djohá. After demonstrating that the Sepharadim adopted and domesticated this figure from the Arabic culture of al-Andalus, I examine the work of different authors and collectors of Djohá tales in the former Yugoslavia and show how the Sephardic mentality differed before and after WWII, particularly in relation to the language, Judeo-Spanish. Most of the examples collected prior to WWII were recorded in Serbian by the followers of Davičo's ideas (Tihomir Djordjević and Žak Konfino). After WWII, however, the tendency was to collect these tales in their original language (Jamila Kolonomos, Matilda Koén-Sarano), usually as part of an organised movement. Particularly interesting with regard to working style is the fieldwork of Koén-Sarano who founded a circle of Sephardic women storytellers coming from various areas within the Sephardic diaspora, including the former Yugoslavia. I analyse her work and strategies from a gender perspective and discuss her role as that of an ideological emissary with a mission to save the heritage of the Sepharadim. Although Koén-Sarano's fieldwork depicts the ongoing efforts of the Sepharadim in Israel, and not those of the former Yugoslavia, I chose to include her work here as it serves to show how methods of collecting and editing (including translations) affect the preservation of Sephardic language and folklore in an era of deliberate and organised efforts to recover the endangered heritage. Hence, it is in the line with the efforts of the post-Holocaust Sephardic authors from the former Yugoslavia, providing a more comprehensive picture.

Through the examination of these three parts, it will become clear why Sephardic folk literature and the Judeo-Spanish language are treated here as endangered material, and the need to preserve this legacy will become apparent. I shall show that having had an awareness that this material was gradually disappearing stimulated the effort of all the authors and collectors studied here to preserve it. The purpose of this book is not only to bring to light the twentieth-century authors, collections and material from the Balkans that for the most part have not been studied, but to contribute to the initiative taken by these and other Sephardic authors to preserve this endangered legacy.

Notes to the Introduction

1. Vidaković-Petrov's book, initially written and published in Serbian, was translated into French by Emmanuel Carlebach in 2012.
2. For the issue of Sephardic literature within diaspora studies, see Wacks 2015.
3. For more information on the history of the Spanish Jews in the Middle Ages, see Baer (1981) and Montes Romero-Camacho (2001); on the expulsion of Jews from the Iberian Peninsula, see Pérez (1993) and Alcalá Galve (1995).
4. For the history of the Judeo-Spanish language and the formation of its *koiné*, see Minervini 1999: 41–54; 2006: 13–34; and, Quintana Rodríguez 2006a and 2006b: 157–81.
5. See Kemal H. Karpat 1974 and 2000; and Levy 1992: 15.
6. For the development of the Sephardic community in Belgrade and Serbia from the sixteenth to the twentieth century, see Vidaković-Petrov 1990: 7–22 and Vučina Simović 2016: 79–169.
7. For a more comprehensive picture of the Bosnian Sepharadim and their history, see Freidenreich Pass 1979, Pinto 1987, García Ripoll 1993: 69–72, Vučina Simović 2013: 41–64 and Kovačević 2014: 35–99.
8. For Macedonian Sepharadim and their history, see Cohen 2003, Dagkas 2003 and Grandakovska 2011.
9. I shall return to the further discussion of the transition period that the Sepharadim went through in the former Yugoslavia at the turn of the twentieth century in *Parts I* and *II* as a fundamental aspect for understanding the standpoints of the authors and collectors examined here.
10. For more information on the development of education among the Sepharadim in the former Yugoslavia, see Veselinović 1998; Cohen 2003: 24–26; 62–64; 67–74; 78–80; 90–95; 114–15; Lebel 2008: 144–49; 232–38; Vučina Simović and Filipović 2009: 100–05; Vučina Simović and Filipović 2011: 565–87; Vučina Simović 2016: 122–28. The latter study by Vučina Simović is of particular interest as it includes a number of newly discovered documents concerning this issue in local languages.
11. In the early 1840s, Ottoman authorities began pressuring the Jewish community to send Jewish students to state educational institutions, such as the Imperial School of Medicine, the Translation Bureau of the Foreign Ministry, or the Imperial *Lycée* in Galatasaray (Istanbul). Therefore, the first organised effort to modernise and transform Ottoman Jewry through education came in fact from the Ottoman state (Levy 1992: 108–12). For more information on the schools of the Alliance, see Rodrigue (1990), Benbassa (1991: 529–60) and Kaspi (2010).
12. In fact, at the turn of the twentieth century, researchers interested in Ladino and its oral tradition, who were not of Sephardic background, were the first to undertake fieldwork among the Sepharadim in the former Ottoman Empire and North Africa. See Subak 1906: 129–85, Luria 1930, Crews 1935; 1979: 91–258. In various of his papers, Christian Liebl (2007: 7–26; 2009: 13–16; 2010: 237–46) examines the fieldwork of Julius Subak and Max Luria, while Samuel Armistead (1978: I, 7–39) and Diego Catalán (2001: I, 66–72) discuss the results of Manuel Manrique de Lara's journey to the Balkans (1911) and Morocco (1915 and 1916) and his fieldwork among the Sepharadim there.
13. For memory works in the Sephardic world, see Romeu Ferré 2012 and 2019.

PART I

❖

The Cultural Work of Haim S. Davičo and Laura Papo: Assimilation Versus Continuity

The leading figures in Sephardic cultural milieu in the former Yugoslavia at the turn of the twentieth century were a man, Haim Samuilo Davičo (1854–1918) from Serbia, and a woman, Laura Papo (1891–1942) from Bosnia. Their Sephardic background and the time period in which they produced their work are not the only traits they have in common. They were both fluent in Judeo-Spanish, their mother tongue, as well as in Serbian, the main language of the countries where they lived. In addition to these, Laura Papo was also fluent in French and spoke some German (E. Papo 2011: 91), while Davičo spoke German and Italian and could read Hebrew (Alkalaj 1925: 78–79; Milošević 1967: 131).[1] What is palpable in both authors is their choice of Sephardic themes as the main focus of their literary work.

Nonetheless, it is their differences, particularly those related to the political and cultural aims of their work, that place them on opposite poles regarding their attitude towards the Judeo-Spanish language and Sephardic heritage. Addressing each author separately, I shall develop in further detail the main differences between them, which can be summarised as follows:

— the social background of Davičo's family is significantly different from that of Laura Papo's. Davičo came from a wealthy and intellectual family, whereas Laura Papo was not born into a privileged family;

— Davičo was educated in Serbian national schools and went on to obtain a higher education degree in Law. Laura Papo, by contrast, received a basic education in French in one of the Alliance's schools;

— Davičo had easier access to education and eventually to becoming a writer. This is because in Davičo's time both education and the profession of a writer among the Sepharadim were limited to the male realm. Laura Papo stood out in her community for being an educated woman and a professional writer, neither of which was common for contemporary Sephardic women;

— Davičo wrote all of his work in Serbian, while Laura Papo opted for Judeo-Spanish;

— Davičo is known for his narrative, while Laura Papo mainly wrote theatre;

— both Davičo and Laura Papo perceived the Judeo-Spanish folk tradition as an important Sephardic cultural identifier and thus incorporated evidence of it in their own work. However, their attitudes towards this heritage differed. Davičo's goal was merely to leave a record of the Judeo-Spanish heritage which had almost disappeared in Serbia. Laura Papo, by contrast, aimed to revitalise the Judeo-Spanish folk tradition (and language) which was still alive in Bosnia in her time but starting to fade away with the new political changes taking place then;

— Davičo spent his life detached from the Sephardic community, whereas Laura Papo lived within this community with whose heritage she identified. As a man, Davičo was able to lead an active public life, becoming politically involved and working as a diplomat. As is the case of (Sephardic) women at this time, Laura Papo had no access to public life. Nevertheless, she gained important acclaim albeit only within her community; and finally,

— Davičo supported assimilation, which also explains his decision to distance himself from the Sephardic community, while Laura Papo advocated the continuation of that very tradition.

The attitudes of these authors, one in favour of assimilation and the other favouring continuation of the existing tradition, are representative of those found among Jewish communities elsewhere in Europe. Davičo's separation from the traditional Sephardic way of life is a phenomenon which emerged among some sectors of the European Jewry prior to Davičo. As Todd M. Endelman points out:

> Suffice it to say that recent social histories of Sephardim in the West and of Ashkenazim in urban commercial centers like London, Amsterdam, and Berlin reveal beyond any shadow of a doubt that transformations in traditional observance were well underway before the Mendelssohnian Enlightenment. (2007: 156)

The Mendelssohnian (Jewish) Enlightenment refers to the Haskalah, a movement which appeared among the European Jewry in the eighteenth century and lasted throughout the nineteenth.[2] This movement advocated better integration into European societies and increasing education in secular studies, ideas Davičo supported. The Haskalah encompassed the idea of social and economic integration and modern acculturation, which eventually resulted in the disintegration of the traditional lifestyle of European Jewry.

As a consequence, the basis of this traditional lifestyle, the Judeo-languages, also suffered changes, the result of which was the creation of two types of bilingualism. One was an internal bilingualism that consisted of the coexistence of two languages, Hebrew and Yiddish for example, both belonging to one ethnic group but functioning differently within the different contexts of the group's life and culture. The other type was an external bilingualism that was created by the coexistence of two languages belonging to different but co-territorial ethnic groups, Yiddish and Polish, or Judeo-Spanish and Serbian for instance, both being employed by members of one of these groups for communication with the members of the other (Miron 1973: 8).

The decision made by each author concerning which language to use as a means of communication in their writings determined their standpoint with regard to Haskalah ideas. Most Yiddish-speaking writers in the nineteenth century excluded Yiddish from their work. Similar to Davičo, who wrote all of his work in Serbian rather than in Judeo-Spanish, Yitskhok Leybush Perets (1852–1915), a Jewish writer from Poland, started his career writing in Polish and later changed to Hebrew (Miron 1973: 11). It was only much later in his life that he started publishing works in Yiddish, something Davičo never came to do with Judeo-Spanish.

Davičo was not the first to advocate Haskalah ideas among the Eastern Mediterranean Sepharadim. An early attempt to promote these ideas among the Ottoman Sephardic audience was David Attias's *La güerta de oro* (hereafter *La güerta*), published in 1778 in Livorno, Italy.[3] This important work by Attias, a port Jew in the term contrived by Lois Dublin (1999), is considered to be the first book in Ladino to advocate secular education, the study of European languages and acquisition of practical knowledge that would prepare the Eastern Sepharadim for the demands of modern life.[4] However, since it was unknown in the Ottoman Empire, *La güerta* had no impact on promoting these ideas. It was not until the second half of the nineteenth century that the turn toward Western Europe and the Jewish Haskalah started to take shape and change Jewish communal life in the Balkans. However, as Michael Studemund-Halévy underscores, 'the *Haskala* did not lead to efforts for assimilation in the Sephardic world, but rather brought forth Sefardic Enlighteners (*personas aklaradas*), who engaged in an active exchange of ideas with the Ashkenazic *maskilim* [Enlighteners]' (2013: 257).[5] Davičo, as I shall document, stands out as the exception as he was the first among the Sepharadim in Serbia (and in the former Yugoslavia as well) not only to promote the idea of assimilation but also to actively put it into practice, thus marking the course for others to follow.

When it comes to Laura Papo, numerous examples of authors who wrote with a similar purpose of maintaining the Sephardic tradition and language can be encountered in her native Bosnia as well as elsewhere in the former Ottoman Empire. Several Sephardic authors in Bosnia, just prior to Laura Papo or contemporary with her, started creating works of theatre, narrative or poetry in Ladino focusing mainly on Sephardic topics and issues, and directing their works to the Sephardic audience only.

For example, Abraham Cappon (1853–1930) and Sabetay Djaen (1886–1947), who were originally from Bulgaria but lived and worked in Bosnia, wrote plays and poems in Judeo-Spanish (Vidaković-Petrov 1990: 98–113; 122–30 and Tauber 2011: 83–85). Abraham (Buki) Romano (1894–1943) wrote Ladino narrative, while poetry in the same language was written by several other authors such as Moise Rafael Atias, known as Zeki-Effendi (1845–1916), and Moshe David Gaon (1889–?).

Despite their different goals, both Davičo and Papo focus their work on their native culture and turn to folk tradition as its most genuine representation. Various methods were employed by these two authors to collect, preserve, disseminate or re-create Judeo-Spanish folk literature. These methods include fieldwork collection (ballads, proverbs and tales), the use of elements of folk literature in their own works (*Landarico*), the re-creation of folk literature (*Don Bueso y su hermana*) and, finally,

FIG. 1.1. Haim S. Davičo, portrait. Jevrejski istorijski muzej, Belgrade, Serbia

the appropriation of elements of other cultures through translations and adaptations (*Ženske šale/Women's Tricks*). Davičo and his work will be analysed first as he was the first of the two to introduce Sephardic topics and motifs, including the folk material, into his work. Following this, I shall examine Laura Papo's efforts to preserve, revitalise and maintain Judeo-Spanish tradition and language through her writings.

1. Haim S. Davičo: An Advocate of Assimilation of the Serbian Sepharadim

The cultural legacy of Haim Samuilo Davičo consists of his literary work (tales and essays), his translations (predominantly from Spanish and mostly of theatre), his theatre reviews and his work as a collector of Sephardic folklore. A good part of his work focuses on his native Judeo-Spanish culture and hence bears valuable witness to the Sephardic community in Serbia at the turn of the twentieth century. This was the time when the Jews in Serbia were undergoing important political, historical, social and cultural changes. Davičo himself witnessed all these significant events.

The existing bibliography on Davičo (mainly in Serbian) offers a mere overview of his life and work rather than an in-depth analysis of his political, cultural and literary ideas. The first article on Davičo was written in 1925 by David A. Alkalaj and has served ever since as the main source of information on Davičo's life. Even the most recent works on Davičo have based their views on the information drawn from Alkalaj's article (see Pavković 2000: 5–17; Nenin 2007: 59; Popović 2010: 237–42).

The first serious attempt to assess Davičo's literary production, focusing on specific literary and cultural traits of his work, was made by Vidaković-Petrov (1990: 113–22; 2009; 2010a), followed by two recent works by Vučina Simović (2015a; 2015b). Hence, to explain Davičo's political tendencies and the value of his cultural work I shall use the information found in these secondary sources as well as in Davičo's own publications (his tales, translations and articles) in various periodicals.

After briefly outlining Davičo's life, I shall focus on two aspects of Davičo's work. The first is related to Davičo's pro-Serbian discourse and to what extent it influenced his work. This aspect is fundamental as it sheds light not only on Davičo's attitude towards his own Judeo-Spanish heritage but also on his choice of topics and the language of his literary work.

The second aspect I examine concerns Davičo's work as a collector of Sephardic folklore and the treatment of this material in his own work. Unlike Laura Papo, Davičo did not attempt to re-activate the Judeo-Spanish tradition and secure its continuation, because he did not perceive this as a necessary task. This attitude can be seen in his choice of Serbian as the language of his work, his supporting the idea of the Sepharadim integrating into Serbian society (expressed in various publications) and, finally, his distancing himself from his community and his heritage. All these points confirm that his aim was merely to preserve a memory of the Judeo-Spanish tradition.

Finally, the nature of the text *Ženske šale* (*Women's Tricks*), which Davičo published in the Serbian newspaper *Videlo* (*The Light*), deserves to be examined closely. The newspaper claims that the text is a folk tale (ATU tale-type 1406) collected from among the Sepharadim in Serbia by Davičo himself.[6] However, as can be seen by a comparison of the Serbian text with Tirso de Molina's seventeenth-century novella *Los tres maridos burlados* (the same tale-type), *Ženske šale* is actually a rather accurate Serbian rendering of Tirso's story (Ž. Jovanović 2014b). The text was most probably translated directly from the original by Davičo himself. Certain Serbian (and some Sephardic) cultural traits of the text should be highlighted as they are the result of Davičo's attempt to acculturate the story to the Serbian environment. This translation technique, known as a domesticating method, aims at securing a fluent strategy, which, according to Lawrence Venuti:

> effaces the linguistic and cultural differences of the foreign text. [...] A fluent strategy performs a labor of acculturation which domesticates the foreign text, making it intelligible and even familiar to the target-language reader, providing him or her with the narcissistic experience of recognizing his or her own culture in a cultural other. (1992: 5)[7]

Moreover, what were the possible motives behind Davičo's decision to present this text as a result of his fieldwork? I shall argue that Davičo's case falls into the category of Sephardic authors who not only collected or re-created elements of the tradition but also created new ones by attributing to the Sephardic culture elements of other traditions through adaptations or translations.

Davičo's Life and Education

Davičo was born on 5 December 1854 as *bohor* (Hebrew for firstborn child) of Samuel (Samuilo) and Ermoza Haim in the heart of the Sephardic neighbourhood in Belgrade known as Yalia (Alkalaj 1925: 77–78).[8] Davičo spent the first years of his life growing up in Belgrade's *judería* (Jewish neighbourhood) surrounded by Sephardic customs and traditions. However, this situation changed when Davičo's father decided to move to another Serbian city, Šabac, just before Davičo was to commence his education in a Sephardic school (Milošević 1967: 131; Vidaković-Petrov 2010a: 314). At that time, Jewish children did not attend Serbian schools (Alkalaj 1925: 78; Vidaković-Petrov 1990: 114 and 2010a: 314). This was closely related to the state's policy regarding Jews and their rights in the country, a policy which underwent several changes during the nineteenth century: from the restrictions imposed on Jews under the rule of Mihailo Obrenović (from 1860 to 1868) to the policy of equal civil rights confirmed by the Serbian constitution of 1888.[9]

Davičo's education is the reason his biography represents a unique case in nineteenth-century Serbia. Although Jews were not allowed to attend Serbian schools when Davičo was a child, his father managed to enroll him in one in Šabac thanks to his connections among the Serbian elite in that town (Alkalaj 1925: 78; Milošević 1967: 131; Vidaković-Petrov 1990: 114; 2010a: 314). This fact suggests that the integration of Davičo's family into Serbian society had already begun before Davičo's efforts.

Once his father had founded a Jewish community in Šabac and a small Jewish school, Davičo also had access to Jewish religious education in Hebrew. It was Serbian school, however, which remained the main centre of education for Davičo, while his Jewish school served merely as an additional and religiously oriented source of learning. This uprooting to a non-Jewish environment both in school and everyday life shaped Davičo's pro-Serbian disposition to a great extent. In his essay 'Slike iz jevrejskog života na Jaliji beogradskoj' ('Scenes from Jewish Life in Belgrade's Yalia'), Davičo confesses that:

> Kada me je škola dovela u dodir sa novim drugovima koji me počeše uvoditi u svoje kuće, trebalo mi je nekoliko godina, da se orjentiram u novim običajima, navikama i ljudima. Za to vreme, retko, gotovo nikad nisam pomislio na jaliju, a mnogo manje, da mi je ikad palo na um, da što o njoj napišem. Istina da su me neki drugovi pozivali i savetovali, da prikupim beleške o jevrejskom životu na jaliji, ali ni to nije bilo kadro, da me prodrma iz moje apatije. (2000: 20)

> (When school put me in touch with new friends [Serbs] who started inviting me into their homes it took me several years to find my way around in the new customs, habits and people. During that time seldom, almost never, had I thought of Yalia and the idea of writing something about it had never even crossed my mind. It is true that some friends encouraged me and advised me to collect notes about Jewish life in Yalia but even that was not enough to shake me out of my apathy.)

From Šabac, the family moved back to Belgrade, where Davičo continued attending Serbian high school and also Jewish school. In 1872, he began his studies of law at

FIG. 1.2. Synagogue Bet Israel, Belgrade. Jevrejski istorijski muzej, Belgrade, Serbia

the Velika škola (School for Higher Education) in Belgrade.[10] Because contemporary Jews were not allowed to take the exam permitting them to practise law, he never actually worked as a lawyer (Vidaković-Petrov 1990: 115). However, Davičo's mastery of several languages, including Serbian, German, Hebrew and Judeo-Spanish, prompted his Serbian friend Jovan Ristić, who was a government minister, to suggest that he start working for the Serbian government in the Ministry of Foreign Affairs (Alkalaj 1925: 78). Soon he was posted to Budapest and from then until his death he worked in several government bodies, such as the Ministry of Economy and the Ministry of Finance, as well as working as a commercial representative of the Serbian government in Munich (Vidaković-Petrov 2010a: 310 n. 2). During World War I, he resided in Geneva, where he died in 1818 (Milošević 1967: 135; Vučina Simović 2015b: 110–13).

Davičo's pro-Serbian Discourse

Davičo's views on how the future of the Sepharadim should unfold with the ongoing changes in the country greatly determined his political, social and literary activities. Davičo's pro-Serbian stand influenced his attitude towards his Judeo-Spanish heritage and eventually led him to distance himself from his own community.

Davičo belonged to that group of Sephardic Jews who supported the idea of the community integrating fully into Serbian society. This entailed their becoming loyal citizens of the country they lived in and adopting the dominant language, — i.e., Serbian. Through his texts Davičo expressed his belief that this process was not only inevitable but also desirable as in this way the Sephardic community would start to benefit from the modernisation Serbia was undergoing and thus catch up with the rest of Europe.

Davičo was not the first one in his family to advocate integration. His grandfather, Haim David, had business relations with the Obrenović family (one of the two ruling dynasties in Serbia in the nineteenth century) and was a close friend of the Prince of Serbia, Miloš Obrenović (1780–1860). In his tale 'Buena', Davičo makes a reference to this link between his family and the Serbian leader. The main plot of the tale does not derive from Davičo's personal experience, but the following comment attributed to one of the fictional characters was likely taken from the family's history: 'Davidov otac Hajim bio je kneževa saraf i bankar, a ujedno, vrlo uvažena ličnost u konaku beogradskog paše' ('David's father, Haim, who was the [Serbian] Prince's accountant and a banker, was at the same time a highly regarded figure in the home of Belgrade's pasha') (Davičo 2000: 96).[11]

Furthermore, Davičo's father had close contacts among the Serbian intellectual elite. He was a close friend of several members of the clergy of the Orthodox Church as well as some renowned Serbian writers of the time, such as Laza Lazarević and Milorad Šapčanin (Alkalaj 1925: 78; Milošević 1967: 131). However, although Davičo's grandfather initiated a partial integration and his father pursued this objective to a further extent, it was Davičo himself and his brother Benko Davičo who were to fully accomplish this goal. By doing so, they marked the course for others to follow.

Davičo's choice of language proved to be crucial in achieving the idea of the Sepharadim becoming fully integrated citizens of Serbia. The results of this linguistic choice can be seen in the writings of other Sephardic authors in Serbia and the surrounding region, such as Isak Samokovlija (1889–1955) from Bosnia or Žak Konfino (1892–1975) from Serbia, who followed Davičo's footsteps and included Sephardic or Jewish topics in their work but wrote in the Serbian language.

Davičo perceived all these changes as a type of practical need, a process that had to be effected for the benefit of the entire (Sephardic and Serbian) community. Several moments from his tales confirm this. For example, in 'Jalijske zimnje noći: Luna' ('Yalia's Winter Nights: Luna'), the secondary character, Andžel, displeased with his Jewish employer and the work he has in the Jewish neighbourhood, complains to his mother and says: 'Dok naučim srpski, potražiću službu kod Morena Katalina' ('After I have learned Serbian I will seek employment with Moreno Katalin')

FIG. 1.3. Isak Samokovlija, follower of Davičo's ideas.
Jevrejski istorijski muzej, Belgrade, Serbia

(Davičo 2000: 47). The message to be inferred here is that as the Sepharadim started to communicate more and more with their surroundings, the knowledge of Serbian became increasingly important in order to expand their possibilities for better life.

In another tale, 'Naumi: jalijska noveleta' ('Naumi: Yalia's Novella'), friends Haim and Aron are having a discussion about the preservation of Sephardic tradition. Haim, who is opposed to assimilation, remarks ironically: 'To da, da je do tebe ti bi već davno želeo, da svi naši molitvenici, pored starog jevrejskog teksta imaju i srpski prevod; znam da je to tvoj davnašnji ideal' ('One thing is clear, if it were up to you, you would have long wished for all our prayer books to have the Serbian translation alongside the old Jewish text. I know that this has been your long-standing ideal') (Davičo 2000: 32). Haim's comment hints at the division which existed in the Sephardic community in Belgrade between those who favoured the ongoing assimilation and those who advocated the retention of a *status quo*. Through Aron's reply to his friend's comment, which is an advocation for assimilation, the author is clearly expressing his own political stand:

> No odričem. Meni je samo žao, što uviđam, da je to vreme u dalekoj budućnosti. Naši državnici nisu dovoljno bezpredrasudni i nacionalni, da bi mogli nužnom ustalnošću privoleti naš podmladak da usvoji državni jezik, kao maternji jezik; a mi opet nemamo toliko patriotizma, da iz sopstvenih pobuda počnemo uvoditi u kuće i van kuća srpski jezik, nego kuburimo sa mrvicama jezika najblagorodnijeg od sviju naroda. (Davičo 2000: 32)

(I don't deny this. I am only sorry to realise that that time will come in the distant future. Our [Serbian] governmental representatives are not sufficiently national and unprejudiced to be able to incite our [Sephardic] progeny by constitutional obligation to adopt the national [Serbian] language as their mother tongue. At the same time, we ourselves [the Sepharadim] lack the patriotism needed to introduce for our own reasons the Serbian language into our homes and outside of them, but rather we struggle with the crumbs of the most glorious language of all.)

It can be inferred from this quote that Davičo's efforts were on two fronts: on the one hand, he wanted to raise consciousness among the Sepharadim of the importance of integrating into the greater, modern Serbian society and on the other, he endeavoured to impel Serbia to do its part as a country to accept the Sepharadim and help them in that process in order to assure the well-being of both. He was mindful that his work could serve as a bridge between the two.

Furthermore, on more than one occasion and through his literary texts, Davičo advocates the Serbian culture and language as a better option than the Sephardic tradition and Judeo-Spanish language: 'Nije nužno da vam kažem da je Naumi Jevrejka. Kada se jednom jevrejskim lepoticama budu nadenula srpska imena, ovo će ime postati umilnije i slađe: Leposava' ('There is no need for me to tell you that Naumi is a Jewish girl. When the moment comes for Jewish beauties to be given Serbian names, such as Leposava [Belle], those names will sound more endearing and sweeter') (Davičo 2000: 29).

Davičo evidently identified himself as being more Serbian than Jewish. This is particularly evident in the way he referred to Jews in some of his writings. In the 1870s, Davičo worked as a secretary of the Jewish community in Belgrade during the presidency of his father (Vučina Simović 2015a: 65). As Andrija Radenić (1992: 27–28) and Ženi Lebl (2001: 153–55) point out, Davičo would use the third-person plural in his documents and writings in general when referring to Jews whilst aligning himself to the Serbian identity. By writing in this way, he consciously distanced himself from his community. A case in point is the document *Iz mrzosti u pakost* (*From Hatred to Envy*) published in 1904 in Belgrade. This twenty-six-page document was signed by Davičo and represents the author's reply to an anti-Semitic text that had been published in the same year in Belgrade by a certain A. S. In the document, Davičo appears as a defender of the Jewish people against the unfair accusations A. S. had made against them.

Nevertheless, what stands out here is that throughout the document he consistently identifies himself with the Serbian nation, disregarding his Sephardic roots. In several places he says 'Mi Srbi' ('We the Serbs'), or 'Naš narod' ('Our nation') referring to Serbia. He even goes so far as to identify himself with the Christian religion: 'I kamo sreće da smo mi čvrsti u svojoj veri kao što su Jevreji u svojoj, naš bi moral daleko bolje stajao nego što danas stoji' ('If only we were as firm in our religion as the Jews are in theirs, our morale would nowadays stand far better than is the case') (Davičo 1904: 24). By taking this stand, it is clear that Davičo counts himself among the Serbs rather than the Jews. One of the reasons could have been that he simply intended to present himself as a neutral observer, thus strengthening his defence of the rights of a group which had been attacked unfairly. In order to convey impartiality, he fails to mention his Jewish background, for as a Jew defending Jews his points might not have been considered unbiased.

Another explanation for his taking this stand could well have been the fact that in spite of his roots he simply did not identify himself as a part of the Sepharadim. This can be seen by the way DaviČo was perceived in some Jewish circles: as an outsider to the community. His tales about the Sepharadim from Yalia were badly received among certain Sephardic groups and gave rise to several threatening letters addressed to him. In 'Buena', DaviČo mentions the existence of several letters of this nature (2000: 108–09). However, only one has been conserved in its translation from Judeo-Spanish to Serbian. The letter is anonymous and is kept in the Archives of Serbia under the classmark VĐ357 (Mihailović 1992: 268; Vučina Simović 2015a: 67).[12] The sentiments expressed in this letter show that DaviČo was seen by some members of the Sephardic community as a traitor to the Jewish faith and the Sephardic traditional way of life:

> Što nijedan stranac do danas pisao nije, učinio si ti. Zar se tako prezrenju izlažu sinovi jevrejski — zar si mogao imati toliko srca, da ih tako osramotiš pred očima čitalaca koji nisu do sada ništa slično o njima čuli. [...] To li smo zar dočekali od prvog jevrejskog činovnika? [...] Već si tako bezobrazan da se usuđuješ kazati, da su zapovedi, što nam naši preci ostaviše smešni. *Teško tebi i tvojoj duši!* (Mihailović 1992: 274)

> (You have written what no foreigner has written to this day. How could you expose Jewish sons to such scorn! How could you have had the heart to shame them in the eyes of the readers who had never before heard anything similar about them! [...] Is this what we were meant to endure from the first ever Jewish diplomat? [...] But you are so contemptuous when you dare claim that the commandments our forebears left for us are ridiculous. *God help you and your soul!*)

The letter seems to have been written by one person (probably on behalf of a group of people), because at one point the author says: 'Dajem ti svoju časnu reč' ('I give you my word') using first-person singular (Mihailović 1992: 274). The same letter accuses DaviČo of not being Jewish: 'Posle toga mi vidimo gde ti pišeš: Jevreji rade ovo ili ono ali se ne uvršćuješ ni u Jevreje ni u Hrišćane. [...] Ti si mangup, jer nemaš ni vere ni narodnosti. Zar tebi nijedna vera nije dobra?' ('Then we can see how you write the following: Jews do this or that but you don't consider yourself either Jewish or Christian. [...] Therefore you are a rogue because you have no religion or nationality. Is no religion good enough for you?') (Mihailović 1992: 274). It is apparent that DaviČo's ideology caused him to have many enemies among his fellow Sepharadim, one consequence of which is this threatening letter he was sent.

The last point worthy of note is that DaviČo's writing, in addition to encouraging his fellow Sepharadim to integrate, entailed another political and cultural aim: namely, to introduce the Sephardic community to the Serbian readership. If DaviČo wanted Jews to accept Serbia and the Serbian language as their own, he also needed to ensure that Serbia would accept them in return. Since the Serbian readership knew barely anything about them, the best way to accomplish this goal was to write tales and essays about their traditions and customs, their poetry and their important days or festivities thus introducing them to the wider readership.

Four indications in his narratives suggest that Davičo also had a Serbian readership in mind when writing these tales. First, he wrote his work in Serbian, the dominant language of the country, making his work accessible to the majority of the population. Second, as a consequence, he took the logical decision to publish his work in Serbian journals and newspapers of the time. Third, he provided parenthetical Serbian translations of the words in Hebrew and Judeo-Spanish (Vidaković-Petrov 2010a: 312). And finally, he compared some events or holy days from Jewish life with similar ones in Serbian culture. For example, in 'Naumi' (2000: 30), he suggests that the annual Jewish fast day commemorating a list of catastrophes, the Ninth of Av (Hebrew *Tish'ah be'ab*), is identical to the Serbian holy day Vidovdan (St Vitus Day) thus drawing a parallel between the two cultures. All this, as Vidaković-Petrov underlines (2010a: 312), indicates that one of Davičo's goals was to present and explain elements of Sephardic culture to Serbian readers who were unfamiliar with this cultural tradition. By doing so, the scene was set for Sephardic culture to be accepted by wider Serbian society.

Davičo had a good understanding of the situation, and he worked towards achieving the integration of the Sepharadim in Serbia, despite this having led to his being rejected by a good part of his fellow Sepharadim. In the end, time proved that he was right in his claim that the Sepharadim could not continue to live in Serbia as they had under the Ottoman Empire and that the integration process was both inevitable and imminent.

Davičo's Fieldwork in Gathering Judeo-Spanish Oral Data

Davičo published all his work in highly regarded Serbian newspapers and journals of the time, mainly in *Otadžbina* (*Fatherland*) and *Delo* (*Work*). Both were monthly periodicals published in Belgrade. The former came out between 1875 and 1892; the latter was launched in 1894 and lasted until 1915. Davičo also collaborated with other newspapers or journals, such as *Videlo* (*The Light*), *Kolo*, *Nova iskra* (*The New Spark*) and *Brankovo kolo* (Vidaković-Petrov 1990: 115; Milošević 1967: 129).[13] Most of the periodicals in which Davičo published his work promoted pro-Serbian ideas (Jovičić 1979).

Furthermore, his contributions were not limited to the Serbian press; some of his work was printed in other newspapers of the region. Such was the case of Sarajevo's *Bosanska vila* (*The Bosnian Fairy*), printed biweekly in the Serbian language (1885–1914), in which Davičo published some of his articles (Davičo 1890: 225–27; Ž. Jovanović 2014b: 987). It is very interesting to note that Davičo published exclusively in newspapers and periodicals in Serbian. Possibilities for him to publish his work in several Jewish (Sephardic) periodicals in the region obviously existed, but he did not use them.

The Judeo-Spanish press started flourishing in the Balkans at the end of the nineteenth century and became one of the main resources for maintaining contact and disseminating news and culture among the Sephardic communities scattered throughout the former Ottoman Empire.[14] The first Sephardic newspaper to appear in the former Yugoslavia, *El Amigo del puevlo* (*The Friend of the People*), was launched in Belgrade in 1888 and continued to be published until 1893.[15] Its intended readers were the Sepharadim from Serbia, Romania and Bulgaria, communities which shared a sense of unity, as was indicated on the cover of the newspaper (Vidaković-Petrov 1990: 56). Although the name of the newspaper was printed in both Ladino and in Serbian (in Cyrillic: *Народни пријатељ*), all articles contained within it were published in the Judeo-Spanish Rashi script.

The other Sephardic newspaper in the former Yugoslavia which existed in Davičo's time was *La alborada* (*The Daybreak*), also published in Judeo-Spanish Rashi script, first in Bulgaria (1898) and then in neighbouring Bosnia (1900–01).[16] Nevertheless, no articles by Davičo can be found in either of these newspapers. The reason may have been the fact that the first Sephardic newspapers in the former Yugoslavia were created exclusively for the needs of the Judeo-Spanish communities in the region: they were published entirely in Ladino Rashi script and therefore were addressing only those who were able to read and understand this script. Davičo's choice of language and his intention to introduce the Sephardic community in Serbia to a wider readership in the country did not fit with the aims of these periodicals and were the reason why he opted to disseminate his work elsewhere.

Davičo wrote four tales and two essays dealing with Sephardic topics and motifs. The two essays were entitled 'Slike iz jevrejskog života na Jaliji beogradskoj' ('Scenes from Jewish life in Belgrade's Yalia', hereafter 'Slike') in 1881, and 'Jedne večeri na Jaliji' ('One Evening in Yalia') in 1895. The four tales all carry as the title the name of a female protagonist: 'Naumi: jalijska noveleta', 1883 ('Naumi: Yalia's Novella', hereafter 'Naumi'), 'Jalijske zimnje noći: Luna', 1888 ('Yalia's Winter Nights: Luna', hereafter 'Luna'), 'Perla: slika iz beogardske jevrejske male', 1891 ('Perla: A Scene from Belgrade's Jewish Quarter', hereafter 'Perla'), and, finally, 'Buena'. The first three appeared in *Otadžbina* and were later reprinted in 1898 together in one book, *Sa Jalije* (*From Yalia*). Davičo completes his series of tales with 'Buena', which was published in instalments in 1913 in *Delo*. All four tales, along with the two mentioned essays, were subsequently published under the title *Priče sa Jalije* (*Tales from Yalia*) in 2000.

Although Davičo was an advocate of the changes taking place in the Sephardic community in Belgrade, supporting its modernisation and integration into Serbian society, he was at the same time fully aware of the consequences this process would have for the Sephardic language, tradition and identity. He became the first Sephardic intellectual in Serbia to understand the necessity of preserving the memory of Sephardic culture in written form. In 'Slike', Davičo declares the need to preserve the memory of that part of the culture which was dying out:

> Združena sećanja iz mog ranog detinjstva, počela su se neodoljivo rojiti u mojoj glavi, i rezultat njihov bio je taj, da su me sklonile, da spasem po mogućstvu nekoliko crta iz običaja i života starog jevrejskog života na jaliji, koje mehanika i saobraćaj preti, da zbriše s lica zemlje. Zato čim dođoh kući, stadoh u mislima prikupljati uspomene na hiljadu nepromenjenih običaja od najstarijih vremena, koji daju 'Pashi' neku osobitu originalnost i svečanost. (Davičo 2000: 21)

(The combined memories from my early childhood started to swarm irresistibly in my head and the result of that was that they compelled me to rescue, if possible, some of the scenes of the customs and life of old Jewish life in Yalia, which mechanisation and traffic threatened to wipe from the face of the earth. So, as soon as I returned home I began gathering in my mind memories of thousands of customs unchanged from the oldest times which give 'Passover' some of its special uniqueness and solemnity.)

This goal to save the memory of a legacy which was on the verge of extinction was accomplished by Davičo in two ways: by introducing elements of Sephardic folk culture and language into his own work and by collecting folk material *in situ*. It should be noted that the scope of his work is not large in either of these cases, but it does hold an immense cultural value as it represents the last remains of the little that the Sephardic community in Serbia saved of their own culture.

Regarding Davičo's first goal, that of introducing elements of Sephardic folk culture in his own works, two practices can be discerned. The first is to introduce Sephardic folk material (in part or in full) in Judeo-Spanish, at the same time as providing its explanation or Serbian translation. For example, when referring to Judeo-Spanish poetry or balladry, Davičo places some lines in Judeo-Spanish alongside their translation to Serbian (Davičo 2000: 33; 66–67; 101–02; 104–05).

The second practice Davičo employed, which was also common to other contemporary authors of the former Yugoslavia like Laura Papo, consists of finding a place for folk literature within the plot of the main work. In this way, folk literature does not function as a mere decorative element or one that exists independently from the main work but rather as one that enriches the plot of a particular work and strengthens its meaning.

Several examples of this can be found in Davičo's tales. In 'Buena', for instance, Davičo describes an old Sephardic custom of making a shroud.[17] While women sewed shrouds and sang ballads, men, separated from the women, would read psalms. Davičo cites two stanzas from a ballad that was sung by women for this particular occasion, providing only two lines in Judeo-Spanish and giving the rest in its Serbian translation: 'Carpintero, carpintero | onde vas con estas tablas?' ('Carpenter, carpenter | where are you taking those boards') (Davičo 2000: 102). These lines partly illustrate the nature of the traditional Spanish *romance* metre: a sixteen-syllable verse consisting of two eight-syllable hemistichs, the first of which remains free while the second has an assonant rhyme (Armistead and Silverman 1960: 231). Although Davičo here provides two eight-syllable hemistichs, it is impossible to draw any conclusions with regard to the assonant rhyme since the rest of the ballad is given in its Serbian translation.

The content of the ballad (hereafter *Carpintero*) reveals the reason why the *romance* was sung for this particular occasion. The carpenter is asked if he might be making a 'sky' or a 'firmament' for a young couple (referring to a *hupá*, a canopy under which a Jewish couple stands during the wedding ceremony, symbolising the sky), a cradle for a child or a dining table. The carpenter discloses that he is not making any of these three but rather a coffin for himself for when his time comes (Davičo 2000: 101–02).

The singing of the *Carpintero* ballad complements the entire event and fits semantically within the context. The making of the coffin is in accord with the sewing of the shroud, both actions embodying the preparation of funeral equipment. The difference is that the former is the work of men, whereas the latter is a typically female job (Vidaković-Petrov: 2009: 403–05). The division mentioned in the type of literature read by men (religious texts) and that of the folk or secular literature transmitted orally by women represents, as Susana Weich-Shahak underlines, a centuries-long trait of Sephardic culture (2009: 274). No other versions of this ballad have been recorded either in the Iberian Peninsula or among other Sephardic communities, and this makes the one found in Davičo's tale even more important.[18]

The other means Davičo used to accomplish his goal of preserving part of the Judeo-Spanish folk tradition was to collect material *in situ*. In the introduction to the Serbian translation of a Judeo-Spanish proverb collection he personally compiled, Davičo comments upon his interest in gathering this material: 'Kada se u meni probudila želja da opisujem Jaliju, ja sam prikupljajući materijal, našao pored zanimljivih običaja i lepe poslovice' ('When a desire to describe Yalia was awakened in me and I was collecting material about it, I came across some beautiful proverbs alongside some interesting customs') (Davičo 1892: 655).

As a compiler, Davičo is mainly known for his collection of Judeo-Spanish proverbs from Serbia. Although he compiled this material in Judeo-Spanish, he only published part of the collection in its translation to Serbian in *Otadžbina* (1892: 654–65). In a brief introduction to this edition of proverbs, Davičo states that he handed over the manuscript containing the proverbs in Judeo-Spanish to a scholar in Budapest whom he does not name:

> Za vreme svog bavljenja u Budim-Pešti napomenuo sam onde jednom naučenjaku, da imam tu zbirku poslovica. On me umoli da mu je ustupim, jer je tada izdavao jedno delo o španjolskim književnicima. Ja mu je ustupih i on je odštampa zasebno, razasla svud po Španiji, i u skoro bude izabran za dopisnog člana španjolske akademije nauka u Madridu. (1892: 655)

> (During my post in Budapest I mentioned to a scholar there that I had this collection of proverbs. He convinced me to hand it over to him because at that time he was preparing an edition of a book about Spanish authors. So I did and then he went and published it as a separate book and distributed it all over Spain and recently he was chosen to be a correspondent of the Spanish Academy for Science in Madrid.)

Davičo's words reveal that he did not give great importance to the material in Judeo-Spanish he had personally collected, as he relinquished it so easily. However, after having seen how successfully the book was received and how widely the publisher was acclaimed, he realised that he had underestimated the value of what he himself had collected. Furthermore, the tone of Davičo's words referring to the nameless scholar ('and then he went and published it as a separate book') shows that he felt that he had been deceived by this person.

The person who took credit for his work and gained recognition was the Budapest Rabbi Meyer Kayserling, who published this collection of proverbs first in his *Refranes o proverbios españoles de los judíos españoles* (1889) and then again a year later in *Biblioteca Española-Portugueza-Judaica: Dictionnaire bibliographique des auteurs juifs, de leurs ouvrages espagnols et portugais et des oeuvres sur et contre les juifs et le judaïsme: avec un aperçu sur la littérature des juifs espagnols et une collection des proverbes espagnols* (1890: 119–40).[19] In the preface to the first edition of proverbs, Kayserling reveals the source of the published material:

> Le recueil de ces proverbes je le dois à mon cher ami m. H. S. Davitcho, Consul de Serbie à Budapest, qui a été secondé dans son travail par ses frères, mrs. David, Benjamin et Jacob, et par son aimable soeur mlle. Rachel, habitant à Belgrade, et j'ai aussi d'obligations envers m. Jacob S. Cohen de Roustchouk, qui a bien voulu me fournir quelques matériaux. (1889: 3)

The information given in the preface indicates that other members of the family were involved in Davičo's fieldwork, namely three of his brothers and his sister. What is not clear is whether he actually collected these proverbs by doing fieldwork with his family members or whether he wrote down proverbs that were kept and cherished among the members of his family.

The collection was arranged in alphabetical order according to topics (*amigos y enemigos*; *amor*; *avaros...*), but whether Davičo or Kayserling was responsible for this arrangement of the collection remains unclear. The latter's words expressed in the preface of his edition suggest that he might have organised the collection in this way:

> Pour ne pas laisser tomber en oubli les proverbes aussi instructifs qu'intéressants dont se servent les juifs de la Serbie et de la Bulgarie j'ai eu l'idée de les offrir pour la première fois au public en les rangeant par ordre alphabétique de matières. (Kayserling 1889: 3)

As noted above, Davičo published in *Otadžbina* only part of this collection in its Serbian translation. As Kayserling points out in his preface, the material published was given to him by Davičo from Serbia and Jacob S. Cohen from Bulgaria (1889: 3). It may well be that Davičo's edition did not include the Judeo-Spanish proverbs from Bulgaria, which had been included in Kayserling's edition. Therefore, it is entirely possible that Davičo's edition in *Otadžbina* did, in fact, encompass the entire proverbial material he compiled with the help of his family. But since Kayserling does not indicate in any way which proverbs were given to him by Davičo and which by Cohen, it is difficult to make any categorical conclusions.

The edition of proverbs published by Davičo was classified according to topics as follows: God; women; children; siblings; relatives; marriage; the home; friends and enemies; neighbours; professions; debt; wealth; poverty; destiny; jokes; love and beauty; gossiping; stinginess; and food and drink (Davičo 1892: 656–65). This division by Davičo overlaps with Kayserling's categories. Davičo's merit should be recognised by republishing these proverbs in the original Judeo-Spanish together with their Serbian translation, under Davičo's name.

Davičo's Text *Ženske Šale* (*Women's Tricks*)

Thus far I have shown different ways in which Davičo collected, conserved and disseminated the Judeo-Spanish oral tradition either through incorporating it into his work or through collecting the material *in situ*. Here, however, I shall discuss a different method he also employed to enrich the Sephardic tradition, which was frequently encountered in the Judeo-Spanish-speaking world at the turn of the twentieth century: the appropriation of elements of other cultures through translations or adaptations. An example of this is the text *Ženske šale* (*Women's Tricks*), which Davičo published in 1885 in the Serbian newspaper *Videlo*, presenting it as a folk tale that he had collected from among the Serbian Sepharadim, when, in fact, it is a translation of the seventeenth-century Spanish novella by Tirso de Molina known as *Los tres maridos burlados*. I discuss the possible reasons for Davičo's presenting this text as the fruit of his fieldwork and in addition offer some details about the translation and the domestication of the text to its environment.

Davičo is believed to have collected a further tale and published it in the Serbian periodical *Videlo*, which came out in Belgrade between 1880 and 1922 (Kostić 1971: 491). In addition to thousands of articles on current political and economic events, *Videlo* included a section of particular note, dedicated to literature and featuring works by both national and foreign authors (the latter translated into Serbian).

On Tuesday, 26 February 1885, *Videlo*'s forty-first issue of the year contained the first instalment of a noteworthy story in eight parts: *Ženske šale–španjolska priča tije Bohore la Komerčere sa beogradske Jalije* (*Women's Tricks–A Spanish Tale by Tija Bohora la Komerčera from Belgrade's Yalia*). The remaining seven parts were published in *Videlo* in the course of the following ten days, in issues 43 and 45–50. It was the newspaper's custom to publish literary works in instalments due to the limited space reserved for them (usually only half a page, sometimes two separate half-pages in the same issue).

The title of the published text indicates the tale's link to the Belgrade Sepharadim. First, it is pointed out that the story published is 'Spanish', an adjective widely used, both by the Sepharadim themselves and Serbs, to denote the Sephardic community in Serbia. Owing to their links with the Iberian Peninsula, the Sepharadim in Serbia were often referred to as Spaniards and their language as Spanish (see, for example, the words of the editor of *Videlo* below). Second, the storyteller's alleged name, Tija Bohora La Komerčera, discloses the Sephardic background of the informant, also discussed in further detail below; and finally, linking the storyteller to Yalia, a Sephardic neighbourhood in Belgrade, was obviously used as a means to confirm the authenticity of the source, i.e., the informant. The owner and editor of *Videlo*, Aleksa Novaković, wanted his readers to believe that this story offers evidence of just how vital their oral history was for Belgrade's Sepharadim. He comments in issue 41:

> Kao primer koliko može predanje da očuva narodnu živu književnost može da služi ova španjolska priča, koja je odolela vremenu od četiri stoleća i održala se, bez sumnje, u onoj vernosti u kakvoj je negda pričana. Želeli bi samo da se što pre prikupe i spasu od propasti ovakvi zanimljivi nabirci nekadanje najslavnije

FIG. 1.4. The front page of *Videlo*, issue from Wednesday, 1 June 1883.
Narodna biblioteka Srbije (National Library of Serbia)

književnosti, jer nam je poznato da je beogradska španjolska kolonija najbolje očuvala ta predanja.

(The following Spanish story can be taken as an example of how oral tradition can keep folk literature alive over the course of four centuries and maintain it, too, in the form in which it once was. We would like to see these interesting examples of what once was great literature collected and saved from extinction as soon as possible, because as far as we are aware it is Belgrade's Spanish community that is best at preserving these stories.)

As can be seen from his words, Novaković not only uses the adjective 'Spanish' to establish that the story published is actually Sephardic but also refers to the Sepharadim as a Spanish community. In both cases, the adjective 'Spanish' would more properly be 'Sephardic'. Despite what Novaković here tells the readers of *Videlo*, I have provided evidence elsewhere that shows that *Ženske šale*, rather than having been preserved through oral transmission and collected by a compiler such as Davičo, is in fact a translation of a *novela* by Tirso de Molina known as *Los tres maridos burlados* (Ž. Jovanović 2014b: 981–1002).

Tirso's story *Los tres maridos burlados* appears in the fifth part ('Cigarral Quinto') of his miscellany, *Cigarrales de Toledo*, published for the first time in 1624 (Tirso de Molina 1996: 456–97). A highly popular and much-cultivated literary genre in Tirso's time and even before, the miscellany is a mixture of different literary forms (poetry, theatre and narrative) not necessarily linked by the same topics or characters.[20]

The tale recounts the story of three good friends, Polonia (married to the cashier Lucas Moreno), Mari Pérez (whose husband, Diego Morales, is a painter) and Hipólita (married to the old and jealous Santillana), who decide to go for a picnic on St Blaise's Day accompanied by their husbands. While enjoying the outing, Hipólita spots something shining in the bushes. Polonia suggests it might be a piece of jewellery. Mari Pérez goes to the bushes and discovers a diamond ring. They start arguing about who should have the ring and, unable to agree, they let their friend, the Count, decide for them. He gives them the task of playing tricks on their husbands over the next month and a half with the promise that whoever plays the best trick on their spouse will be declared the winner.

Each of them then plays a different trick on her husband. Polonia convinces her husband that he has died, Mari Pérez makes her husband believe that their house has moved during his absence and Hipólita tricks her husband into becoming a monk after getting him drunk. All three have help from their family members, friends or servants. The tale ends on an ambiguous note, since the Count is unable to choose a winner. In the end, while they do not share the ring (given that the Count has misplaced it), they are each rewarded equally with money he gives them, and each is satisfied with what she has attained.

Even a cursory reading of the tale *Ženske šale* reveals a strong similarity to Tirso's *Los tres maridos burlados*, and a closer examination and comparison with Tirso's text leads to the conclusion that this published Sephardic story is in fact a translation of Tirso's *novela* (a story which fits into ATU's tale-type 1406).[21] No further examples of this tale-type have been recorded thus far among the Sepharadim, although, in addition to Tirso's tale, there are two other examples of this tale-type known in Spanish Golden Age literature.[22]

The translator, who evidently worked from the original text, could well have been Davičo himself, whose name appears linked to the story as its compiler. In issue 41 of *Videlo*, below the tale's title appear the words: 'Recorded by H. S. D'. It is logical to believe that these letters refer to Haim Samuilo Davičo. Although *Videlo* does not provide a list of its contributors, Davičo was evidently one of its most active ones (Alkalaj 1925: 79; Milošević 1967: 129; Vidaković-Petrov 1990: 115). It is likely that he came to publish in *Videlo* due to his close friendship with Stojan Novaković, one of the leaders of the Srpska napredna stranka (Serbian Progressive Party), which produced the periodical.

There are other reasons for believing that H. S. D. stands for Haim Samuilo Davičo, not least being the fact that it was not unusual for his works to appear in a newspaper linked to him merely by his initials. On 15 September 1900, he published an article in *Bosanska vila* on Jovan Dimović, an eminent Serbian teacher in Trieste, Italy, and indicated his authorship only by his initials. Moreover, this newspaper usefully provides a list of contributors, which reveals that H. S. D. indeed stands for Haim Samuilo Davičo (Davičo 1900: 225–27). Finally, so far as I have been able to discover, there are no other contributors to the newspaper *Videlo* who have these same initials.

Davičo's roles as writer and collector have so far been highlighted, but he was also well known for his translation work. According to Alkalaj (1925: 78), at the age of seven Davičo was already translating from Hebrew. As an adult, he was the first in Serbia to translate Spanish literature directly from the original. His brother Benko stated the following in a letter to Ángel Pulido Fernández:

> Gracias a las traducciones de mi hermano, el Sr. H. S. Davitcho, antiguo consulo general de Serbia a Trieste, en el Teatro Nacional de aqui se represendan, á mas de todas las joyas del Teatro Español, imprimidas fin hoy, mas de 10 dramas de Echegaray, el cual, sin saberlo, esta influendo á la drama original serba. (Pulido Fernández 1905: 402)[23]

> (Thanks to the translations of my brother, Mr H. S. Davitcho, the former general consul of Serbia in Trieste, more than ten of Echegaray's plays are performed here in the National Theatre along with all the jewels of the Spanish theatre published to this day, influencing, without realising it, Serbian original drama.)

Davičo translated the works of Juan Eugenio Hartzenbusch, Jacinto Benavente, Ramón de Campoamor and José Echegaray and was highly respected in Serbian intellectual circles as a theatre critic, writer and translator (Vidaković-Petrov 1990: 121; Ž. Jovanović 2014b: 990–92). He translated from several languages, including German, Spanish and Italian.

As a Sephardic Jew, Davičo was fluent in Judeo-Spanish and, thanks to the education he received in Serbian schools and at the Faculty of Law at the Velika škola, he spoke perfect Serbian. His close friend, Stojan Novaković, admired the elegance and purity of his Serbian language (Milošević 1967: 130). In addition, Jasna Stojanović (2005: 266; 279–83) points out that Davičo translated two of Cervantes's *entremeses*: *Opsenarije* (*El retablo de las maravillas*), published in *Delo* (Servantes Saavedra 1905a), and *Sudija za bračne parnice* (*El juez de los divorcios*), which appeared in *Nova iskra* (Servantes Saavedra 1905b). Furthermore, he provided assistance to Đorđe Popović-Daničar while the latter was translating *Don Quixote* into Serbian. This list of works and authors translated or read by Davičo suggests that he was not only familiar with the Spanish Golden Age and contemporary literature, but also that he possessed all the necessary skills to carry out the difficult task of translating a Spanish Golden-Age work, such as Tirso de Molina's *novela*.

While we have abundant information about Davičo, little is known about the person alleged to have been the storyteller here, other than that she was called Tija Bohora la Komerčera, and, according to the title of the story as published in *Videlo*, she lived in the Sephardic area of Belgrade known as Yalia. Significantly, however, I have found another reference to this very person in one of Davičo's own tales, 'Luna', in which the author states that she lived in a different Serbian town called Smederevo and was well known for her expertise in traditional medicine. In this tale, in which she appears under a slightly different form of her name (Tija Bohora de los Komerčos), she tries to cure a young man from Yalia who falls seriously ill:

> Kad je sunce otskočilo, raznese se po mahali glas, da je Mordehaja nečastivi posednuo. I doista istog dana su otputovala dva crkvenjaka, jedan u Smederevo, da dovede **tija Bohoru de los Komerčos**, a drugi u Požarevac po čuvenu vidaricu Bohoru de Jošua. (Davičo 2000: 57; [my emphasis])

> (When the sun came out, a rumour spread throughout the entire neighbourhood that Mordehaja had been possessed by the *guerco* [Devil]. That very day the two pious men left, one for Smederevo to seek out **Tija Bohora de los Komerčos**, and the other for Požarevac to fetch the well-known healer Bohora de Jošua.)

The noun *tijo/a* (masculine/feminine) does not, of course, merely indicate kinship bonds (uncle/aunt), but was widely used by the Sepharadim (as well as the Spanish) as an honorific title for an older person. The word *bohor/bohora* denotes a family's first-born child and in many cases, as Joseph Nehama observes (1977: 93), serves as a nickname, while *la Komerčera* is equally rich in potential meaning. *Komerčere/ra* exists as a surname among the Sepharadim, and it is not unusual for names or surnames in Judeo-Spanish to be preceded by the definite article. However, in this particular case, I suggest that *Komerčera* could even be a nickname designating, perhaps, a merchant's wife or a female merchant, as seems probable from its etymological link to the word *komerčante* ('merchant').

Bearing in mind that Davičo cites Tija Bohora on two different occasions, she was most likely someone Davičo and other members of the Sephardic community in Serbia knew well and appreciated as an expert in traditional medicine and a keeper of folk wisdom. It is highly possible that he named her as the alleged storyteller to add credibility to the idea of his undertaking fieldwork and thus to the authenticity of the story published. It is also feasible that she was just an invented character, a product of Davičo's imagination.

A further possibility, of course, is that Tija Bohora, assuming she existed in her own right, translated the text and passed it on to Davičo. However, this is less likely since, according to Mihailo B. Milošević (1967: 135), Judeo-Spanish was still the predominant language spoken by the Sepharadim in Davičo's time: 'U 19. veku beogradski Jevreji još su pretežno govorili španski u kući i u međusobnom saobraćaju van kuće. Davičo ih poziva da nauče srpski' ('In the nineteenth century Belgrade's Jews still spoke mainly Spanish in their homes and to communicate among themselves when outside; Davičo encourages them to learn Serbian'). It is true that the most recent studies on language shift in the Sephardic community in Belgrade show that by the end of the 1860s Serbian started to infiltrate different areas of Jewish life, especially among the younger members of the community (Vučina Simović and Filipović 2009: 133–41; Vučina Simović 2016). However, the linguistic competence of Spanish Jews in Serbian is in doubt, at least until the end of the nineteenth century. Hence, Sepharadim possesing a high linguistic competence in Serbian were not readily found at that time. Tija Bohora is even less likely to have spoken Serbian as, based on the meaning of *tija*, she would have belonged to the older generation of Spanish Jews.

Although the title *Ženske šale* accurately summarises the content of the story, it evidently does not come from Tirso, for the Spanish author called his work a *novela* without providing a specific title for it. Tirso's tale is commonly held to be titled *Los tres maridos burlados*; however, this title was added by modern critics, not the author himself. So, the title in the Serbian translation, *Ženske šale*, was probably added by the translator or editor. Which edition of Tirso's *Los tres maridos burlados* Davičo used for his work is uncertain, given that there were several complete editions of the *Cigarrales de Toledo* available by the time this translation was made, and there were also a significant number of separate editions of the *novela* which concerns us, both in Spanish and in French translation.[24]

The question that arises here is what could have prompted Davičo to present a tale which derives from Spanish Golden-Age written literature as a Sephardic folk tale. Firstly, although the tale was taken from a written source, its folk background is unquestionable. 'The Three Clever Wives' Wager' (ATU1406) is a worldwide folk tale and has been orally transmitted as such at least since the Middle Ages (Uther 2004: II, 198–99). Different medieval tale collections confirm both its international character and its existence as early as the thirteenth century when the first versions were recorded in what are now France and Germany (Raas 1983: 9–10). In addition to this, the hoaxes that the women play on their husbands are well-known motifs in oral tradition, as Stith Thompson's *Motif Index of Folk Literature* (1966) shows:

— 'Wife makes her husband believe he is dead' (J2311.0.1.);

— 'Naked person made to believe that he is clothed' (J2312);

— 'Layman made to believe that he is a monk' (J2314); or 'woman has husband made monk while he is drunk so as to get rid of him' (K1536); and,

— 'Husband made to believe that his house has moved during his absence. The wife and her confederates transform the house into an inn with tables, signs, drinkers, etc. The husband cannot find his house' (J2316).[25]

Tirso's tale contains most of these motifs and resembles an authentic folk tale in its structure. This is why Davičo's readers would probably have believed that *Ženske šale* was indeed an authentic Sephardic folk tale. Nevertheless, this tale-type seems to be completely unknown in the Sephardic world as no examples of it have been recorded thus far among any of the communities of Spanish Jews (Haboucha 1992).

Secondly, it should be noted that adaptations or translations of original works from Spanish and other languages were a frequent occurrence in the Judeo-Spanish speaking world. As Elena Romero points out:

> Del *corpus* hasta ahora conocido podemos deslindar de entrada el lote de las novelas que la cultura general, la moderna erudición de forma esporádica o las mismas indicaciones de portada nos reflejan que son traducciones. Todo lo demás queda sujeto a duda sobre si se trata o no de originales en judeoespañol, ya que ni siquiera fórmulas como 'por', 'escrito por', 'escrito especialmente' y otras similares resultan ser concluyentes. Así pues, sólo una investigación minuciosa podrá determinar o no la originalidad de esas obras. (1992: 239)[26]

Thus, taking elements from other cultures or traditions and presenting them as authentically Sephardic through adaptations or translations was a widespread phenomenon in the Ladino-speaking world. Borovaya (2012: 140) goes even further and claims that 'all Ladino novels — including those that claim to be original works — borrowed elements from foreign-language texts', which is why she describes all Ladino novels as rewritings and refers to their creators as rewriters. Hence it may seem at first that the case of *Ženske šale* fits perfectly within this stream.

However, in my view, Davičo's act conceals much more than seems apparent at first glance. *Ženske šale* is one of the first texts published in the Serbian language which aimed at presenting the Sephardic community in Belgrade to a wider readership. It is also Davičo's first known translation from Spanish to Serbian. Before this text came out, Davičo had only published two literary works about the Sephardic community in Belgrade, 'Slike' (1881) and 'Naumi' (1883). Both texts appeared in the periodical *Otadžbina*, which contained articles mostly on literature and science; the lack of articles on political, economic or current affairs must have limited the scope of the journal's readership.

By contrast, *Videlo*, where *Ženske šale* was published, acted as the economic, political and literary newspaper of the Srpska Napredna Stranka (Serbian Progressive Party), whose members were also known as the Young Conservatives. At the turn of the twentieth century, the Young Conservatives represented one of the two opposition tendencies to the Liberals (the other being the Radicals), who led the Serbian Parliament at the time and who viewed themselves as the spokesmen of the Serbian nation (Stokes 1990: 178–79). Although Davičo was a close friend of the leader of the Liberals, Jovan Ristić, who had introduced Davičo into the Serbian Ministry of Foreign Affairs, Davičo was politically much closer to the ideas of the Young Conservatives. Their standpoint was that Parliament should be run by the educated adherents of the new and more progressive standards of the West rather than by representatives of the Serbian traditional culture, whom they considered backward peasantry, which was the stand defended by the Liberals (Stokes 1990: 182). Most of the leaders of the Progressive Party were, in fact, educated abroad.

Davičo supported the idea of Serbia following the modern and progressive mind of Western Europe. In that sense, he encouraged his fellow Sepharadim to integrate into Serbian society and join the country on its path to modernisation.

At least two of the leaders of the Young Conservatives were Davičo's close friends: Stojan Novaković and Milan Đ. Milićević. The former, according to Milošević (1967: 130), was a great admirer of Davičo's cultural work and his refined style in the Serbian language, while Milićević's literary and ethnographic work is what inspired Davičo to publish his own collection of Judeo-Spanish proverbs (Davičo 1982: 654). Milićević was also one of the founders of the Srpska književna zadruga (The Association of Writers of Serbia), a place frequented by contemporary intellectuals, and which is where the two men probably met.

In order to express and promote their political ideas and their political programme, the Young Conservatives launched *Videlo*. The first issue came out on 14 January 1880 and marked the beginning of what would be the newspaper's most fruitful period, which lasted until 1896, when its publication came to a halt (Stokes 1990: 179). The newspaper was relaunched on two more occasions (1906–08 and 1921–22). It initially appeared three times a week, on Wednesdays, Fridays and Sundays; then daily, except for Mondays; and, in its latter stages, on Thursdays and Sundays only (Kostić 1971: 491). The range of topics included in the newspaper, such as history, political and economic issues, current affairs or literature, ensured that the newspaper would reach a wide scope of readers, particularly those who supported the party's political agenda.

Bearing in mind the political nature of this newspaper, which also became a vehicle for the Young Conservatives' allies, the Radicals, it comes as no surprise that Davičo, who supported the ideas of the party, chose to publish his text here and present it as an example of how thriving and vigorous the Sephardic community in Belgrade was. *Videlo* represented an ideal place to initiate the introduction of the Judeo-Spanish community to a wider readership in Serbia and thus take a first step towards this idea of the Sepharadim integrating into Serbian society and being accepted by wider society.

Davičo aimed to achieve this by creating a positive image of the Sephardic community, depicting it as traditional with a rich oral literature that was very much alive. The words quoted earlier by *Videlo*'s editor Novaković support this hypothesis. Furthermore, the choice of this tale-type was by no means accidental. A comic tale with a happy ending which recounted innocent tricks played by women on their husbands constituted a perfect tool to achieve the proposed goal.

Finally, while the Serbian text is to be regarded as a translation of a Spanish Golden-Age *novela* and not as an authentic, Judeo-Spanish, orally-transmitted version of the ATU1406 tale-type, its existence clearly shows that there continued to be deep awareness of the bonds between the Sepharadim and Spain in the minds of Spanish Jews in Serbia and the Balkan region, which formed an integral and important part of their identity. Davičo's choice of presenting the tale of a Spanish author, Tirso, as Sephardic indicates how strongly the Sepharadim were linked to the Iberian Peninsula in his mind.

It should nonetheless be noted that while some parts faithfully translate Tirso's text, other parts are adaptations rather than translations and are characterised by deletions and by changes deliberately made to make the content more familiar to the Serbian readership at which this Serbian version is aimed. Unlike a foreignising (or exoticising) translation, which aims at retaining features of the source text and source-language culture, the domesticating (or naturalising) translation, of which Davičo's text is an example, aims to make the target text seem as accessible and familiar as possible to target language readers, especially on the cultural level (Venuti 1992: 5; Haywood, Hervey and Thompson 2009: 270). Thus I shall examine here the main features of Davičo's acculturation of Tirso's novella to the Serbian environment.

Cultural Transplantation: Deletions of Localising References

Various degrees of cultural transplantation were carried out by Davičo in his translation. In translation studies, the term cultural transplantation designates the replacement of source-cultural details from the source text with cultural details drawn from the target culture in the target text (Haywood, Hervey and Thompson 2009: 269–70). Tirso's novella, for example, is characterised by a large number of references to contemporary Spanish life, making the use of localising and topographical details one of the tale's most notable characteristics. As Guillermo Guastavino Gallent puts it: 'Lo primero que salta a la vista en el relato tirsiano es la radical españolización de los temas y más aún la madrileñización del ambiente' (1959: 689). There is no doubt that it was Tirso's intention to make the story familiar and acceptable to his readers by setting the action of the tale in contemporary Madrid:

> En Madrid — hija heredera emancipada de nuestra Imperial Toledo, que habiéndola puesto en estado, y casado sucesivamente con cuatro monarcas del mundo (uno, Carlos Quinto, y tres Filipos), agora que se ve Corte, menos cortesana y obediente que debiera, quebrantando el cuarto mandamiento, le usurpa, con los vecinos que cada día le soborna, la autoridad de padre tan digno de ser venerado — vivían pocos tiempos ha tres mujeres hermosas, discretas y casadas. (Tirso de Molina 1996: 456–57)[27]

A reader of Tirso's period would have been able to relate the tale quickly to a familiar place and to recognise, in addition, a number of well-known events or facts of near-contemporary Spanish history and society: for example, the move by the royal court from Toledo to Madrid, which, as a result, became Spain's capital in 1561, or the names of the first four Habsburgs to reign as kings of Spain. Such references, perhaps of interest and relevance to readers in Tirso's Spain, are not, however, essential to the tale itself, and would have had little or no relevance almost three centuries later for Serbian readers. Understandably, therefore, the translator omits such information and starts the tale instead simply with the words: 'U Madridu življahu tri lepe i vrlo dosetljive žene' ('In Madrid there lived three beautiful and very witty women') (Davičo 1885: 41).[28]

Moreover, although the Serbian translation preserves Madrid as a key location within the tale, it omits several of the other places mentioned. For instance, introducing the St Blaise's Day picnic, Tirso says: 'Concertaron para el día de San Blas, que se acercaba, salir al sol y a ver al Rey, que se decía iba a Nuestra Señora de Atocha aquella tarde' (457–58). Our Lady of Atocha, an important place of worship, would be an appropriate church for the King to visit on a feast day. As Luis Vázquez Fernández points out: 'Eran frecuentes las visitas reales a Nuestra Señora de Atocha, para dar gracias, o solicitar ayuda' (1996: 458 n. 1065). In the translation, however, the specific reference to this location disappears: 'Padne im na pamet da na Sv. Blaza izađu u polje da vide kralja, jer se bio preneo glas da će kralj tog dana pred veče izaći' ('It occurred to them to go out and about on St Blaise's Day to see the King because there was a rumour going around that the King would be going out that afternoon') (Davičo 1885: 41).

Other references of this kind have also been left out in the Serbian translation. What follows is a selection of examples of such omissions. Thus, for instance, in Tirso, when Lucas Moreno questions his own sanity, he mentions Nuncio in Toledo, a well-known mental institution at the time (469). And when Mari Pérez wants to buy a door that she will later use to convert her house into an inn, she sends her brother to the market of the Plazuela de la Cebada (471). This is because, as Vázquez Fernández comments, 'en tiempos de Tirso se vendían toda suerte de objetos, sobre todo puertas, los jueves' (1996: 471 n. 1088). Then, in Tirso, when the painter complains about having to go to fetch the midwife, he mentions the long distance between his house in Lavapiés and the Puerta de Fuencarral, where the midwife lives (472–73).

Not only does the Serbian translation contain none of these references, but they are also not replaced by the names of any equivalent Serbian local places, streets or institutions. Thus Nuncio is simply translated as a madhouse, the Plazuela de la Cebada becomes a market, and it is stressed, without specifics, that the painter and the midwife lived at the opposite ends of the town. The reason for such changes could well be that, since the translator had preserved Madrid as the setting for the story, he could hardly use the names of Serbian local places and streets without sounding implausible and indeed contradictory.

Translation of Latin Words and Expressions

Tirso sometimes uses Latin words and expressions to convey his meaning. The translator deals with these in different ways. For instance, when Santillana runs away from Lucas Moreno, pretending to have seen a ghost, he exclaims: '¡*Abrenuncio*, espíritu maligno! ¡No debo a Lucas Moreno sino seis reales que me ganó a los bolos el otro día; pero *quod non ponitur non solvitur*!' (465). According to Vázquez Fernández, *abrenuncio* (exclamation meaning 'far be it from me'), employed during exorcisms, is a word frequently used by Tirso in his plays (1996: 465 n. 1075). In the Serbian text, the word *abrenuncio* is translated as Satan, whilst *espíritu maligno* appears as Beelzebub (Hebrew *Ba'al Zebûb*). According to popular Jewish belief, Beelzebub is the leader of the demons (Kohler 1902: II, 629–30).

The translator's use of the word Beelzebub, a symbolic word embodied in Jewish culture, to translate *espíritu maligno* may indicate a Jewish background of the translator, as a non-Jew would probably have employed a different term of reference. As for the Latin saying *quod non ponitur non solvitur* ('nothing ventured, nothing gained'), the translator has chosen to eliminate it completely from the text without compensating for the omission or offering any alternative in its place (Davičo 1885: 41).

In another instance, the Serbian text provides a direct translation of a Latin sentence used by Tirso rather than preserving the words in the sourcework. Thus, in Tirso, to defend himself from the monks, Santillana exclaims: '¡Fugite, partes adversae!' (490). The Serbian translation, on the other hand, simply transfers the meaning of the phrase into Serbian without indicating that the source-work used is Latin: 'Begajte od mene pogane duše.' ('Get away from me, you evil souls') (Davičo 1885: 49).

Domestication of the Tale

As explained earlier, a domesticating or naturalising translation aims at adapting the source text to the cultural expectations of readers in the target language in order to bridge the (cultural) differences that may obstruct an easy reading and comprehension of the source text. Davičo's translation contains a number of examples which illustrate the acculturation of Tirso's text to the Serbian context.

For example, there is no doubt that the season in which Tirso's story is set is crucial to its significance. The story takes place in the period immediately prior to Lent and is depicted in Tirso's tale as a very lively period of the year in which there are many celebrations. Tirso highlights a number of well-known, symbolic dates, all relevant to the story. Some of these are part of the Catholic Church calendar (St Blaise's Day), whereas others pertain to carnival festivities. For instance, the day when the three women agree to make fools of their husbands is *Jueves de Compadres*, a day when women traditionally play tricks on their husbands, whilst a week later (on *Jueves de Comadres*) the latter have the opportunity to take revenge on their wives (Vázquez Fernández 1996: 67).

None of these celebrations preceding Lent have any place in Jewish (or Serbian) culture and an authentic Sephardic transmission of the tale would probably have omitted or adapted them, as occurred with similar Christian references in many Judeo-Spanish ballads of Hispanic origin.[29] As this is a translation made from the original written text, however, some Christian details are kept; as a result the translation only partly captures the atmosphere created in Tirso's tale.

The picnic originally takes place on St Blaise's Day, which, according to the Serbian translation, falls on a *mrsni četvrtak* (non-fasting Thursday). Consequently, it is celebrated with feasting and the consumption of large amounts of meat, which is forbidden during Lent. Since celebrating Godfellows Thursday, with its associated symbolism, is not a recognised part of Serbian custom and tradition, the translator selects *mrsni četvrtak* to transmit the joy and festivities that are characteristic of that particular day, for this Serbian term indicates a religious holiday that is a day for feasting without restrictions on eating and drinking:

> Pa kako taj dan padaše na mrsni četvrtak (koji se svetkuje bolje no uskrs, i ako nije u kalendaru zabeležen crvenim slovima), to se složiše da ponesu od kuće sve što treba, da se tog dana što slavnije provedu u kakvoj javnoj bašti. (Davičo 1885: 41)

> (And since that day [St Blaise's Day] fell on a non-fasting Thursday (which is celebrated even more than Easter although it is not marked in red letters on the church calendar), they agreed to bring from home everything they needed to have a great time in some public garden.)

A particularly interesting feature of the Serbian translation is Davičo's usage of proper names and types of food and currencies, which tend to differ considerably across cultures. The names of the main characters have been preserved just as they appear in the Spanish source. However, at times for comic effects, the Spanish names of certain secondary characters have been adapted to better suit the Serbian context. For example, in Tirso's story, the painter attempts to convince a young servant that the inn is a house that belongs to him with the words:

> — Yo no busco posada que no sea mía (dijo el pintor), sino que me dejen entrar en mi casa, y me diga el que hace mandón en ella quién en hora y media la ha dado el nuevo oficio de hostellería, habiéndole costado su dinero a Diego de Morales.
> — De *Parras* debía de ser. (476)

Tirso links the characters' surnames with fruit trees so as to produce wordplay. Morales derives from the noun *moral*, which *inter alia* means mulberry tree, whereas the name Parras comes from *parra*, which is a grapevine. He then uses the wordplay to achieve comic effect. The Serbian translation, by contrast, reads:

> 'Ne tražim ja [Dijego de Morales] tuđ stan, nego svoj sopstveni, i koji je to drznuo da pretvori za sat i po u mehanu kuću, koju je pošteno isplatio Dijego de Morales.'
> 'Bolje kažite de Lozanić.' (Davičo 1885: 45)

> (— I [Diego de Morales] am not looking for someone else's house, but my own. And who is it who has dared transform into an inn, and in an hour and a half, the very house that was honestly bought by Diego de Morales.
> — You mean by de Lozanić.)

As indicated, the Serbian translation replaces Parras by de Lozanić. The choice is a comic one for two reasons. First, Lozanić derives from the word *loza*, which in Serbian means grapevine, the same as the Spanish word *parra*, and the surname ending *ić* is added to make it sound Serbian. At the same time, the Spanish preposition *de*, which in Tirso's case is used to designate possession (bought by...), has been maintained. Although the preposition does not exist in Serbian in this form, it can feature as part of a name (foreign names, in particular), usually to suggest an aristocratic background. Hence we are presented with an imaginary innkeeper whose name has noble overtones: de Lozanić. Although the word play is slightly different in the Serbian translation, the comic effect is taken over and used in the very same place as in the Spanish source-tale. The translator also makes changes where types of food are concerned. In Tirso's work, convinced that he is dead, Lucas Moreno decides to dine and drink plentifully before going to bed:

> En fin, el pobre *ánima en pena*, sin averiguar si comían o no los del otro mundo, abrió un escritorio y dio tras una gaveta de bocados de mermelada, acompañándola con bizcochos y ciruelas de Génova, que ayudó a pasar con los empellones de una bota, cuya alma le había infundido la Membrilla. (466–67)

Serbian readers would doubtless have struggled to visualise such things as sponge fingers or Genoese prunes, mentioned in the Spanish text, as these were not common foods in Serbia, so the translator chose something likely to be more familiar to them: potted ham hock. Cooked pork shank in aspic is a Serbian delicacy, which is usually prepared for important religious holidays, such as Christmas or *Slava* (a family patron saint's day): 'Ostavši sam, ova duša u mukama, otvori dolac, i nerazmišljajući mnogo, da li se na onom svetu jede ili ne, izvadi kolenicu sa pihtijom i stade stojeći i hodajući jesti' ('Once alone, this tortured soul opened a cupboard and, without considering much whether beings from the World Beyond consume food or not, he took out a potted ham hock and started eating it while standing and walking around') (Davičo 1885: 45).

The translator also changes the currencies mentioned in the original text. Tirso uses *reales* and *escudos* on several occasions throughout his story, both of which refer to coins in circulation in Spain at the time (461; 465; 496). The translator, however, prefers to refer to Serbian coins, such as *groš* instead of *real* and *dinar* instead of *escudo*.

In summary, Davičo used several means to collect, conserve, disseminate and re-create Judeo-Spanish folk tradition. First, he collected elements of his native culture from among his fellow Sepharadim, translated them into Serbian and then published them in different periodicals. A part of the compiled material was published in its original language, Judeo-Spanish (his proverb collection, for example). But the credit is not Davičo's, for he chose to publish all his work in Serbian. It is rather the merit of others, Kayserling for instance, who were more aware than Davičo of the immense value of such material compiled in its original language.

Second, by choosing to write about topics and motifs related to the Judeo-Spanish tradition, Davičo started incorporating in his own work ballads, poems, proverbs or tales that were circulating in his community when he was a child. When interpolating them, he made sure to convey the meaning and the role they had for the Sepharadim in Belgrade by describing the occasion or situation when they were usually performed or mentioned.

Finally, there was an attempt by Davičo to create new elements of the tradition by taking elements from other cultures and presenting them as Sephardic. This was the case of the text *Ženske šale* where Davičo tried to accomplish this goal through translation and adaptation of Tirso de Molina's novella *Los tres maridos burlados* which he presented as the fruit of his fieldwork. This phenomenon of translating and adapting works from other traditions was widespread in the Judeo-Spanish speaking world of the time.

However, in Davičo's case, this act conceals a political and cultural aim which was to introduce his community to the general readership in Serbia. For that reason, he chose an influential newspaper of the time, *Videlo*, as a place to publish the result of his alleged fieldwork while making various changes to the text in order to domesticate the story to its general environment.

Davičo's choice of assimilation, which entailed the language shift from Judeo-Spanish to Serbian, is in complete contrast to Laura Papo's attitudes. The latter advocated the continuity of the Sephardic tradition and endeavoured to preserve it and recover it by addressing her work to her community rather than the general audience in Bosnia. For this reason, Laura Papo opted for Judeo-Spanish as a means of communication rather than Serbian or French. I examine all these viewpoints maintained by Laura Papo in the following chapters.

2. Laura Papo: A Vindicator of Continuation and Recovery of the Judeo-Spanish Language and Culture

Laura Papo, known as Bohoreta, was undoubtedly the leading figure in the Bosnian Sephardic cultural scene in the first half of the twentieth century thanks to her multifaceted work. She wrote different literary genres including theatre, narrative (tales, essays and newspaper articles) and poetry, all of which were relatively new in the Sephardic literary panorama.[30] What makes her work even more remarkable is the fact that she was the first ever female Sephardic playwright. In addition, she personally directed those pieces of hers in which her sisters played roles. Furthermore, she translated or adapted works from Serbo-Croatian, French and German to Judeo-Spanish (E. Papo 2012: 131–32; 143). And finally, she was well known for gathering folk material *in situ*.

There exists a facsimile edition of Laura Papo's work in three volumes prepared by Sejdalija Gušić, Edina Spahić and Ana Cecilia Prenz Kopušar.[31] The original manuscripts are kept in the Istorijski muzej grada Sarajeva (The Historical Museum of Sarajevo) in Bosnia. Thus far only two plays by Laura Papo have been published in an annotated scholarly edition: *Esterka* (L. Papo 2012) and *Avia de ser* (E. Papo 2016: 339–64). In addition, Nela Kovačević (2018b) published several tales by Laura Papo, some of which had previously appeared in two Bosnian Jewish periodicals, *Jevrejski život* (*Jewish Life*) and *Jevrejski glas* (*The Jewish Voice*).[32]

With regard to secondary sources, most of the works on Laura Papo have appeared in recent years and, rather than providing a detailed examination of her work, tend to focus on general points such as her life, the titles of her publications or the existing bibliography (Čampara 1967; Vidaković-Petrov 1990: 105–09; Kovačević 2010; 2018a: 19–42; E. Papo 2011; 2012; 2013b). There exist three works focusing on specific aspects of Laura Papo's work: in her edition of Laura Papo's play *Esterka*, Ana Cecilia Prenz Kopušar (2012: 3–19) includes an introduction in which she provides an analysis of the play; Kovačević (2014) focuses on the portrayal of the Sephardic woman in Laura Papo's narrative in her doctoral thesis from the Universidad de Granada, Spain; and, in her book on Laura Papo, Jagoda Večerina Tomaić (2016) offers a descriptive rather than an analytical investigation of Laura

FIG. 1.5. Laura Papo, portrait.
Jevrejski istorijski muzej, Belgrade, Serbia

Papo's work and thus fails to shed light on relevant historical, social and literary issues related to Laura Papo and her work.[33]

It is important to place Laura Papo's educational background and the fact that she was a female author in the historical and cultural context of her time. An examination of Laura Papo's efforts to preserve, develop, disseminate and re-create Sephardic folklore will be contrasted to Davičo's work and his attitudes and aims. The two methods Laura Papo used to accomplish her goals were collecting the folk material *in situ*, and introducing this material in her own work. Special emphasis will be laid upon this second practice with regard to balladry as her work exemplifies different ways in which this particular genre of folk literature was treated.

For example, Laura Papo's most common practice was to introduce a ballad in its traditional (Sephardic) form, i.e., sung, in a Sephardic context depicted in a play. Her *Avia de ser*, 1930 (*Once upon a Time*), contains several ballads such as *Landarico*, *La mujer engañada*, *La partida del esposo*, and *La doncella guerrera* which are set in the Sephardic female context of the play and are used with a specific didactic function. I examine the case of *Landarico* to exemplify this.

Likewise, folklore serves Laura Papo as a starting point, a source of inspiration, which she then enlarges upon, thus creating something different. Laura Papo's practice of re-creating folk literature is also analysed here with the example of the ballad *Don Bueso y su hermana* (hereafter *Don Bueso*) which in Laura Papo's play *Avia de ser* becomes a tale. Both of these ballad examples, *Landarico* and *Don Bueso*, display the variety of techniques employed by Laura Papo to incorporate ballads into her work. At the same time, these examples underscore the context and the function that oral literature played in the life of the Bosnian Sepharadim.

Laura Papo and the Education of Women among the Sepharadim

Laura Levy (Papo's maiden name) was born in 1891 in Sarajevo into a modest traditional Sephardic family as the oldest child of Juda Isak León Levy and Ester Levy — hence her nickname and her literary pseudonym 'Bohoreta'. Her father worked as a merchant and her mother, like most Sephardic women of the time, was in charge of the upkeep of the house and raising the children (E. Papo 2011: 89). Laura Papo had four sisters and two brothers. In 1916, she married Daniel Papo, a fellow Sephardi from Sarajevo, and had two sons by him, León and Koki, both of whom were killed during WWII. Laura Papo never came to learn about the cruel fate of her sons as she herself passed away in 1942 in a hospital run by Catholic nuns in Sarajevo while hiding from the Croatian Nazis, Ustashas (E. Papo 2011: 105).

As an educated woman, a polyglot and a writer, Laura Papo was avant-garde for her time, when it was rare to encounter a woman who possessed an education and had a profession. After her husband was institutionalised for mental illness, she was forced to live the life of an *agunah* (a Hebrew word meaning 'anchored'). This term designates a woman who is chained to a husband who refuses or is unable to grant her a divorce, a *get*, in Jewish religious law. It was most likely this situation that led her to use her education to take on the role of the breadwinner.

One of the crucial moments in Laura Papo's life, which enabled her to develop intellectually, took place (in 1897?) when the family decided to move to Istanbul in the pursuit of a better life (Kovačević 2014: 104).[34] This change of city proved to be essential for Laura Papo's future vocation as a writer as it was in Istanbul that she attended one of the Alliance's schools for girls. In Laura Papo's time, the incorporation of Sephardic girls into the educational system was still in its early stages, as schooling continued to be a predominately male realm, thus maintaining a *status quo* which had characterised all Sephardic communities for centuries.[35]

As the new education became a privilege accessible only to the middle and upper Sephardic classes, Laura Papo's family was in no financial position to sponsor their daughter's education in one of the Alliance's schools. Furthermore, in keeping with traditional values, Laura Papo's parents preferred to invest the little money they had in the education of their son, Isak, rather than their daughters, in spite of the fact that, unlike Laura, Isak did not show a great interest in learning (E. Papo 2011: 91). It was the Sephardic community of Istanbul which granted Laura a scholarship for her exceptional talent and intelligence. This act by the community of Istanbul was a clear sign that the Eastern Sepharadim were starting to embrace new values coming from the West, one of these being the education of girls.

FIG. 1.6. Laura Papo and her sons.
Jevrejski istorijski muzej, Belgrade, Serbia

Thanks to this generous help, Laura Papo became fluent in French and German at the Alliance while at the same time gaining valuable knowledge in various subjects such as history, mathematics, geography and literature. The latter was to become one of her strongest passions. It seems that it was at this time that Laura Papo changed the name given to her by her parents at birth, Luna, to Laura, deeming that Laura was more in accord with westernisation: 'en la atmósfera "afrancesada" de la escuela de la Alliance, un nombre como Luna podía generar dificultades de integración a la sociedad, más aún cuando se trataba de una inmigrante de Bosnia' (E. Papo 2011: 90).

In addition to the education received at this school in Istanbul, in 1928 Laura Papo went to Paris, where she completed a course for which she gained a *Diplôme supérieur d'Études Françaises*, awarded by the Alliance (E. Papo 2011: 102). In her essay, *La mužer sefardi de Bosna*, 1932 (*Bosnian Sephardic Women*), Laura Papo underscores that for the women of the past, to be able to read and write was something of great merit: 'las pokas mužeres ke meresieron a saver meldar "ladino" hueron envidiadas komo oj no se envidia a "milioneras" '('Those few women who got to learn to read "Ladino" were envied more than "millionaires" are envied today') (L. Papo 2005: 162). Reading and writing continued to be highly appreciated skills in Laura Papo's time, and her education, her ability to read and write, helped her natural gift to flower.

Furthermore, it was precisely through her education at the Alliance's school in Istanbul that Laura Papo became acquainted with Western European literary genres, such as the theatre, the novel and journalism, which had no previous existence among the Sepharadim:

> A mediados del siglo XIX comenzaron a soplar vientos nuevos en el tradicional mundo sefardí: entraba el influjo de Occidente. Surgieron entonces los llamados *géneros adoptados*, sin tradición en la literatura judía precedente y que empezaron a cultivarse con un claro afán de emulación por las literaturas occidentales: se escribieron novelas y poesía de autor a la manera europea; surgieron aquí y allá grupos de teatro de aficionados que producían textos teatrales para su propio consumo y adaptaban o traducían las obras de otras literaturas; y proliferaron las publicaciones periódicas. (Díaz-Mas 2006: 194)

This knowledge of new literary genres began to bear fruit when Laura Papo decided to write literary works. Although Laura Papo also wrote tales and poetry, for various reasons she chose to write mainly for the theatre. Firstly, Sephardic theatrical life in Sarajevo began to flourish at the turn of the twentieth century with several theatre troupes (El Progreso, La Lira and La Matatia) performing secular plays in Judeo-Spanish for important occasions or holidays (Vidaković-Petrov 1997: 155). Hence Sarajevo quickly became a renowned theatre centre of the time. For the staging of her work, Laura Papo collaborated with the amateur theatre troupe La Matatia. Founded in Sarajevo in 1923, La Matatia represented a cultural society of working Jewish youth, with a very active drama section. They organised nights of Sephardic folklore as part of their activities (Vidaković-Petrov 1990: 52–53). The popularity that the theatre enjoyed in her time undoubtedly prompted Laura Papo to choose this genre of literature as an effective way of transmitting and promoting her ideas.

Secondly, Laura Papo's first forays into the art of literature were theatre pieces she composed for her family with the sole purpose of entertaining them and in which her sisters performed (E. Papo 2011: 92; 95). Word of these intimate performances spread rapidly around Sarajevo. For that reason, La Benevolencia, a Sarajevo Jewish institution which promoted Jewish education and culture, commissioned Laura Papo to write a play to be performed at one of their charity auctions (E. Papo 2011: 95).[36] A portrayal of that performance and Laura Papo's sisters' participation in it can be found in the novel *Balada o Bohoreti* (*The Ballad of Bohoreta*) by Gordana Kuić, Laura Papo's niece.

Kuić wrote several novels about the history of Laura Papo's family based on true events and the memories of her mother, Blanka Levy-Kuić, who was Laura Papo's sister. The novels provide an interesting and revealing insight into many crucial moments in the lives of Laura Papo's sisters and Laura herself. The *Balada o Bohoreti* is entirely dedicated to the figure of Laura Papo. Kuić describes these theatrical performances as a kind of family venture in which each of Laura's sisters was assigned a specific role:

> Sastavila sam scenario jednog kratkog komada za Blanki i Riki da ga izvedu na Purimskoj zabavi. Naslov je *La Molinera i la Karvonera, kantika francesa adaptada*

FIG. 1.7. *Lira*, Jewish Singing Society, Bosnia.
Jevrejski istorijski muzej, Belgrade, Serbia

en espanjol (Mlinarica i ugljarica, francuska pesmica prilagođena španskom). [...]
Kostime je sašila Nina. [...] Rikica stalno dodaje nove korake njihovom plesu,
a Blanki samo šapuće: '*Tristi di mi!* Teško meni, kako ću ja!?' Rikica, ozbiljni
koreograf, strogo pogleda Blankicu i kaže: '*Estu es kulaj... ansina*, ovo je lako...
Evo, ovako!'[...] Klara svira na klaviru. (2010: 293–94)[37]

(I [Laura Papo] have written a script for a short theatre piece to be performed
at the Purim celebrations by Blanki and Riki. The title is *La Molinera i la
Karvonera, kantika francesa adaptada en espanjol* (*The Miller's Wife and the Coalman's
Wife, French Song Adapted to Spanish*). [...] The costumes were sewn by Nina. [...]
Rikica is constantly adding new steps to their dance routine and Blanki does
nothing but whisper '*Tristi di mi!* Poor me, how will I do it!?' Rikica, a serious
choreographer, gave her a strict look and said: '*Estu es kulaj... ansina*, This is
easy... like this!'[...] Klara will play the piano.)

Thirdly, the topics of Laura Papo's plays fit perfectly into the mainstream of
contemporary Sephardic theatre. According to Romero (1992: 283–85), two categories of plays can be discerned in the first half of the twentieth century: plays
which deal with communal problems and those of everyday life (*de contenido*

FIG. 1.8. Laura Papo and her sisters.
Jevrejski istorijski muzej, Belgrade, Serbia]

costumbrista), and plays which depict the break with traditional values and the appearance of new lifestyles brought by modern times (*de comedia nueva*).[38] Laura Papo cultivated both types of plays, often mixing elements of both: 'Sus estampas y obras de costumbres incluyen mensajes sociales en la misma medida que sus piezas sociales están colmadas de elementos folklóricos' (E. Papo 2011: 103).

Finally, it seems plausible that by choosing to write theatre in the language of her home and dealing with Sephardic topics, Laura Papo intended to reach all members of her community regardless of their sex, age or education. It should be borne in mind that at the time not all Sepharadim in Bosnia spoke fluent Serbian or any other language aside from Judeo–Spanish. Laura Papo makes reference to this situation in several of her plays.

One of the characters in her play written in 1933, *Shuegra ni da barro buena: pedaso en tres aktos, retrato social de muestros dias* (*No Mother-in-Law is Good, Not Even if Made of Clay: A Piece in Three Acts, Social Portrait of Our Days*), a female gypsy learned some Judeo-Spanish so she could predict the future to elderly Sephardic ladies who spoke only Judeo-Spanish (E. Papo 2011: 91 n. 6). In another play, *Madrastra el nombre le abasta* (*Stepmother, Enough Said*), a scene takes place in which two Serbian villagers are trying to talk to Tia Merkada but misunderstandings in communication occur because she is not fluent in Serbian (E. Papo 2011: 91 n. 7). In addition, Laura Papo's plays were written to be performed rather than read and thus even those who were illiterate could enjoy her theatre. Hence writing theatre became a vehicle which allowed her to express and transmit her standpoint regarding the preservation of the language and culture of her home and her community in a way that was accessible to everyone, including those who might not have had access to a written work.

Changing Reality in the Lives of the Sepharadim in Bosnia

The topics that Laura Papo chose for her works, such as the customs and traditions of her community, the end of isolation, the problems of everyday life, and the role of Sephardic women in society (both the Sephardic and Bosnian), were closely related to ongoing changes in the life of the Sepharadim at the turn of the twentieth century. These circumstances prompted Laura Papo to turn her eyes to her own community and reflect on the consequences these changes would have on Sephardic cultural heritage and identity.

In her text, 'Por esto akea vieža no se kižo murir' ('That is Why That Old Lady Refused to Die'), published in the *Jevrejski glas* (1929: 9–10), Laura Papo pinpoints that this 'tipo de viežas de un tiempo son raros. Por la ley de la natura kale ke dispareskan. Me esforzo para enfikar en la memoria algun retrato de estas mužeres de un tiempo' ('The type of lady from the past is difficult to find. It is Nature's law that they disappear. My aim is to preserve the memory of these women of the past'). *Jevrejski glas* was one of the leading contemporary Jewish newspapers in the area. It appeared in Sarajevo from 20 January 1928 until 1941. Most of the articles were published in Serbo-Croatian although there were texts, such as this one by Laura Papo, that were written in Judeo-Spanish (Vidaković-Petrov 2013: 69–96).

Nonetheless, the Europeanisation of Bosnia brought radical changes for its entire population, and this included the Sepharadim: the long isolation was broken and the integration into a larger society affected not only Sephardic men but also Sephardic women.[39] The latter abandoned the realm of the home and started gaining an education. Consequently, they began to adopt the main language of the country at the cost of their mother tongue, which altered their role as the main keepers of Sephardic tradition.

Laura Papo's family was also embracing these newly created circumstances in Bosnia. As her niece Kuić describes in another biographical novel of the family, *The Scent of Rain in the Balkans* (2004), both Laura Papo and her sisters can be seen as examples of the multiple changes occurring in the Sephardic community at the turn of the twentieth century. First, they dressed in the Western way, in complete contrast to their mother, who dressed in the traditional way. Although Laura Papo did wear, at the beginning of her marriage, the traditional headdress by which a

Sephardic married woman was identified, she also adopted the Western style of dress and soon stopped wearing it (E. Papo 2011: 92). Second, Laura Papo and her sisters travelled abroad, to European cities, something that was unusual for Sephardic women of that time. Third, they chose to have professions, and they spoke other languages in addition to Judeo-Spanish. Finally, three of Laura Papo's sisters married Christians, at a time when mixing with other religions or ethnicities was not a common occurrence among the Sepharadim.

Although Laura Papo embraced all these changes, the aims of her work were just the opposite of Davičo's. She opted to address her work only to the Sephardic community by writing in Judeo-Spanish and choosing topics concerning the community. By doing so, she endeavoured not only to preserve and collect the evidence of that tradition but also to secure its survival.

Laura Papo's Fieldwork in Collecting Oral Data

Seeing all these changes that were affecting the Sephardic traditional life, and not wanting to remain passive when confronted with the possibility of the disappearance of a way of life dear to her, Laura Papo took upon herself the role of an ideological emissary with the mission to preserve and, if possible, reactivate the cultural heritage of the Bosnian Sepharadim through her writings. She was only seventeen when in 1908 she wrote her first play, *Elvira*, which curiously did not have either Bosnia or Jews as the subject matter (Večerina Tomaić 2016: 113). She wrote this play in French, which at that time was considered to be a prestigious language, especially among the Sepharadim.[40] However, as she matured and became aware of the importance of her own cultural heritage, she decided to write in the language of her home, Judeo-Spanish. She considered this to be fundamental in order to preserve the traditions of her community in the face of the changes taking place. As Kalmi Baruh points out:

> I believe that there is a need to paint an extraordinary portrait of Mrs Laura Papo in order to understand the essence of her, let us call it, publication work. In her education, she was an exception among our Spanish women, and her modesty to a great extent gives character to her writing. [...] Her modesty determined both her form and motifs, and what is most important, the language [Judeo-Spanish] of her work. She also was familiar with the Castilian language, and as a pupil of *Alliance*, spoke French very well; nevertheless, her diction did not embrace any of those two, in our view, artificial sources. She drew from the language of her home. Our women are, after all, the most faithful keepers of our mother tongue. (2007: 135–36; trans. Tatjana Jovićević)

Like Davičo, Laura Papo endeavoured to accomplish this task of collecting, preserving and developing the Judeo-Spanish folk tradition in two ways: by compiling the folk material *in situ*, and by incorporating elements of this material in her plays and thus disseminating it. Eliezer Papo provides an insight as to just how Laura Papo went about doing so:

> Empezó a publicar retratos de personas comunes, ancianos y ancianas de antaño, 'tipos antiguos' que, en su opinión, encarnaban la forma de vida judeo-

española, los valores y concepciones de la sociedad judeo-española tradicional, sus anécdotas y recopilaciones folclóricas sobre las costumbres y juegos en desaparición. (2011: 102)

Laura Papo's work as a collector is comprised of a short compilation of ballads which she gathered in 1917 from among the members of her community. She managed to collect sixteen ballads by interviewing at least four people, all originally from Sarajevo: Flora Abinum, forty-six years old (*Bernal Francés*, M9; *Silvana*, P1), Señora Eskenazy, thirty-five years old (*Virgilios*, F8), Esther Levi, forty-six years old (*Hero y Leandro*, F2; *Parto en lejas tierras*, L2; *Morena me llaman*, AA45) and Gioia Theodorus Levi, sixty-five years old (*Las hermanas reina y cautiva*, H1, two versions; *La princesa y el segador*, Q4; *El villano vil*, Q6; *El infante cautivo*, H16; *Roldán al pie de la torre*, B2; *El raptor pordiosero*, O3; *Don Bueso y su hermana*, H2).[41] In addition to these, there are two more ballads (*La cabalgada de Peranzules*, H8 and *La hermosica*) where the name of the teller(s) is omitted.[42] Consequently, there might have been more informants. The manuscript containing these ballads is kept in the Historijski arhiv Sarajeva (Sarajevo's Historical Archives) and has been published in part or in full on several occasions.[43]

Laura Papo's particular interest in and appreciation of Sephardic balladry was most probably stimulated by her encounter with a renowned ballad collector from Spain, Manuel Manrique de Lara, who in 1911 visited the Sephardic communities in the Eastern Mediterranean. The Junta para Ampliación de Estudios, a progressive Spanish institution dedicated to the encouragement of research, granted a scholarship to Manrique de Lara to carry out this extensive fieldwork in the countries of the Ottoman Empire as a part of a larger project of ballad collection initiated in Spain by Ramón Menéndez Pidal.[44] Laura Papo's admiration for Manrique de Lara and his work can be seen in the fact that she followed his example and started collecting ballads herself in her own community. Her great respect for him is also evident in her references to him in some of her works (see the quotation below).

In Sarajevo, Manrique de Lara interviewed several Sephardic Jews, one of them being the nineteen-year old Laura Levy (Papo's maiden name). On that occasion, Laura Papo was able to provide Manrique de Lara with a number of ballads. This fact shows us that she herself was a loyal keeper of the Sephardic *romancero* tradition.[45] It is to this contact with a Spaniard that Laura Papo attributes her understanding of the cultural value of the Sephardic *romancero*:

> Kon razon diši Don Manuel Manrique de Lara kon el kual tuve el onor de kolavorar en su romansero sefardi: ke estas romanses tan antikas y tan guardadas onde mozotros les azen el efekto de un buqueto de klaveles y rozas en un kampo de jervas malas. Kuanto puede maraviar ansina un kante el kual en la tiera madre en Espanja ya disparesio. A este señor de Lara no se le topava palavras para maraviarse por los biervos antikos kontenidos en muestras romances! (L. Papo 2005: 166)

> (Don Manuel Manrique de Lara, with whom I had the honour of working on his Sephardic ballad collection, has a point when he says that these ballads, that are so old and cherished among us, seem like a bouquet of carnations and roses in a field of weeds. A song that had already disappeared in its motherland Spain

> still manages to delight us immensely. This señor de Lara could not find words to express his amazement with the very old words contained in our ballads!)

According to Eliezer Papo (2011: 94), Laura Papo's ballad collection was not intended for the Jewish audience but rather for scholars abroad who might be interested in Sephardic (Spanish) balladry. He made this assumption about the aim of the collection because the information about the informants was not given in Judeo-Spanish or Serbo-Croatian but in German. He may well be right as her ballad collection was one of the ways for Laura Papo to disseminate her cultural heritage. An example of this can be found in a letter she wrote in 1928 while studying in Paris. The closing of the letter, 'Agradesca Usted saludos respetuosos de su alumna' ('Kind regards from your student'), suggests that it was addressed to one of her professors in France to whom she offered her ballad collection as material worthy of being researched:

> Deseo comunicar a Usted este facto, que onde nosotros se cantan romances de la idat media. A uno de sus colegas tengo que remeter mi chico romancero que recoge [sic] en mis dias jobenes, porque onde nosotros durmen estos tresores de folklor. Sé muy bien que, en Francia uno tiene senso entendimiento para todo loque es hermoso. Si a Usted le pueden gustar estos cantares anticos, volveré a mi casa le envierra a Usted mis romances. (Nezirović 1986: 117)

> (I would like to draw your attention to the fact that medieval ballads are still sung among us. I need to send to one of your colleagues my modest ballad collection which I compiled when I was young because these folk treasures sleep among us. I know very well that people in France have appreciation for anything that's beautiful. If you think that these old songs might be of interest to you, I could send my ballads to you once I return home.)

Furthermore, Muhamed Nezirović mentions that in the same letter Laura Papo transcribed the ballad *Amadil* (1986: 116). Eliezer Papo (2011: 103 n. 35) maintains that it is a version of the ballad Laura Papo inserted in her play *Esterka*, where it is called *Tres ermanicas* (ballad-type *Hero y Leandro*, F2). I have been unable to consult the original letter and verify the lines of the ballad, but Eliezer Papo's opinion seems at the very least doubtful to me as a character by the name Amadil does not appear in *Hero y Leandro*, whereas in *La vuelta del marido* (I1) the protagonist is called Amadil or Amadí. Moreover, a version of the latter ballad appears in the third act of Laura Papo's play *Esterka* with the following opening lines: 'Arvolera, mi arvolera, tan | galana, tan gjentil' ('Grove, my grove, so | graceful, so delicate') (L. Papo 2012: 86). Therefore, it is highly probable that the ballad referred to by Laura Papo in her letter to her professor in France is the one in the third act of her play *Esterka*, known as *La vuelta del marido*, and not, as Eliezer Papo claims, the ballad *Hero y Leandro* which appears in the first act.

In addition to collecting the folk material *in situ*, Laura Papo also incorporated elements of it into her theatre. Bearing in mind Laura Papo's interest in the Sephardic *romancero*, it comes as no surprise that traces of those songs appear in her plays on a number of occasions. A good example is the previously mentioned play she wrote in 1930, *Esterka: ritrato social de nuestros dias en 3 actos* (*Esterka: A Social Portrait of Our Days in Three Acts*). Although the play revolves around the everyday problems of a modest Sephardic family, it contains abundant description of customs and folk tradition. With regard to this, Naftali Bata Gedalja wrote a review of the play after its performance in Belgrade in 1931. The review, published in the *Jevrejski glas*, states the following:

> Ako od čitavog sefardskog folklora, specijalno balkanskog, ostane samo *Esterka*, ona sama po sebi je već dovoljna, da nam da jednu dovoljno jasnu predstavu o govoru i načinu života naših starih u onim boljim prošlim vremenima, kada je bilo više ljubavi, više sloge i saglasnosti u radu i patrijahalnom životu. (1931: 2)

> (If nothing more were to remain of Sephardic folklore, particularly of that from the Balkans, but the play *Esterka*, it would be enough to give us a sufficiently clear idea of a language and a way of life of our forebears in those worthier times, when there was more love, more harmony and rapport in work and patriarchal life.)

Three ballads appear in the play, two in the first act (*La princesa y el segador*, Q4 [+ *Delgadina*, P2]; *Hero y Leandro*, F2), and one in the third (*La vuelta del marido*, I1). Eliezer Papo (2011: 103 n. 35) and Prenz Kopušar (2012: 11) cite a fourth one in the third act which they call *La blanca niña*. However, the latter shows no formal traits of a ballad and is in fact a very rare lyrical song. There are four versions from Bosnia published by Samuel M. Elazar (1987: 141; 292–93; 334); one of them (1987: 334) was told to him by Nina Škoro-Levi, Laura Papo's sister.

Laura Papo uses ballads not only to evoke past times when ballads were sung at home as part of everyday life, household chores or different Jewish festivities, but also to pinpoint their didactic role within Sephardic society. After hearing *Hero y Leandro* in the play *Esterka*, the characters Linda, Esterka and the *abuela* comment on the nature of this poetry: 'ESTERKA Ves Linda, esto te es la pedagogia entera en dos palavras, kuantos livros se gastan, i al kavo venimos a loke dizen los viežos!' ('ESTERKA You see Linda, the entire pedagogy in just two words. So many books written but still we go back to what the elders said') (L. Papo 2012: 46).

Likewise, her play *Avia de ser: escena de la vida de un tiempo kon romansas en un akto* (*Once Upon A Time: A Scene from Past Times with Ballads in One Act*), written in 1930, mainly consists of medieval Hispanic ballads: *Don Bueso y su hermana*, H2; *Landarico*, M8; *La mujer engañada*, L13; *La partida del esposo*, I6 [+ *La vuelta del hijo maldecido*, X6]; *La doncella guerrera*, X4.[46] Laura Papo uses ballads here to show the didactic role they had among the Sepharadim and to illustrate that these forms of folk literature were sources of education for Sephardic girls who at that time received no formal education. This point will be analysed using the examples of *Don Bueso* and *Landarico* in the following two chapters.

However, not only ballads feature in her plays. A folk tale or a proverb can also appear as a source of her theatre, as was the case with *Shuegra ni da barro buena* (*No Mother-in-Law is Good, Not Even if Made of Clay*). The title of the play, *Shuegra ni da barro buena*, refers to a well-known proverb in Sephardic culture which implies that a relationship between a woman and her mother-in-law is not always an easy one (Saporta y Beja 1978: 180). The proverb most likely derives from a well-known Judeo-Spanish tale-type, ★★903C 'Not Even in Pictures', an oicotype, several examples of which have been collected from among the Sepharadim (Haboucha 1992: 379–80).[47]

The tale can be summarised in the following way: a young bride who has never met her deceased mother-in-law listens to her friends' constant complaints about theirs. Puzzled, she suggests that her husband order a clay bust of his mother, and he is more than happy to do so. When the sculpture arrives, it is given an honoured place in the couple's living room. Each day, however, the wife finds that she must move it around while cleaning the house. Soon she tires of the chore and of the bust. Throwing it to the floor, she shatters it into a thousand pieces while acknowledging the truth behind the saying that all mothers-in-law cause trouble, even if they are made of clay (Haboucha 1992: 379).

Significantly, this tale-type, as well as the proverb itself, has been recorded in two cultures only: the Sephardic and the Spanish. The Castilian equivalent of this proverb appears as early as 1627 in Gonzalo Correas's *Vocabulario de refranes* and reads: 'Suegra, ninguna buena: hícela de azúcar, y amargóme; hícela de barro, y descalabróme' (1967: 295). Moreover, there are several examples of the **903C tale-type recorded in Spanish Golden-Age literature (Chevalier 1983: 258), and a number of examples of this tale-type in the Sephardic world, a subject I shall deal with in *Part II*. Here, however, I intend to examine two ballad-types in more detail, *Don Bueso* and *Landarico*, and the way in which they are employed by Laura Papo in her play *Avia de ser*.

Laura Papo's Play *Avia de ser*

Sephardic authors from the former Yugoslavia did not limit themselves to merely reproducing folklore in the same form in which it had appeared in the tradition. Sometimes they re-created the folk material by including a number of elements borrowed from oral tradition but rewritten and reinterpreted. This was the case for Laura Papo's re-creation of the medieval Hispanic ballad *Don Bueso y su hermana*, H2, which appears in her play *Avia de ser* (hereafter *AS*).

AS was written as a one-act play in 1930 and marked the beginning of the most productive period in Laura Papo's creative life. Two manuscripts of it have been preserved. The first manuscript is a preliminary version of the play consisting of fourteen pages with two subtitles: *Evocacion* (*Recollection*) and *Stampa, scena de la vida de un tiempo* (*A Portrait: A Scene from Past Times*) (E. Papo 2012: 139–40). The second manuscript represents the complete version of the play which consists of twenty-two pages and a further scene added at the end, the inclusion of which seems not to have been initially planned (E. Papo 2012: 140). The title remains the same, *AS*, but the subtitle changes, *Escena de la vida de un tiempo kon romansas en un akto* (*A Scene from Past Times with Ballads in One Act*).

At the beginning of the first page, the names of the main characters are given ('la Madre, Rahelika, Sarika — sus dos ižas', 'the Mother, Rahelika, Sarika — her two daughters') along with information regarding the place and the date of the composition of the play: Sarajevo, 18 February 1930. On the last page appears the date when the play was completed: 26 February 1930. Both manuscripts are

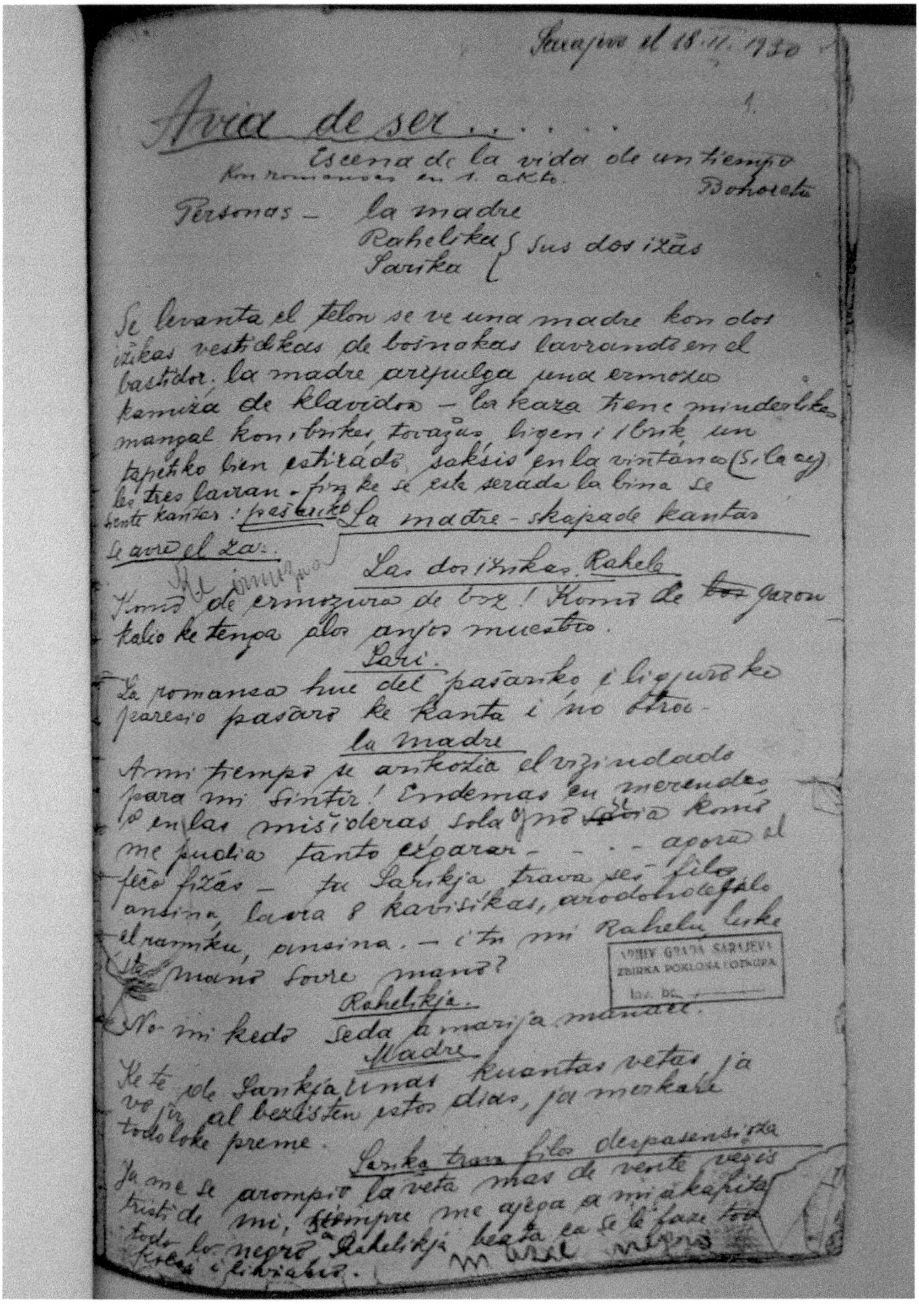

FIG. 1.9. First page of Laura Papo's manuscript *Avia de ser*.

in Judeo-Spanish Latin script in which influences of the Serbo-Croatian graphic system can be seen.

Two editions of the play have appeared in recent years. In 2015, Sejdalija Gušić, Spahić Edina and Ana Cecilia Prenz Kopušar prepared a facsimile edition of various of Laura Papo's plays, including this one, while in 2016 Eliezer Papo published an annotated scholarly edition of the play. For the purposes of this book, I have consulted the original manuscript kept in the Historijski arhiv Sarajeva under the classmark O-BP-168.

AS has no particular plot; it simply depicts a mother and her two daughters embroidering at home, the daughters all the while listening to the tales and ballads their mother is telling them. Ballads formed part of the everyday life of Sephardic women which was centred around the home and household chores. *AS* depicts just such a scene, and therefore the telling of ballads constitutes an important part of the play. In this way, Laura Papo provides an insight into one of the key places where the ballads were performed among the Sepharadim (in the home environment) and what they were used for (to entertain and to teach). The play represents an authentic *escena costumbrista* which contains the following elements taken from daily life:

— women in their domestic environment doing household chores;

— folk literature being transmitted orally (ballads and tales are being recited/sung aloud); and

— transmission of this literature from one generation to another (the mother is conveying age-old lore to her daughters).

Laura Papo's treatment of *Don Bueso y su hermana* (hereafter *Don Bueso*) is representative of how she uses the *romancero* as a base to create a folkloric *pastiche* which mixes elements of different kinds. In Laura Papo's work, this ballad becomes a tale in which the author introduces elements which are not found in the ballad. Two points can be discerned here. First, these newly added elements are described in great detail because the Sephardic audience, who knew the ballad well, was not familiar with them. And second, when Laura Papo introduces the ballad she does so partly in its poetic form, citing lines from it, and partly summarising it in prose. Although the text contains a number of folk motifs documented in Thompson's catalogue (1966), the end result is a fictitious tale which, as far as I have been able to ascertain, has not been recorded in any tradition.

Laura Papo's Re-Creation of *Don Bueso*: A Ballad Becomes a Tale

Don Bueso is a medieval Hispanic ballad which recounts the story of a Christian girl being kidnapped by the Muslims and taken into captivity, from which she was rescued years later by her own brother, even though they do not at first recognise each other. The starting point of the peninsular versions is usually years after the abduction when the brother comes across his sister washing clothes in the river or sea, which is then followed by her rescue and return home (Díaz-Mas 2005: 434–39).

The earliest references to the ballad have been documented from the fifteenth and sixteenth centuries and confirm that it most certainly dates to at least the late Middle Ages (Anahory Librowicz 1980: 40; Piñero Ramírez 2001: 111). In the oral tradition, the ballad still exists in its hexasyllabic form, which could explain why it was left out in the old chapbooks: 'El menosprecio de los recolectores del siglo XVI por los romances dodecasílabos explicaría la ausencia de fuentes antiguas impresas' (Anahory Librowicz 1980: 40). Furthermore, the fact that this ballad was very popular among the Sepharadim supports the theory of the ballad's medieval origins. The Sepharadim probably learned the ballad in Spain prior to their expulsion in 1492.[48] However, the possibility that *marrano* Jews who emigrated to the Ottoman Empire after the expulsion might have contributed this ballad to the corpus of Sephardic balladry cannot be ruled out.[49]

Ramón Menéndez Pidal (1956: 89–173) has demonstrated that its origins lie in the thirteenth-century Austrian epic *Kudrunslied*, a fact that has been confirmed by more recent studies (Anahory Librowicz 1980: 40; Piñero Ramírez 2001: 110–11; Pomeroy 2005: 235). According to Samuel G. Armistead and Joseph H. Silverman, the Austrian epic could have been introduced in Spain through the French *chanson* (1962: 62–65). Although the origin of the Spanish ballad lies outside of Spain, it was not long before it was adapted and domesticated to its new environment. This can be seen in the setting which depicts the frequent medieval frontier conflicts between Christians and Muslims in Iberia.[50]

As stated earlier, the peninsular versions usually omit the first episode which relates the abduction of the girl. The Sephardic versions, by contrast, tend to include this initial episode and the girl's misfortunate fate during her captivity: she is taken to the Islamic kingdom where she is given to the Queen who, jealous of her beauty and fearing that the King (or her son) might fall in love with her, condemns her to hard labour in order to tarnish her beauty (Pomeroy 2005: 236–39). Curiously, all these elements appear in *Kudrun* as well, which indicates that the Sephardic versions are more archaic and therefore closer to the Austrian source, preserving all the elements which have disappeared in the Spanish versions but which are described in the Austrian source.

Numerous examples collected in Bosnia indicate that *Don Bueso* was a very popular ballad fostered among the Sepharadim in that country (Armistead, Silverman and Šljivić-Šimšić 1971: 73–74; Armistead 1978: I, 269–76; III, 86–99). Therefore, it comes as no surprise that when Laura Papo decided to write a play which depicts the importance and the function of ballads in the everyday life of the Bosnian Sepharadim, as is the case of *AS*, she logically introduced *Don Bueso*.

But, unlike other ballads in the play which appear in their traditional form, here *Don Bueso* serves Laura Papo as a base on which to create a tale which she then enriches with additional elements. Further, the plot of the ballad is rendered partly as a narrative and partly as a poem.

This practice of converting a ballad plot into a tale is not an isolated case in the Sephardic or Hispanic cultures. Another example is that of the ballad *Delgadina*, P2, the story of a father who tries to seduce his daughter.[51] There are examples of this story being told as a tale rather than a ballad. Tamar Alexander-Frizer (2008: 350–52), for instance, interviewed Ester Levy, a Sephardic woman from Israel, who knew the ballad well. In addition to providing a version of the ballad, Levy also told her interviewer a narrative version of it. Although the story was amplified when told as a tale, no new relevant elements were added to the story and the tale summarises the events as depicted in the ballad.

This, however, is not the case with Laura Papo's tale. As stated above, the main characters of Laura Papo's play *AS* are a Mother and her two daughters, Sara and Rahela. They are depicted doing household chores, which allows for the introduction of folk literature as part of the everyday life of Sephardic women. To pass the time, the daughters ask their mother to tell them a tale: 'RAHELA Kontimos una kunseža, sintiendola, lavraremos kon mas gusto!' ('RAHELA Let's tell a story, listening to it will entertain us while we work') (*AS* fol. 3). *Konseža* or *kunseža* is the term that is used in the Judeo-Spanish speaking world to designate a folk tale (Díaz-Mas 2006: 172).

To make the story sound authentically Sephardic, the mother starts the tale with 'Avia de ser' ('Once upon a time'), a typical opening formula not only of Sephardic fairy tales but also of any type of folk tale (Alexander-Frizer 2008: 14–15). The story can be summarised in the following way: a beautiful girl, Sol, the only daughter of the Christian King and Queen, had two Muslim slaves, Zaide and Sultana. Every morning she went with them to wash her face in the garden well, decorated by her father with gold and silver. Carrying the barrel of rose and jasmine water, the slaves noticed the sapphires and emeralds covering it. One day Sol realised that the precious stones were missing. Although she suspected that the slaves had taken them, fearing they would be punished she chose to remain silent. Days later when Sol once again went to the well accompanied by her two slaves, she was suddenly seized roughly and abducted: the slaves had conspired with a fellow Muslim to kidnap her (L. Papo *AS* fols. 3–9).

In Laura Papo's version of the story, recounted by the mother to her daughters, the moment of the abduction marks a change in the mode of narration. Up until this point the story is told in prose. However, from this instant on, the story follows the plot of *Don Bueso*, the mother mixing prose and lines from the ballad as she tells the story in her own words: the *Moro* makes Sol his slave and takes her to his Queen who, fearing that her husband might take her as his mistress, forces Sol to do hard labour for seven years until one day she encounters a knight, i.e., her brother, who takes her with him. It is only when they arrive at their destination that the girl recognises the landscape and the knight realises that Sol is his lost sister and takes her to their parents (L. Papo *AS* fols 3–9).

Laura Papo creates here a tale by mixing elements from different sources, thus creating a narrative unrecorded in any tradition, Hispanic, Sephardic or Balkan, in a form such as this. The tale combines different folk motifs such as the evil maids (K2252), a princess being abducted (R10.1), a well made of precious stones (D1500.11.1), a girl being rescued from the place of her captivity (R111.2), a girl being rescued by her brother (R166). Other elements such as the meeting at the river or the sea, the captive girl washing clothes, concern over the girl's honour, the recognition of brother and sister, the arrival of a daughter instead of a daughter-in-law, which all appear in the ballad, represent frequent motifs found in traditional poetry.[52] This use of folk literature shows that Laura Papo did not limit herself to merely reproducing the text of oral literature in the form with which she was familiar. She also reinterpreted it, thereby creating something new.

From the outset, the tale establishes a series of contrasts on various levels: social, religious and moral. Social opposition is reflected in the status of the characters. Sol is a princess whereas Zaide and Sultania are at the same time maids and slaves. The difference between these characters is also established through their religion: Sol is Christian while Zaide and Sultania are Muslims. This is not only clearly stated in the tale but is also indicated by their names. Likewise, the story establishes the differences in personality between these characters based on their religion. Sol is not only beautiful but, being Christian, she is blessed with virtues such as generosity, goodness and perseverance. Both maids, by contrast, are depicted as envious, greedy, selfish and evil. This differentiation between Christians and Muslims is further developed in the depiction of the treatment Sol is exposed to in the Muslim kingdom, particularly the way the Muslim Queen treats her.

It is highly probable that Laura Papo gave the name of Sol to the protagonist in her narrative version of *Don Bueso* drawing from another narrative poem known among the Sepharadim as *Sol la Sadicca* ('Sol, the Saint'). The latter recounts the true story of Sol Hachuel, who in 1834 was decapitated by the order of the Moroccan Sultan for alleged apostasy from Islam (see Vance 2011). The name of a true historical figure is thus preserved for posterity.

In *Sol la Sadicca*, the protagonist is depicted as a heroine who is sentenced to death for refusing to renounce her Jewish religion and convert to Islam so that she can marry a Muslim King (see Anahory-Librowicz 1988: 97–98 n. 40; 98–100 n. 41; Alexander 2004). Thus, the poem shares an important point with *Don Bueso*: a non-Muslim female protagonist who shows resilience to Muslim rule and emerges from the conflict as a moral winner. In *Don Bueso*, the Christian main character is rescued and returns to her family and her homeland; in *Sol la Sadicca*, the Jewish protagonist, although sentenced to death, is seen as victorious for not succumbing under pressure and staying firm in her beliefs.

Although *Sol la Saddica* is rooted in the Moroccan Sephardic tradition, the story itself circulated in the East in the Sephardic press where it was published as a novel recounting the aforesaid event of the nineteenth century. Thus, Laura Papo could very well have been familiar with the story of Sol.

The temporal setting of Laura Papo's tale is the same as in *Don Bueso*: the action takes place in medieval frontier Iberia. As in other versions of the ballad, Granada appears as the place of birth of the princess. This Andalusi city became a common reference in many frontier ballads. As Díaz-Mas underscores:

> Entre los romances viejos que los sefardíes llevaron en su bagaje cultural hacia el exilio había un puñado de temas fronterizos en los que la mención de la ciudad andalusí [Granada] no era infrecuente. Además, en los decenios inmediatos posteriores a la Expulsión — durante los cuales el aislamiento de los judíos con respecto a la Península no fue, como sabemos, tan absoluto que impidiese la llegada de noticias y textos de la literatura española del momento — se desarrolló con vigor la moda del Romancero morisco, en muchos de cuyos textos se menciona *Granada* como escenario tópico. (1989: 191)[53]

The idea of maintaining the time and place of the ballad has significance for the Sepharadim: it evokes the time when they were living in Spain and thus contains an element of nostalgia. At the same time, the mention of Granada reminds the Sepharadim that 1492, the year in which the Christians reconquered Granada from the Muslims, was also the year the Jews were expelled from Spain.

The tale does not contain elements of judaisation: the characters are Muslims who are orientalised and Christians depicted as virtuous.[54] This was achieved through the introduction of elements hitherto unseen in the ballad: the good-hearted character of Sol, who loves her slaves as if they were her sisters and protects them from punishment, whereas the maids are represented as evil. Furthermore, Laura Papo's characters from the play, the daughters listening to their Mother telling the tale, seem to identify themselves with the Christians from the ballad. This is evident from the message the Mother is trying to convey to her daughters and the daugthers' reaction to it. She tells them the tale not only to entertain them but also to warn them not to trust people, particulary men. In this ballad, this danger comes from *Moros*: 'SARA No se spante por mozotros, mana!; RAHELA Mozotros no bivimos en tiera de Moros!' ('SARA Don't you worry about us, mom!; RAHELA We don't live in the land of *Moros*!'). From this it can be inferred that the daughters identify with the Christians, particularly with the female protagonist.

This episode in Laura Papo's play indicates the function folk literature had among the Sepharadim: the elderly tell stories or ballads to young people to entertain them and to educate them. Here, in addition, both the performance and the reception were limited to the female environment. I shall examine these points in more detail in the following section, where I analyse Davičo's and Laura Papo's treatment of another Hispanic ballad, *Landarico*.

3. *Landarico* in the Works of Davičo and Laura Papo

Both Davičo and Laura Papo deploy the same ballad in their work.[55] This ballad of Hispanic origin is known among scholars as *Landarico*. The topic of the ballad is female infidelity: it is the story of a queen who is punished for committing adultery. The numerous versions collected attest to the great popularity this ballad enjoyed among the Sepharadim.[56] Further proof of this is that each of these two Sephardic authors from the former Yugoslavia makes use of this ballad on more than one occasion.

Davičo uses the ballad in 'Naumi' (1883), the first tale he wrote about the Sephardic community in Belgrade, and in the last, 'Buena' (1913). In Laura Papo's case, this ballad appears as a part of her play, *Avia de ser* (*AS*), and in her essay, *La mužer sefardi de Bosna.* The interpretation of the ballad and the Sephardic context in which this *romance* was set differ with each author. Davičo's and Laura Papo's interpretations of *Landarico,* which derive directly from the tradition, confirm Diego Catalán's theory of a ballad being an open system:

> El romance tradicional es un sistema abierto (no un organismo o estructura cerrada), tanto verbalmente, como poéticamente, como temáticamente, y su evolución depende de la adaptación de ese sistema abierto o subsistema (poema) al ambiente, al sistema lingüístico, estético y ético del grupo humano en que se canta, en que se reproduce. El cambio es claramente ecosistématico. (1972: 205)

The survival of medieval Spanish ballads such as *Landarico* among the Sepharadim nearly up to the present day has been possible precisely because these ballads have received different interpretations at different times and in different places. They were adapted in order to better fit the social, cultural and psychological needs of those who fostered them. In other words, if ballads had not had anything to convey to the Sepharadim, they would have stopped transmitting and performing them.

The first point I aim to analyse here concerns the interpretation and role this *romance* had among the Serbian and Bosnian Sepharadim — as seen in the works of these two authors — while underscoring a specific context linked to this ballad. The specificity of the treatment of this ballad by Davičo and Laura Papo has its roots in the folk tradition of the Bosnian and Serbian Sephardic communities respectively. This point will be highlighted in contrast with other Sephardic communities as well as Hispanic tradition.

The second point concerns the manner in which these two authors use elements of folk literature (in this case, a ballad) for the purposes of their own literary works. *Landarico* appears in both authors in its unchanged traditional form (in part or in full) but set within the plot of the main work of each author. Davičo renders the ballad into Serbian. Laura Papo, by contrast, introduces it in its original language, Judeo-Spanish.

Two main goals can be discerned behind the decision of these authors to use oral literature in this way. The first was to collect and save valuable folk material and prompt its continued dissemination through a written source. Up until then, this literature was kept alive exclusively through oral transmission. The second goal was to use these existing forms of folk literature to reinforce the main idea of their own works. This is achieved by drawing a parallel between the folklore conveyed in these literary forms and the main idea of their own stories, conveyed through the fate of their characters.

This treatment of folk literature encompasses several features of relevance here as it reveals diverse facts of cultural importance. For example, Davičo stresses the occasions on which some ballads were sung in his (Sephardic) community and how they were perceived by their listeners. Laura Papo, on the other hand, depicts how ballads were performed among the Bosnian Sepharadim and for what they were used.

I shall start with peninsular versions of *Landarico* for an obvious reason: this is a medieval Spanish ballad, and the Sepharadim initially learned it before abandoning the Peninsula. It is first necessary to explain the original meaning of the ballad, the condemnation of adulteresses and thereby women, in order to appreciate the changes the ballad underwent, as found in the examples collected from among the Sephardic communities of Serbia and Bosnia. These changes, which are reflected in the treatment of the ballad by Davičo and Laura Papo, are a result of the dynamic and fluid nature of the oral discourse which 'presumes variation on all levels — transformations which, when seen collectively, represent diverse re-workings of the ballad material by the ballad transmitters' (Catarella 1990: 332). In this connection, I intend to examine *Landarico* and the way it was deployed by Davičo and Laura Papo as a 'female cultural expression, i.e. as functioning through and for women' (Catarella 1990: 332). Likewise, I shall use the differences in the perception of the ballad's plot in the works of these two authors to show that gendered performances and versions can also be unstable and thus allow for different potential viewpoints and identifications.

The material used in the case of the Iberian tradition includes the oldest extant version of the ballad from the sixteenth century and some twentieth-century versions collected throughout Spain and Portugal. In the case of Sephardic tradition, special emphasis will be placed upon versions of the ballad from Bosnia and Serbia (most of which are kept in the Fundación Ramón Menéndez Pidal, Madrid). Versions from other Sephardic communities will also be taken into account (Armistead, Silverman and Anahory Librowicz 1977: 124–25; Benmayor 1979: 68–77; Anahory Librowicz 1980: 61–64). All examples collected from among the Sepharadim date either from the late nineteenth or the twentieth century.

Therefore, the comparison will include both synchronic and diachronic analysis. Its aim is to point out the originality and uniqueness of the Sephardic versions used by Davičo and Laura Papo (and hence the Serbian and Bosnian Sephardic communities) compared to the Iberian tradition and other Sephardic communities.

Landarico in the Peninsular Tradition

The only known Spanish version of *Landarico* prior to modern times is the sixteenth-century version found in the chapbook collection of the National Library of Prague.[57] However, this ballad has almost certainly existed since the Middle Ages. The fact that the Sepharadim, who left Spain in 1492, knew the ballad well indicates its existence in the Iberian tradition before that date.

In modern times, only a few versions have been collected in Spain and Portugal. Rina Benmayor (1979: 72–73) published a version compiled by Gonzalo Menéndez Pidal in 1926 in Bohoyo (Ávila) from forty-three-year-old Eustaquia González.[58] In the Fundación Ramón Menéndez Pidal in Madrid, I have consulted two more versions: one collected by Ramón Menéndez Pidal from fifty-four-year-old Rosario González, also from Bohoyo, and the other collected by Jenaro Ramos Hernández in 1905 in Torrejoncillo (Cáceres). The name of the informant of the latter appears merely as La Jermosa. Paul Bénichou (1968: 104–05) cites the existence (not the texts) of more versions collected by Menéndez Pidal and his wife María Goyri. However, I have not been able to consult the file containing these versions as its whereabouts are unknown. With regard to Portuguese tradition, I have looked at a version from Baçal collected and published by Francisco Manuel Alves (1938: 562) and one from Vinhais compiled and published by Firmino A. Martins (1938: 22–23).[59]

In order to facilitate the identification of different ballad-types, both Hispanic and pan-Hispanic ballads were accorded certain reference numbers in various catalogues. Thus in Catalán's *Catálogo general del romancero pan-hispánico*, *Landarico* appears as item TITU0426 (1984: 1, 233).[60] Armistead classifies the Sephardic versions of the ballad as M8 (1978: II, 64–73). Manuel da Costa Fontes, who looks at balladry tradition in Portuguese, maintains the same letter as Armistead, which is used by both to designate various ballads about the adulteress, but assigns it a different number: M4 (1997: 1, 179–80).

The events depicted in the ballad are based on a historical event: the tragic death of King Chilperic I (539–584). The latter was killed by an unknown assassin while returning from hunting one evening in Chelles. The murderer disappeared in the night and was never found (Armand 2008: 181–207). Curiously, in the eyes of the King's subjects, his wife Fredegund and her lover Landri were guilty of killing the King. This interpretation not only became part of oral tradition but was also disseminated by medieval chronicles which added further information to the story that thus far has not been acknowledged as historical fact (Armand 2008: 182–84).

A case in point are two Latin medieval chronicles, the anonymous *Gesta regum francorum* (c. 1100) and *De gestis francorum* by the monk Aimoin Floriacense (c. 960–c. 1010), which recount the event in the following way: One day, King Chilperic enters the Queen's chambers and finds her taking a bath. Taking her unawares, he approaches her from behind and strikes her with a stick. The Queen, convinced it is her lover who is joking with her, says imprudently: 'Quare sic facis Landarice' ('What are you doing, Landri?'), only to discover that it is the King and not her paramour who is standing behind her. The King leaves her chambers without uttering a word. Terrified of possible punishment, the Queen sends for her lover, who shows remorse for having been involved with the Queen: 'Tam mala hora te viderunt oculi mei' ('I curse the moment when I set my eyes on you'). However, Fredegund composes herself and suggests killing the King. Upon his return from hunting, the King is assassinated by the Queen's accomplices and she and her lover spread the rumour that the killer is the King's nephew, the sovereign of Austrasia (Menéndez Pelayo 1916: XII, 489–91; Armand 2008: 183–84).[61]

There are two reasons why Menéndez y Pelayo cites both chronicles as possible sources for the Hispanic ballad: they both precede the ballad, and the similarity between the way the event is portrayed in these works and the sixteenth-century Hispanic ballad suggests that the origins of the latter are to be found in an erudite source (1916: XII, 488–92). This has been confirmed by later studies of *Landarico* (Bénichou 1968: 103–04; Vidaković-Petrov 1990: 166–69 and Díaz-Mas 2005: 295). The sixteenth-century ballad contains the same facts as the chronicles discussed. All the events depicted in it occur in the same way: the King surprises the Queen;

mistaking him for her lover, she unwittingly reveals her adultery: 'Está quedo, Landarico' (Díaz-Mas 2005: 296); the King leaves without uttering a word; the Queen seeks help from her lover; the latter expresses remorse for having become involved with her: 'En mal punto y en mala hora | mis ojos te han mirado' (Díaz-Mas 2005: 296); nonetheless, the Queen convinces him of the necessity of having the King killed, a deed they carry out; in the end, the lovers go unpunished (Díaz-Mas 2005: 295–97). This denouement of the ballad goes against the norms of oral tradition in which such guilty parties are exposed to condemnation and punishment, especially in the case of an adulteress. Moreover, this ending to the events is another indication that the old version of the *romance* was most probably based on written sources.

The name of the lover that appears in Latin texts is Landaricus. This, again according to Menéndez y Pelayo, eliminates French texts as the possible source for the Spanish ballad since French *juglares* had changed the name to Landri or Landrix (1916: XII, 492). It is curious to note that the story of a queen who commits adultery is known among scholars not by her name but by that of her lover, Landarico. The reason is that the name of the Queen (as well as the King), which appears in Latin texts, was omitted in the ballad even though she is the central figure of the story. She is addressed only by her royal title. It is solely the name of the lover that has been preserved. This can be seen in the sixteenth-century version, where he is called Landarico. In twentieth-century versions, the Queen continues to be nameless whereas the lover is still referred to as Landarico (or some close form of that name).

This ballad, like so many others, has survived the test of time, and in the twentieth century a number of versions have been collected in Spain (Catalonia, Castile and Extremadura) and Portugal (Piñero Ramírez 2008: 395). This number, however, is not so great in comparison with the number of Sephardic versions compiled both in North Africa and the Eastern Mediterranean. This ballad was to gain more popularity in the Sephardic diaspora than it had in Spain judging by the number of versions collected.

The examples from the Iberian Peninsula show how the oral tradition has introduced new elements and changes to the plot of the ballad over the course of centuries. In modern Iberian versions — that is, in those from the twentieth century — two novelties can be discerned compared to how the story was depicted in the Latin chronicles or the sixteenth-century ballad. The first is the mention of children. When the Queen reveals her adultery, she also reveals that two of her sons were fathered by her lover and that she bestows upon them more privileged treatment:

> Los del rey visten de seda, | los tuyos seda y bordado;
> los del rey gastan espada, | los tuyos puñal dorado;
> los del rey montan en mula | y los tuyos a caballo;
> los del rey comen en mesa | y los tuyos a mi lado.
>   (Díaz-Mas 2005: 298)

The question arises as to how such an open favouring of some of her children over the others could have gone unnoticed. In my view, this element was clearly introduced to intensify the Queen's guilt. She is not only an adulteress, but she is also depicted as a bad mother who attempts to secure better treatment for her illegitimate children than for her legitimate ones, thus inverting what was traditionally imposed by law as expressed in *Las siete partidas* by Alfonso the Learned (Burns 2001: IV, 948–55). This reference to her children and the unequal treatment they receive appears in both Spanish and pan-Hispanic versions of the ballad, which leads Benmayor (1979: 74) to conclude that it must have formed part of the peninsular ballad before the Jews had left Spain.

The second novelty concerns the denouement of the ballad. In the sixteenth-century version, the Queen and her lover elude punishment by killing the King. The modern versions, by contrast, make sure that the guilty parties receive their due: once the affair has been revealed, they are both sentenced to death. This ending is more in keeping with the code of ethics prevalent in Hispanic balladry, in which the death penalty for the adulteress is almost a *sine qua non*: 'Only the terrible retribution with which the adulteress is threatened — if not actually punished — rings true to Hispanic balladry's inexorable judicial code' (Armistead and Silverman 1971: 223). With this solution to the events, the ballad seeks to assert male authority and convey a clear didactic message that adultery committed by a woman warrants strict punishment.

Landarico in the Sephardic Tradition

Landarico is one of the most popular ballads fostered among the Sepharadim both in the former Ottoman Empire and in North Africa. The Sephardic tradition has remained faithful to the peninsular interpretation of the ballad in most aspects. The Queen is sentenced to death by beheading, a well-known folk motif (Q421.0.2) and thus the typical punishment reserved for an adulteress in folk literature.[62] The recognition of male authority is thereby clearly emphasised.

The differences consist of adding more details in the description of the privileges the lover's sons enjoy and the omission of the figure of the lover. The latter is only mentioned in the words of the Queen when she imprudently reveals her secret, but he does not participate in the development of the plot. The main idea focuses on the adulteress being punished, thus confirming the aforementioned didactic role of the ballad: '–– Perdón, perdón, siñor el rey, | esfueño lo ha pasado. | El rey esvainó su espada, | la caveza le cortava ('–– Pardon, pardon, Sir King, | it was a dream. | The King unsheathed his sword, | her head he cut off') (Benmayor 1979: 69 n. 6c). This is what Teresa Catarella defines as the mythic move in the narrative trajectory of the ballad, in which the primary linguistic and thematic relationships are solved according to the conventional archetypes of the patriarchy (1990: 340).

This, however, was not the case of Bosnian and Serbian versions of the ballad in which the lover plays an active part and appears in dialogues. As a result, *Landarico* receives a different interpretation in the works of Davičo and Laura Papo which reflects the changes that these two Sephardic communities had introduced to the plot and the function of the ballad.

Landarico in the Works of Davičo

Davičo uses *Landarico* on two occasions, in his tales 'Naumi' and 'Buena'. All Davičo's tales about the Sephardic community of Belgrade have as a title the name of a female protagonist. This indicates that the emphasis is on Sephardic women and their position in the Sephardic culture. Davičo's use of *Landarico* is closely related to this idea.

As a child, Davičo was exposed to various forms of Sephardic folk literature. According to Alkalaj, the ballad tradition in particular left a strong impact on him as he frequently saw them being performed: 'Još detetom [Davičo] slušao je u kući svoga dede, čuvenog ćir-Haima Daviča, anegdote i priče iz prošlosti mahalske i uživao u romacama i baladama koje su na španskom, na čuvenim *tajfas* (večerinke) izvijale razne *tijas* Mirjame, Blanke i druge' ('During his childhood, he [Davičo] had had the opportunity, in the home of his grandfather — the renowned Mr. Haim Davičo — to listen to anecdotes and tales from Yalia's past and enjoy Spanish ballads and songs at the legendary *tajfas* (evening gatherings) performed by different *tijas* by the names of Mirjam, Blanka or the like') (1925: 80).

In Alkalaj's account, it is evident that it was women who performed ballads, that they were the guardians of balladry and transmitters of the legacy. Davičo also pointed out that it was a *tija* who was the source of his tale *Ženske šale*, thereby bolstering the point of female transmission and the fact that most informants of folk literature among the Sepharadim are, in fact, women.[63] Since ballads formed an inseparable part of the Sephardic culture and everyday life, Davičo could not write about his community without taking them into account. The function played by ballads among the Sepharadim is skillfully illustrated in Davičo's use of *Landarico*.

I shall start with 'Buena' as here more emphasis is given to *Landarico*, which appears in its complete form. The ballad was rendered into Serbian with a couple of verses in Judeo-Spanish at the very end. In his other tale, 'Naumi', Davičo only makes a reference to the ballad through quoting two lines in Judeo-Spanish, which he also translates to Serbian to ensure that the readers understand the message. Since *Landarico* is unknown in Serbian culture, Serbian readers might otherwise have been unable to make the link between the meaning of the two lines and the fate of Davičo's characters. I aim to highlight the meaning of the ballad as it appears in Davičo and how the ballad connects to the main idea of his tales.

At the heart of 'Buena' lies an emotional story of two young couples in love: David and Reina on the one hand, and Rufo and Buena on the other hand. These young people long to spend their lives together, but they are confronted by the opposition of their families. In his story, Davičo depicts these family and social conflicts, which seem to constitute an insurmountable obstacle to the realisation of the couples' love.

These conflicts emerge from the changes that the Sephardic community is experiencing and which divide the community into two factions: those who defend traditional values at all costs, which implies children obeying their parents' wishes, and those who are trying to follow the pace of the times by allowing their children to make their own choices. This conflict is, for example, portrayed in the scene in which Juda, Buena's father, goes to see his brother Haim, in order to arrange a marriage of convenience between his daughter and Haim's son, David. Juda insists on the marriage taking place in spite of the fact that Buena and David are not in love with each other. His brother Haim, nonetheless, defends a more open and modern view on the subject: 'Veridba je stvar dopadanja dvoje mladih. Roditelji mogu tu da savetuju, ali ne treba da prisiljuju i nameću' ('Engagement is a matter of two people sharing feelings for each other. Parents can offer their advice on this matter but they shouldn't force or impose their will') (Davičo 2000: 98).

Davičo very cleverly uses the obstacles that these young people are facing to highlight the conflicts within the Sephardic community as it is poised between old and new values, between East and West: 'I zbilja, u mahali beše od nekog vremena nastupio prevrat. Evropski duh poče istiskivati istočnjački' ('And indeed, a change has been coming to the neighbourhood for some time. The [Western] European spirit began replacing the Oriental one') (Davičo 2000: 107).

Davičo's attitude of open-mindedness, which is evident in his writing, defines his position in this conflict. All four of his tales about the Sephardic community in Belgrade include a love plot, usually with a tragic denouement. This is owing to the situation of women in traditional societies, such as the Sephardic one, in which their life choices were determined by the wishes and expectations of men — that is, their fathers or husbands.[64] Davičo's attitude in favour of individual freedom of choice is seen in the way he portrays his female characters, showing great sympathy and comprehension for their situation. In keeping with this idea, he uses *Landarico* to show that the lack of freedom of choice usually results in a tragic ending as depicted in the ballad.

The moment Davičo chooses to introduce *Landarico* in his tale is very suggestive. The community is commemorating the Ninth of Av. This day in the Jewish calendar marks the memory of the destruction of both the First and Second Temple in Jerusalem. Over the course of time, other tragedies were added to the commemoration of this day; for example, the expulsion of the Jews from Spain in 1492 was one of them (Danon 1996: 69). However, a tragedy of a personal nature could also be associated with it. Thus *romances de endechar* (lament ballads) came to form part of a rich repertoire of texts performed for this day:

> Para aumentar el ambiente de general tristeza es costumbre reunirse a entonar cantos tristes, ya sean los poemas paralitúrgicos relativos a la caída de Jerusalén (quinot), ya las endechas que vienen a recordar a los difuntos de cada familia, ya cualquier otro cantar triste que narre un hecho desgraciado y sea capaz de conmover a los oyentes; y entre estos cantares tristes se incluyen un buen número de *romances*. (Díaz-Mas 1981: 100)

This atmosphere of sadness and melancholy proved to be ideal for Tija Mirjam, one of the secondary characters of this tale, to sing ballads which in their core recount the tragic destiny of young women about to marry men they do not love. But how does *Landarico* fit into this idea of doomed love? And why would the Belgrade Sepharadim, according to Davičo, have associated the ballad about adultery with the Ninth of Av?

Landarico is clearly known both in Spain and in Sephardic communities, with the exception of those of Serbia and Bosnia, as a ballad that condemns adultery and punishes the adulteress. This constitutes the main message conveyed by the twentieth-century versions. In addition, the ballad contains several aspects which depict the female protagonist as not only an unfaithful wife but also a bad mother, who shows no compunction in treating some of her children better than others depending on who their father is.

In Davičo's interpretation, by contrast, the Queen's actions are understood differently, and they are therefore perceived with more understanding and empathy. The ballad becomes a story of an unhappy or miserable woman who had to renounce her true (first) love to marry a man she did not love: 'Estáte, estáte, Anderlino, | tú mi primer namorado' ('Be still, be still, Anderlino | my first love') (Benmayor 1979: 68 n. 6a). The excuse for the Queen's behaviour is to be found precisely in the fact that she was not allowed to marry her first love. The moral message therefore points in a different direction: the ballad works as a symbol of resistance against prearranged marriages which force young women to marry against their will. By writing about young people who cannot fulfill their love for the same reason, Davičo's tale also embodies a criticism of the negation of free will.

We have no information about whether Davičo collected the ballad from the community or if it came from memories of his childhood. Its content does not differ from most Sephardic versions: in keeping with the code of ethics the adulteress is punished for her actions. But it is the reaction of those who are listening to the ballad, particularly the two young couples who are fighting the opposition of their parents, which reveals the perception of the ballad as seen in Davičo:

> Nesrećna sudba junakinje balade izmamljivaše suze, uzdahe i jecanja. Junakinje i junaci ove priče [David, Reina, Rufo and Buena] ćutahu, ne jecahu niti uzdisahu, ali srca njihova setna ali presretna, kucahu silno i zaklinjahu se da ih nikakva sila neće rastaviti... (Davičo 2000: 105–06)

> (The tragic fate of the ballad's protagonist provoked tears, sighs and moans. The heroes and heroines of this tale [David, Reina, Rufo and Buena] kept silent, they didn't moan or sigh but their sad yet joyful hearts were beating hard and they swore that no fate would separate them...)

The reaction is one of empathy and understanding for the Queen's actions and sadness for her fate. The characters of Davičo's tale identify themselves and their fate with that of the Queen as they fear that they, too, will be forced to renounce their true loves. Davičo's exploration of alternative narratives and representation of the Queen being contemplated as victim corresponds to the 'unconscious rejection of patriarchal codes but the conscious pseudo-adherence to them' (Catarella 1990: 341).

As noted, the ballad, according to Davičo's account, is performed for the Ninth of Av. The link between this ballad and *Tish'ah be'ab* emerged thanks to this different interpretation of the ballad's events which depicts the adulteress as a victim of circumstances rather than a transgressor. Her tragic fate, coerced as she is into renouncing her true love and marrying someone else, followed by her terrible punishment (beheading) for keeping that love alive in spite of being married, links the Queen's story perfectly to this day which commemorates national and personal tragedies. Without this change in the perception of the female character, this ballad would have no place within this Jewish holy day.

Davičo rightly calls this ballad Spanish, thus indicating its origin. But the usage and the place it received among the Sepharadim from Belgrade, as described by Davičo, show how the ballad was domesticated by the Spanish Jews. By giving it a different meaning and by associating it with the Ninth of Av, the ballad underwent a process of cultural adaptation to its environment. In other words, the ballad was judaised. There are reasons to think that Davičo's account of this ballad derives from oral sources. The fact that he links the ballad to the Ninth of Av in two different tales leads me to believe that he was documenting elements of oral tradition in his community rather than adapting the ballad to the needs of the plot of his tales. There are other examples in the Sephardic tradition similar to *Landarico*. One of them is *Parto en tierras lejas*, L2, which only in the Bosnian Sephardic tradition became a lament sung for the Ninth of Av (L. Papo 2005: 157 and Vidaković-Petrov 2014: 318).

This new understanding of the ballad fits perfectly within the plot of Davičo's tale in which young couples struggle against the pressure of traditional values to preserve their love. Davičo underlines the similarity between the Queen's fate in the ballad and that of his own characters. The ballad adds force to the Sephardic context in which the plot of Davičo's tale unfolds. At the same time, it shows the role that folklore played in the everyday life of the Sepharadim.

In 'Naumi', written thirty years before the publication of 'Buena', *Landarico* is used for the first time. On that occasion, Davičo introduces only two lines from the ballad, which were sufficient for him to convey his message to prospective readers. The tale's plot revolves around a tragic love story between Naumi, a young Sephardic girl, and her sweetheart, David. In spite of the love they feel for each other, these two people are unable to be together because Naumi's parents have chosen another suitor for their daughter: a rich Jewish man from another Serbian city. In desperation, Naumi attempts suicide to avoid the destiny that awaits her, only to fail. She eventually dies of grief, thus underlining just how tragic the consequences of taking traditional customs to the extreme can be.

The tale again takes place during the Ninth of Av. By setting the plot of his tale then, Davičo hints at a tragic outcome of the story. Once again he links the fate of his character, in this case Naumi, and the Queen from the ballad with this day of mourning in Jewish tradition. However, this time Davičo uses the ballad in a slightly different way.

As stated above, Naumi's parents choose a wealthy man as the ideal husband for their daughter and force her to marry him. To oppose the idea of wealth being the deciding factor when choosing a spouse, Davičo quotes these two lines from the ballad: 'Mas te quero, mas te amo | que al rey con su fonsado' ('I care for you, I love you more | than I love the King with all his wealth') (Davičo 2000: 33). This is the moment in the ballad when the Queen expresses her feelings for her lover without realising that the King is standing behind her. The meaning of these lines, as shown above, is to underscore that true feelings are more valuable than material wealth. Davičo provides a Serbian translation of the lines and clarifies the link between the ballad and the plot of his own tale by rendering the word *fonsado* meaning the king's guards or army as the king's wealth or treasure.

These lines were not included in the version of the ballad which Davičo introduces in 'Buena'. Although in the latter tale the main idea is also to underline that young people should not be forced to marry against their will, there is no reference whatsoever to this conflict of material values versus true love. In 'Buena', the confrontation is between traditional and modern values and hence these lines would not have the same functional role there as they do here. In 'Naumi', Davičo draws a clear parallel between the main character of the ballad, the Queen, and Naumi, the protagonist of his tale. Both characters reject material values and try to overcome the circumstances imposed upon them, each in her own way. Hence they are seen as victims who long for something they cannot achieve.

The lines quoted do not appear in any of the Spanish or Sephardic versions of the ballad that I have been able to consult. However, similar verses can be found in the Portuguese version from Baçal: 'mais te quero, Andarilho, | do qu'ó rei com ser coroado' (I love you more Andarilho, | than I love the King with his crown') (Alves 1938: 562), suggesting that this version belongs to the same tradition as Davičo's. The fact that Davičo introduces two different versions of *Landarico* in his tales is, in my view, a clear indication that they derive from two different sources.

In summary, on two occasions Davičo turns to *Landarico* to draw similarities between its content and that of his tales. This is a ballad which condemns adultery as an act that goes against family values. But in Davičo's interpretation, it becomes a story where the condemned protagonist is contemplated with more understanding and sympathy. Here the Queen is perceived more as a victim of circumstances for having to renounce her true love and marry someone else. Davičo uses this idea to draw parallels between the ballad's plot and the destiny of his own characters. Thus, his use of *Landarico* serves to support the main idea of his own tales.

Landarico in the Works of Laura Papo

Laura Papo knew *Landarico* well as she herself was a transmitter of this *romansa* (Judeo-Spanish for ballad). When interviewed by Manrique de Lara, she recited this ballad precisely. Furthermore, like Davičo, she made use of it in two of her own works: in *Avia de ser* (*AS*), and in *La mužer sefardi de Bosna*. However, she introduces the ballad in its original language, Judeo-Spanish, unlike Davičo, who renders it in Serbian.

In Laura Papo's *AS*, *Landarico* is used to initiate discussion between the main characters of the play, a mother and daughters, regarding the interpretation of the events depicted in the ballad. The ballad is here performed by a woman for a female audience in a typically female context (performing household chores in the home). The sex of the performer and recipients and the performance context legitimise women's interpretation of the events described, in addition to exemplifying the didactic and entertaining purposes of ballads.

The first ballad in the play is *Don Bueso*. But rather than singing, the mother tells it to her daughters as a tale. Hence *Landarico* is the first ballad to appear in Laura Papo's play in its traditional form — that is, in lines which are sung. We know that the ballad was sung during the performance of the play for several reasons. First, Laura Papo's plays were usually commissioned by the Sephardic community to be performed on a particular occasion. Laura Papo's sisters were given the roles of playing the piano, singing ballads and dancing. Second, the manuscript indicates that some lines of the ballad, such as [the King] 'Topo la reina en kavejos, | ke a penjar se los ija [*sic*]' ('[the King] Came upon the Queen with her hair down, | getting ready to brush it') (*AS* fol. 9), were to be sung twice; or there is a stage direction indicating *kanta* ('singing') (*AS* fol. 9). Finally, the characters of the play, the daughters, encourage their mother to sing: 'SARA Agora mos va kantar la [romansa] de Andarleto' ('SARA Why don't you sing us now the one about Andarleto') (*AS* fol. 9).

The last quotation reveals two facts: first, the ballad was also known among Spanish Jews by the name of the lover, which in Sephardic versions is not Landarico but Andarleto. This was the most widely spread name of the lover among the Sepharadim (Armistead 1978: II, 64; III, 331). In addition, within the play, both daughters make comments indicating that they knew the ballad well because they had obviously heard it before: 'RAHELA Akea romansa dela reina ke enganjo al marido' ('RAHELA That ballad about the Queen who deceived her husband') (*AS* fol. 9). Rahela's and Sara's request for this ballad could suggest that the ballad must have been frequently sung among the Bosnian Sepharadim and thus was well known to the audience.

The mother proceeds to sing the ballad. The daughters listen to her carefully. The verses go up to the point when the Queen imprudently reveals that she has a lover. Unaware that the King is standing behind her, she adds that two of her sons are her lover's and the other two the King's. This is the moment when the mother ceases singing and then summarises the rest of the ballad's plot in her own words: the Queen turns around and sees her husband and knows that for this fatal indiscretion she is going to die (*AS* fols 9–10).

The daughters immediately express empathy with the Queen and her fate: 'RAHELA Tristi di ea, kruel negro, otraves no kalio ke la mate' ('RAHELA Poor her, what a cruel man; still she didn't deserve to be killed') (*AS* fol. 10). So does the mother, thus underlining that women are weak emotionally: 'LA MADRE I el korason de la mužer es siempre flako' ('MOTHER And a woman's heart is always weak') (*AS* fol. 10). But the latter makes sure that her daughters understand that the Queen got her due at the end. This reinforces the original idea of the ballad that adultery is wrong and warrants punishment: 'LA MADRE Luke buško — akeo topo' ('MOTHER She got what she deserved') (*AS* fol. 10).

Sara, one of the daughters, attempts to defend the Queen by saying that her only crime is having been in love: 'SARA I si namoro, mira tu fečos agora' ('SARA But she only fell in love and look what happened') (*AS* fol. 10). Her mother is quick to reply and point out that if a woman is married, and especially if she has children, she should not seek a lover: 'LA MADRE Onde vites tu mužer kazada, afižada —

namorarse, ni si vea ni si sienta!' ('MOTHER Where did you see a married woman with children — fall in love, such a travesty is unthinkable!') (*AS* fol. 10). So far, the ballad contains no new elements which would alter how it was widely understood.

However, unlike most versions, in the Bosnian tradition, the ballad does not end here. An addition at the end changes its perception. The ballad ends at the exact place in the narrative most likely to incorporate or to openly express the ideology of the singer about the topic of the ballad as highlighted by Catalán: 'Más notables aún son las modificaciones que se producen al final del romance. Según suele ocurrir, la adaptación del poema al sistema ético y estético de la sociedad en que se canta se manifiesta sobre todo en la inestabilidad del desenlace' (1972: 193). Catarella (1990: 340) also underscores this fact. After having examined two ballad-types, *La vuelta del marido* and *Albaniña*, the theme of the latter also dealing with the unfaithful wife, Catarella emphasises the instability and the ambivalence of the versions, particularly in their endings, even when the performers are only women.

So when the Queen is condemned to death, the audience (here the daughters) is expected to sympathise with the King (Vidaković-Petrov 2014: 325). The Queen has not only betrayed her husband but she has also favoured the children she has had by her lover. Why then do the daughters express their compassion for the Queen?

A ballad's content (and its main idea) can be modified by either replacing or adding/omitting elements (Catalán 1972: 192). In the case of *Landarico*, in the Bosnian Sephardic tradition, the shift was carried out through an addition. The female singers of this ballad introduced not one but two significant additions compared to other Iberian or Sephardic versions, a fact of which Laura Papo was well aware. These additions change the interpretation of the ballad's ending.

The mother ends the story of the ballad by including two more lines illustrating the dialogue the Queen is conducting with her lover. After realising that she is going to be punished for her adultery, the Queen summons her lover for help. But he replies: 'Para mi topi remedio, para vos | andate buškaldo' ('I found a solution for myself | as for you, go and find yours') (*AS* fol. 10).

This dialogue between the Queen and her lover in Laura Papo's version is incomplete. The Queen only says: 'Andarleto, mi Andarleto | mi pulido enamorado' ('Andarleto, my Andarleto | my handsome lover') (*AS* fol. 10). Laura Papo omits the part where the Queen explains that the adultery has been revealed and that she is threatened with death. It is precisely this confession by the Queen which provokes the lover's reply known in the Bosnian versions. The omitted part, however, would not have caused any confusion for her audience. *Landarico* was one of the most popular ballads among the Bosnian Sepharadim, and all versions collected in Bosnia contain this development of events.

In twentieth-century balladry, dialogue has become a dominant trait. This was not the case in the *romancero viejo* in which the presence of dialogue was minor and less significant for the ballad's plot. According to Catalán, the greater importance played by direct speech in modern balladry can be attributed to the fact that one episode or dialogue tends to acquire a dominant position within the ballad (1972: 203). In this way, the idea conveyed by this particular dialogue becomes the main theme of the entire ballad.

In Bosnian versions of *Landarico*, the final dialogue between the Queen and her lover, which Laura Papo only partially transmits in her play, appears as the dominant part of the ballad; it is here that the main idea is conveyed. This kind of dialogue between men and women is frequent in folk literature because it allows men and women to express their different views on love, family life and gender relations:

> They tell the same stories but change them in subtle but clear ways according to their different male and female points of view. One cannot directly observe this process of feminizing and masculinizing stories because the retelling takes place over a long period of time, storytellers do not always remember from whom they first heard a particular tale. (Taggart 1990: 13)

In Hispanic balladry, a good example of this is the ballad *La princesa y el segador*, Q4, which was performed by both sexes. However, the ideas and beliefs that women express in their rendition of this ballad differ considerably from those expressed by men.

The ballad recounts the story of a young woman of noble background who engages in sexual relations with a harvester. Beatriz Gómez Acuña has shown how the development of the ballad's plot is conditioned by the sex of the singer (2002: 183–96). In versions sung by women, the female protagonist seduces the harvester, assumes an active sexual role and then rewards him with money. The versions rendered by men, on the other hand, depict the harvester in a typically masculine role: he controls the sexual act and uses the woman for his own pleasure. These versions most often end with the death of the harvester caused by the perfidy of the seductress. But, as I stated earlier, not all versions performed by women follow the same pattern; they too can have different variants and endings. These differences can range from legitimising the established values of a dominant male social order to rejecting that order or simply exploring alternatives. This is the case of *Landarico* in the Bosnian tradition compared to other Sephardic communities.

So after the outcome of the dialogue between the Queen and her lover, the mother in Laura Papo's play underscores the new idea of the ballad's ending: 'LA MADRE Veš luke son lus ombres! El Dio no de kreerlos!' ('MOTHER Do you see what men are like! God forbid you trust them!') (*AS* fol. 10). The added message is that women should beware of the deceiving nature of men. The mother's comment works as an inference to the closing dialogue between the Queen and her lover in the ballad which changes the focus of the *romance*. Now in addition to condemning female adultery, the ballad condemns the deceptive nature of men.

This last idea was condoned by the tradition which Laura Papo transmits faithfully here. The corpus of recorded versions from Sarajevo (and some from Belgrade) corroborates this fact. I have consulted the following versions of *Landarico* from Bosnia and Serbia: 1) Leo Wienner published a version he collected from an informant in Belgrade, who was originally from Bosnia (1903: 262–63 n. 11); 2) in 1911, Manrique de Lara recorded versions of *Landarico* from sixty-five-year-old Ester Abinum Altaraz from Sarajevo and twenty-four-year-old Pascua Oserovics de Alcalay from Belgrade (both kept in the Fundación Ramón Menéndez Pidal in Madrid); 3) *Jevrejski glas* published a version of *Landarico* on 26 April 1940 told by Sara, the wife of Moše Papo (this is the only information provided by the newspaper); 4) Kalmi Baruh published a version of the ballad from Sarajevo (1933: 277); 5) Samuel Elazar published three versions of the ballad, one of them being the one that appeared in *Jevrejski glas* and two new versions (1987: 40–41; 259–61).

All these versions make reference to the dialogue between the Queen and her lover as seen in Laura Papo. A case in point is the version recounted by Abinum Altaraz, in which this dialogue reads: '[the Queen] Anderleto, Anderleto | el rey me quiere matar. | [the paramour] Para mí topé [*sic*] remedio | i para vos andad buscadvos' ('[the Queen] Anderleto, Anderleto | the King wants to kill me. | [the paramour] I found a solution for myself | and as for you, go and find yours'). Moreover, in the version collected by Wienner and the one told by Oserovics de Alcalay (which I cite below), this dialogue is carried even further: the lover not only leaves the Queen to her fate, but he also rebukes her for having taken a lover while being a married woman:

> [the Queen] Andarlieto, Andarlieto, [...]
>> dame tú a mé un consejo, | que el rey mos tiene amenazados.
> [the paramour] Para mé, todo remedio; | para te, ve buscátelo.
>> Como tienes rey por marido, | ¿qué te busca el amorado?
> [the Queen] Andarlieto, Andarlieto, [...]
>> tell me what to do, | the King is threatening us.
> [the paramour] I found a solution for myself | as for you, go and find yours.
>> Since the King is your husband | why did you look for a lover?

In some of these versions, the dialogue between the Queen and her lover called for the addition of a metatextual comment at the end of the ballad designed to make sure that the audience interpreted the ballad correctly (Vidaković-Petrov 2014: 325). It reads: '¡Mal añada a las mujeres | que en los hombres se confían!; | los falsos y mentirosos, | echados a la malina' ('God help women | who trust men!; | they are deceitful and liars | given to maliciousness').[65] The mother's words about the untrustworthy nature of men in Laura Papo's play have their source in this addition approved by Bosnian tradition.

In Davičo, by contrast, there is no reference to the treachery of the Queen's lover. This is closely related to the way the ballad is presented in Davičo's work: it neither aims to condemn the adulteress (and hence women) nor to criticise men, whereas in Laura Papo both women and men are denounced. Davičo's and Laura Papo's examples of *Landarico* illustrate both Catalán's theory of ballads being an open system and Catarella's view regarding the instability and ambivalence of gendered ballad performances and versions.

However, the reinterpretation which we find in Laura Papo should not be considered a completely new element introduced by the Bosnian Sepharadim but rather as a pre-existing element that has been developed further by this community. I believe that this idea of men's deceitful nature appears in the old version of the ballad. As noted, in the sixteenth-century version, the Queen also seeks help from her lover after the adultery has been revealed. Instead of offering her his help and support, the paramour expresses his remorse for having ever become involved with her. This idea, however, was not taken further in the old version (there is no mention of him abandoning her), but it must have served as a source for the additions in Bosnian versions of the ballad. This brings me to another point: can gender be said to play a role in the addition of these parts?

The added dialogue and the metatextual comment at the end of *Landarico* clearly express the female perspective of events and were probably introduced by female singers of the ballad.[66] The fact that women became the principal informants in the modern oral tradition of Hispanic (Sephardic) balladry conditions to a great extent the point of view, ideologies and perceptions expressed in ballads. As Catarella highlights, 'it is predominately women who retain, rework and transmit ballads and from whom the overwhelming majority of ballad versions have been collected' (1990: 331). Owing to this fact, the *romancero* contains a strong female voice as, according to Ian Michael, the ballad was the one means by which ordinary women could convey their feelings and ambitions and which they themselves re-created and passed down (1993: 101).[67] However, this point should not be taken literally as gendered ballad performances and versions can also vary: from women accepting the patriarchal view to rejecting it unconsciously, although consciously adhering to the rules (Catarella 1990: 341).

I have already mentioned the case of *La princesa y el segador* in Hispanic tradition, to which we can add Catalán's view that 'los romances [hispánicos] que actualmente se cantan o recitan representan, sin duda, un enjuiciamiento del mundo referencial que ha de considerarse en buena parte como expresión de una perspectiva femenina' (1984: 1, 21). Regarding the Sephardic tradition, Susana Weich-Shahak (2009: 274) and Paloma Díaz-Mas (2009a: 81–101) also insist on a close connection between gender and genre: while the role of men was to transmit the liturgy and the regularly performed paraliturgical repertoire in Hebrew, it was the women who transmitted the *romances* and *cantigas*. Consequently, the voice of women is strongly present in Sephardic balladry.

This has clearly been the case of *Landarico*. The original text sought to assert male authority by punishing the adulteress. According to Catarella (1990: 340), this represents the mythic move in ballads' narrative trajectories: the *romance* affirms the values of the prevailing social order. Although Bosnian tradition does not sanction the adultery or favouring of illegitimate children over legitimate ones, it does change the status of the female character from a clear transgressor to a woman who is misled by male deception (Vidaković-Petrov 2014: 325). Thus a perfidious woman is rendered into one who can be led astray. This is what Catarella defines as the transformative move in which new episodes, motifs and characters are developed and a new narrative direction is established in compliance with the wishes of the speakers and the characters in the ballad (1990: 340).

The change in interpretation of the ballad undoubtedly determined the target audience. In Davičo, this ballad underwent a change of context of performance entailing a partial shift in interpretation. The ballad, as noted, was performed for the Ninth of Av. The occasion on which it was performed and the message it conveyed called for the presence of a general audience consisting of both men and women.

Since versions of *Landarico* in Bosnia contain a message directed to women, who are presented here as victims of male deception, the ballad was sung by women for a mostly female audience who were potential victims. This custom is depicted perfectly in Laura Papo's play with the mother singing the ballad to her daughters. Furthermore, the occasion is exclusively female: the home environment where women are alone doing their household chores.

This is by no means an isolated case in Sephardic balladry. Another example is *Delgadina*, P2. This ballad of Hispanic origin deals with the topic of incest and recounts the story of a father who tries to force himself on his daughter. For having rejected him, the daughter is punished by being locked up in a tower and deprived of water. She eventually dies of thirst (Benmayor 1979: 139–42; Ž. Jovanović 2013: 292–93).

Among the Sepharadim, this ballad was performed by elderly women for young women to teach them how to react properly if they were faced with a similar situation (Alexander-Frizer 2008: 352). The ballad should provide a defense mechanism for these young women, a strategy to which they should adhere in order to avoid a worse fate. To accomplish this aim, the ballad is directed to an audience whose members are potential victims of male aggression, and the composition of that audience is therefore gender-determined. Although this story represents a voice against the father's authority and his ability to control his daughter's destiny, and therefore against men in general, it excludes male presence (see Ž. Jovanović 2013: 296–97).[68]

Performing different forms of folk literature was one of the ways for elderly women to pass certain lessons on to young girls. Laura Papo emphasises this educational role of *Landarico* in her text *La mužer sefardi de Bosna*:

> avia las romanses ke las alegrava i konsolava a las solas y entre gente [a las mujeres]. La romansa di Andarleto era la mas estimada de nuestras nonas, porke aki se demoštrava ki los ombres son negros, ke no preme kreerlos. [...] Mis fižikjas, no kreaš a los ombres (2005: 164).

> (There were ballads which used to cheer us up and comfort us when we [women] were both alone and with others. The Andarleto ballad was one of the most appreciated among our grandmothers because it shows that men are bad, that they are not trustworthy. My dear daughters, don't trust men)

This idea of using ballads as an educational tool is put into practice in the play. The mother uses *Landarico* as an *exemplum a contrario*, that is telling her daughters what they should not do. Firstly, they should not commit adultery; and, secondly, they should not put their trust in men. The last message is a specific trait of the Bosnian and Serbian Sepharadim, and it has not been documented in relation to the ballads studied here among other Sephardic communities or in Spain or Portugal.

Davičo's and Laura Papo's versions of this ballad not only have different aims and interpretations but also different social uses. In Laura Papo, the ballad serves to entertain the listeners (women only) at their household chores while conveying a didactic message. In Davičo, the ballad is performed during a time of sorrow, the Ninth of Av. This shows how the ballad was adapted to its environment, which enabled its survival over the course of centuries. These versions of *Landarico* differ

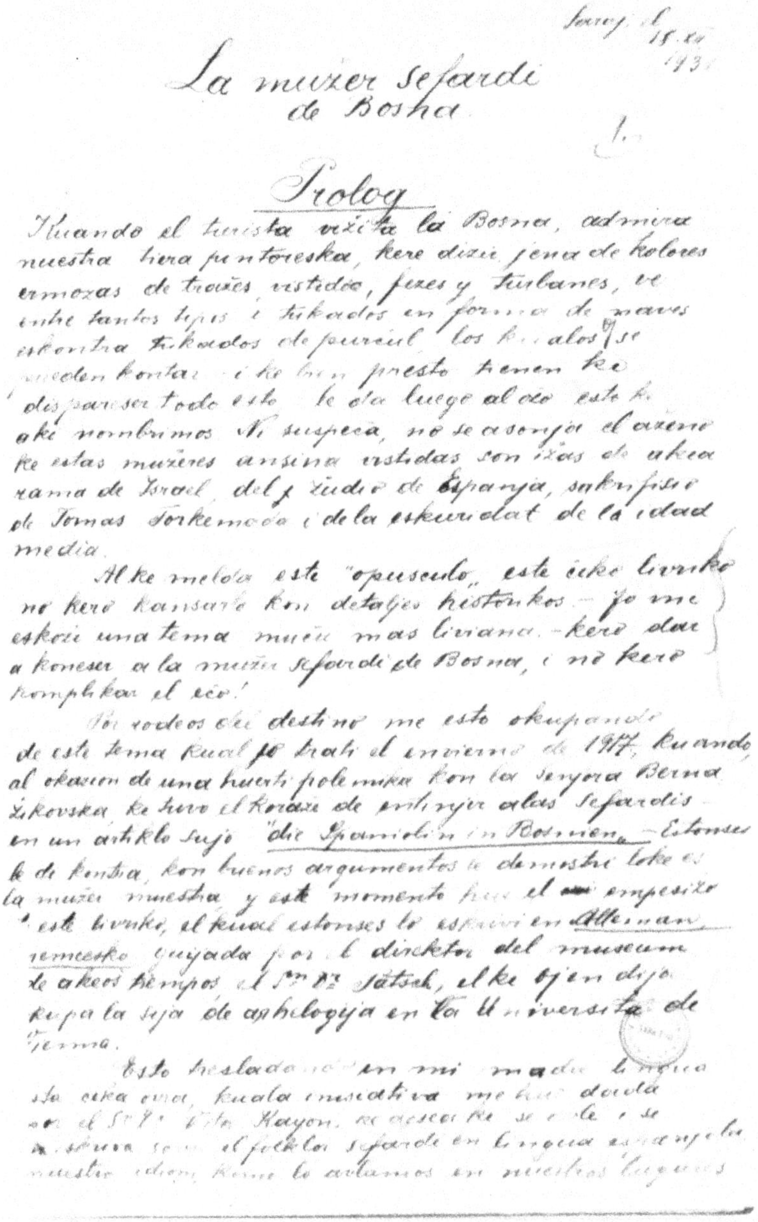

La mužer sefardi
de Bosna

1.

Prolog

Kuando el turista vižita la Bosna, admira
nuestra tiera pintoreska, kere dizir jena de kolores
ermozas de trožes, vistidos, fezes y turbanes, ve
entre tantos tipos i tokados en forma de naves
ekontra tokados de pursel los kualos se
pueden kontar i ke bien presto tienen ke
disparesér todo esto le da luego al ožo esto ke
aki nombrimos. Ni suspeča, no se asonja el aženo
ke estas mužeres ansina vistidas son ižas de akea
rama de Israel, del žudio de Espanja, sakrifisio
de Tomas Torkemada i de la eskuridat de la idad
media.

Al ke meldo este "opusculo" este čiko livriko
no kero kansarlo kon detaljes historikos. Jo me
eskoži una tema muču mas liviana. Kero dar
a koneser a la mužer sefardi de Bosna, i no kero
komplikar el ečo!

Por rodeos del destino me esto okupando
de este tema kual jo trati el invierno de 1917, kuando
al okasion de una huerti polemika kon la senjora Berna
Žikovska ke tuvo el koraže de entinjar a las Sefardis
en un artiklo sujo "die Spaniolin in Bosnien". Estonses
le di kontra, kon buenos argumentos le demostri loke es
la mužer nuestra y este momento fue el empesižo
este livriko, el kual estonses lo eskrivi en Aleman
nemecko ujada por el direktor del museum
de akeos tiempos el Sr Dr Pätsch, el ke ojen dijo
kupa la sija de arheologija en la Universita de
Vienna.

Esto treslado en mi madre lingua
... kuala insiativa me fue dada
... Kayon ...
... el folklor sefardi en lingua espanjola
nuestro ... komo lo avlamos en nuestros lugares

Fig. 1.10. First page of Laura Papo's *La mužer sefardi de Bosna*.
From the private collection of Eliezer Papo

from those collected among other Sephardic communities both in their reception and their roles. This demonstrates that one single yet geographically dispersed ethnic group could come up with a different interpretation of the same ballad topic. At the same time, that very same ballad can play a different role and function according to the occasion for which it is performed and the audience for which it is intended.

4. Conclusions to Part I

The various practices of collecting, preserving, recovering and disseminating Sephardic folk literature prior to WWII by two Sephardic authors, Haim S. Davičo from Serbia and Laura Papo Bohoreta from Bosnia, have been examined in *Part I*. These practices include fieldwork collection (ballads, tales and proverbs), the use of elements of folk literature in their own works, the re-creation of folk literature and, finally, the appropriation of elements of other cultures through translations and adaptations. These practices were not exclusive to these two authors but rather form part of a larger picture that characterised the Judeo-Spanish speaking world at the turn of the twentieth century.

Although some of these practices are common to both authors, the political and cultural aims of their work differed and exemplified the conflict existing at the turn of the twentieth century between modernity and tradition, assimilation and continuity. Davičo supported the idea of the Sephardic community assimilating into the larger Serbian society, which entailed the adoption of Serbian as their first language to the detriment of Judeo-Spanish. He perceived this process to be desirable and beneficial for the community as a whole as in this way the Sepharadim would join Serbia on its way to modernisation and westernisation. This is why Davičo chose Serbian as his means of communication and published all of his work in Serbian newspapers and periodicals of the time. This fact influenced his use of Sephardic folk literature, which in his work appears for the most part rendered into Serbian.

Laura Papo, by contrast, endeavoured to recover the Sephardic tradition and language by writing all of her work in Judeo-Spanish and thus directing it to the members of the Sephardic community in Bosnia and elsewhere rather than to the general audience. Unlike Davičo, whose aim was to preserve the memory of the Sephardic legacy, Laura Papo's efforts were focused on securing the continuation of the tradition and the language.

Both authors employ folk literature not only to show the function that it played in the everyday life of the Sepharadim but also to reinforce the message of their own works. They introduce Sephardic folk material in part or in full and place it within the plot of the main work. Likewise, both Davičo and Laura Papo carried out fieldwork; the former collecting proverbs and the latter ballads. In addition, I have pointed out another method of enriching the Sephardic tradition through the appropriation of elements of other cultures through translations or adaptations, a phenomenon that was widely spread across Judeo-Spanish speaking world. This was the case of Davičo's text *Ženske šale* which, rather than having been preserved through oral transmission and collected through fieldwork by Davičo, is a translation of the novella *Los tres maridos burlados* by Tirso de Molina. However, by rendering Tirso's story into Serbian, Davičo's success in enriching the Sephardic tradition is rather questionable. This tale has never entered the corpus of Sephardic traditional narrative nor does it exist in Judeo-Spanish, but its existence in the Serbian language thanks to Davičo's work adds value to the Serbian rather than Sephardic tradition.

Davičo's other goal, that of using this tale to introduce the Sephardic community of Belgrade to the wider readership, was, on the other hand, carried out successfully, both by his choice of *Videlo,* a periodical with a large impact and scope of readers, as a place to publish it, as well as his choice of type of tale, a comic story whose humorous content contributed to the favorable picture of the Sephardic spirit and tradition.

Some of these practices continued to be fostered after WWII, such as fieldwork collection or introducing folk material in the original works. Others changed or disappeared. However, the aims and the efforts of the Sephardic authors after WWII were mainly focused on the recovery of the legacy and the revitalisation of the language. This will be the focus of *Part II*, where I examine the works of two authors from Bosnia, Gina Camhy and Isak Papo, both from the second half of the twentieth century.

Notes to Part I

1. For an account of Davičo's life, see Alkalaj 1925: 74–85; Milošević 1967: 129–35; Vidaković-Petrov 1990: 113–22; 2010a: 307–16; Mihailović 1992: 249–76; Ž. Jovanović 2014b: 981–1002, and Vučina Simović 2015a: 61–77; 2015b: 109–21. For an account of Laura Papo's life, see E. Papo 2011: 89–107; Prenz Kopušar 2012: 3–19; Večerina Tomaić 2016: 22–34 & Kovačević 2018: 19–36.
2. For more information on this, see Feiner 2002 and 2010.
3. Attias's *La güerta* has been published recently by Ángel Berenguer Amador (2017). Also, on Attias's work, see Borovaya 2012: 10 and 2017: 233–38.
4. The term *port Jew* is used to designate western Jews from port communities who, due to their engagement in maritime commerce, are highly integrated into civilian society and are therefore more inclined to embrace secularisation and the Enlightenment.
5. For more information on the Sephardic *maskilim*, see Studemund-Hálevy 2013: 255–80 and Bornes Varol 2013: 281–94.
6. I use Hans-Jörg Uther's revision of Antti Aarne and Stith Thompson's tale-type numbers and hence the abbreviation ATU. See Uther 2004.
7. On this, also see Venuti 1995: 20–39 and Munday 2001.
8. Yalia comes from a Turkish word *yali* meaning strand or bank, in this case the bank of the Danube which was the area Belgrade's community of Spanish Jews inhabited (Milošević 1967: 130; Vidaković-Petrov 2010a: 311).
9. In 1878, the accords signed at the Berlin Conference not only secured Serbia its independence but also contained a clause securing equal rights for Jews. This was then confirmed by the Serbian constitution in 1888 when Jews were given full rights, most of which they already enjoyed by that time (Vučina Simović and Filipović 2009: 107; Vidaković-Petrov 2010a: 309).
10. Founded in 1863, the Velika škola was composed of three faculties: Law, Philosophy and Engineering. It represented the highest institution of education in Serbia at that time.
11. *Pasha* is an honorific title, formerly the highest title of Turkish civil and military officials (Koén-Sarano 2004a: 346).

12. VĐ stands for Vladimir Đorđević's Fund. The letter was printed on at least two occasions; see Mihailović 1992: 274–75, & Lebl 2001: 418 n. 364.

13. *Kolo* designates a type of Serbian national dance, and Branko is a given name for a man. Hence, *Brankovo kolo* means *Branko's kolo*.

14. For an account of the Judeo-Spanish press in the former Yugoslavia, see Vidaković-Petrov 2013: 69–96.

15. In the only catalogue of the Judeo-Spanish press, *El Amigo del puevlo* appears as item number 30. See Gaon 1965: 23–24.

16. On this, see Vidaković-Petrov 1990: 56–60; 2013: 78–87, and Tauber 2011: 39–43.

17. For other testimonies about the custom of making the shroud among the Balkan Sepharadim, see Molho 1950: 178 and Laura Papo 2005: 235.

18. Also, for the example of another ballad, *Escogiendo novia*, ballad-type S15 (Armistead 1978), and the way Davičo uses it in his work, see Vidaković-Petrov 2010b: 295–315.

19. Five years later, R. Foulché-Delbosc (1895: 312–52) published most of these proverbs alongside others that he had personally collected in Turkey and Greece. However, since he had left some out, Kayserling (1897: 82) decided to publish the missing twenty-three proverbs in the same journal.

20. For further information on miscellanies, see Alcalá Galán 1996: 11–20 and Bradbury 2010 and 2017.

21. On this, see Ž. Jovanović 2014b.

22. To consult these two texts, see Sánchez de Vercial 1961: 238–39 and Soons 1976: 76–81.

23. It was Pulido Fernández's book *Españoles sin patria y la raza sefardí* (1905) that drew Spain's attention to the Sepharadim at home and abroad. Likewise, it prompted various scholars to carry out fieldwork among them in the Eastern Mediterranean and North Africa.

24. For more information on the different editions of Tirso's miscellany to appear, both complete and partial, see Vázquez Fernández 1996: 73–82.

25. Unless otherwise stated, all reference numbers to folk motifs are taken from Thomspon's catalogue (1966).

26. On this, see also Alpert 2009: 13–36.

27. All the quotations from Tirso's novella are taken from the following edition: Tirso de Molina, *Cigarrales de Toledo*, ed. by Luis Vázquez Fernández, 216 (Madrid: Clásicos Castalia, 1996). For future references, only page numbers will be provided in parenthesis.

28. The number following the year of publication refers not to the page (as the leaves of the newspaper *Videlo* are not numbered) but to the issues in which the tale was published.

29. For examples of de-Christianisation in Sephardic balladry, see Armistead and Silverman 1965: 21–38.

30. For a complete list of Laura Papo's works, see E. Papo 2012.

31. The first volume (2015) includes the following plays: *Ožos mios*; *Avia de ser*; *La pasiensia vale mučo* and *Tiempos pasados*; the second volume (2016) contains three plays: *Shuegra ni de baro buena*; *Hermandat* and *Esterka*; and, the third (2017), which was done in collaboration with Fuad Ohranović, includes tales, essays, poems and ballads: *La mužer sefardi de Bosna*; 'Al ocasion del jubileo de combate, lavoro y succeso'; 'Dotas'; 'Davičon el hamal'; 'La molinera y la karvonera'; 'Huanita'; 'Madres'; 'Violetas'; 'Flor amurčada'; 'Duspues de las hadras'; 'Tija Rahelona de Sason'; 'Tija Merkada de Jahilo Finzi'; 'La Paparoza de tio Kako Monteira'; *Romansas* and *letters*.

32. The following tales appear in this volume: 'Madres', 'Morena', 'Linda — Rikordo di Oriente', 'Al ocasion del jubileo de combate lavoro i suceso', 'Por esto akea vieža no se kižo murir', 'Tija Rahelona de Sasson', 'Tija Merkada di Jahilo Finci'. On Laura Papo's tales appearing in the Jewish press of her time, see Eliezer Papo 2012.

33. Kovačević's thesis is available online: <http://digibug.ugr.es/bitstream/10481/35123/1/24328698. pdf> [accessed 19 March 2019].

34. The exact year of the family's move to Istanbul is unclear. Kovačević first cites 1897, but later in her work she mentions both 1898 and 1899 as the possible date of the move (2014: 103; 104). Eliezer Papo, on the other hand, cites 1900 as the year when the family went to Istanbul (2011: 89).

35. For a more detailed account of education among the Sepharadim in both pre-modern and

modern times, see Laskier 1982: 191–212; Rodrigue 1990; Arie 1990: 87–106; Benbassa 1991: 529–60; Levy 1992: 108–15; Díaz-Mas 2006: 79–85, and Díaz-Mas and Sánchez-Pérez 2010: 13–25.

36. For more information on La Benevolencia and its aims, see Vidaković-Petrov 1990: 49–50 and E. Papo 2011: 95 n. 22.

37. Blanka, Rikica, Nina and Klara were the names of Laura Papo's sisters.

38. Also on this, see Valentín 2010: 293–303.

39. For the modernisation of Bosnia following the Austro-Hungarian occupation in 1878 and later annexation in 1908 by the same power, see Lovrenović 2001: 147–57 and Hoare 2007: 70–99.

40. Little is known about the play *Elvira* as it has only recently been discovered. Večerina Tomaić (2016: 113–16) dedicates few pages to it in her book.

41. The titles of the ballads and their reference numbers are all taken from Armistead's catalogue of the Judeo-Spanish balladry (1978). It should be noted that in this case not all titles indicate ballads (*romances*). Although Laura Papo classifies them as such (she calls her collection *romancero*), *Morena me llaman*, for example, is a lyrical song.

42. I was not able to classify *La hermosica* which seems to be a rare ballad indeed. In fact, no other versions of the ballad apart from the one by Laura Papo have been known to exist either among other Sephardic communities or in the Iberian Peninsula.

43. See Nezirović 1986: 115–30 and E. Papo 2012: 124–25, nn. 3–5.

44. For a more detailed account of the project of ballad collection in Spain and elsewhere, see the two monumental volumes by Diego Catalán (2001). For an account of Manrique de Lara's journey to the Balkans, see Armistead 1978: I, 18–22 and Catalán 2001: I, 66–72.

45. For a complete list of the ballads Laura Papo told to Manrique de Lara, see Armistead (1978: III, 90). Likewise, Manrique de Lara interviewed Gioya Tódoros (Todros) Leví, who was also one of Laura Papo's informants. In Laura Papo's writing, the name is spelled differently as Gioia Theodorus Levi.

46. *La vuelta del hijo maldecido* is not of Hispanic but Greek origin, and it shows the influences of the Balkan culture on the Sepharadim. See Armistead and Silverman 1982: 151–68.

47. The term oicotype was coined by Carl W. von Sydow, who borrowed the word from botanical science. When applied to folklore, the term designates: 'Local forms of a tale type, folksong, or a proverb, with "local" defined in either geographical or cultural terms. [...] The concept "oicotype" differs from the notion of subtype in that the "oicotype" is tied by definition to a very specific locale' (Von Sydow 1965: 219–20). Two asterics in front of the number designate an oicotype.

48. For a bibliography on Sephardic examples of the ballad, see Armistead, Silverman and Anahory Librowicz 1977: 78–81; Benmayor 1979: 195–97 and Anahory Librowicz 1981: 42.

49. On this, see Armistead and Silverman 1960: 235.

50. On *romances fronterizos*, see Yiacoup 2015.

51. For more information on this ballad, see Gutiérrez Estévez 1981: I, 69–352 and Ž. Jovanović 2013: 287–312. I shall return to this ballad in the next chapter.

52. For a detailed description of these motifs in relation to *Don Bueso*, see Piñero Ramírez 2001: 116–31.

53. For more information on the different roles the mention of Granada has in Sephardic balladry, see Díaz-Mas 1989: 191–200.

54. This depiction of Muslims in *Don Bueso* coincides with what Edward W. Said defined in his *Orientalism* (1978) as a method of practical and cultural discrimination (in Western scholarship) that was applied to non-European societies and peoples in order to establish European imperial domination.

55. This chapter is derived from my article published in *Abenámar: Cuadernos de la Fundación Ramón Menéndez Pidal*. See Ž. Jovanović 2018a: 43–66.

56. For recorded versions of the ballad, both peninsular and Sephardic, see Fontes 1997: I, 179–80; Benamayor 1979: 76 and Armistead 1978: II, 64–73. 'Peninsular' here refers to Spanish, Catalan and Portuguese versions of the ballad.

57. Marcelino Menéndez y Pelayo (1912?: IX, 219–20) was the first to publish the ballad, which was later re-edited by R. Foulché-Delbosc (1924: 463–64 n. 76) and Ramón Menéndez Pidal (1960: I,

331–32). Most recent collections of Hispanic *romancero* usually include the oldest version of the ballad and other versions collected in the twentieth century. See Stefano 1993: 192–93; Díaz-Mas 2005: 295–99 & Piñero Ramírez 2008: 393–97. On different collections of old chapbooks, see Rodríguez Moñino (1997). It is here that a reference to a chapbook containing the *pliego suelto* with *Landarico* appears (Rodríguez Moñino 1997: 552 n. 655).

58. The same version was later printed in Díaz-Mas (2005: 298–99).

59. Also, see Leite de Vasconcellos (1958) and Pires da Cruz (1988).

60. TITU is the 'denominación del romance y número indentificador' (Catalán and others 1984: I, 221).

61. For more information on the King's wife, Fredegund, see Bernet 2012.

62. See Hélène Cixous's article translated into English on beheading as a form of female castration (1981: 41–55). Cixous initially published this article in 1976 in French and developed her arguments in her later works. See Cixous 1980 and 1989.

63. Also on this, see Catarella 1990: 331 and Armistead 1996: 13–26.

64. On this, see a feminist article by Gayle Rubin 1975: 157–210.

65. The lines are taken from the version given by Oserovics de Alcalay. The added comment has the form of a saying, which is a frequent way to end a ballad. Sayings such as this one can easily be applied to other ballads having a similar plot due to the didactic message they contain. For example, this particular saying appears in the Bosnian versions of another ballad, *La vuelta del marido*, II.3. See Armistead 1978: I, 319–30, and Armistead, Silverman and Šljivić-Šimšić 1971: 46.

66. For more information on the question of women and the *romancero*, see Guerra Castellanos 1971, Odd 1983 and Gómez Acuña 2002.

67. Also on this, see Menéndez Pidal 1953: II, 372–74; Petersen 1982: 76; Mariscal de Rhett 1987: 655–56.

68. For more information on discursive strategies which include different forms of oral literature used by women to openly express their views and experience, see Buxó Rey 1988 and Harding 2003: 268–91.

PART II

Gina Camhy and Isak Papo: Efforts to Revitalise the Sephardic Language and Tradition of Bosnia in the Aftermath of WWII

The works of Gina Camhy (1909–1990) and Isak Papo (1912–1996), both originally from Bosnia, exemplify acts of memorialisation and thus fit perfectly within the mainstream of literature written both by the Sephardic and Ashkenazi Jews in the aftermath of WWII. As Jonathan Schorsch has noted, memory work — autobiographies, biographies, novels, tales or epistolary collections — has moved to centre stage in the collective Jewish psyche and represents an attempt to (re)invent one's past and find one's place (2007: 83). The importance of this sense of identity among the Sepharadim and their need to safeguard it is echoed in the Sephardic proverb, 'Sin memoria no ay avenir' ('Without memory there is no future'), which urges that survival is contingent upon safeguarding the past.

Memory works in the Judeo-Spanish speaking world first emerged towards the end of the nineteenth century, as seen in the works of Haim Davičo and Laura Papo, and were prompted by historical and political circumstances taking place in the Balkans prior to WWII. These events included the creation of the new Balkan states, which encouraged the Sepharadim to assimilate and embrace education in mixed-sex secular schools to the detriment of traditional religious single-sex education. Consequently, the Sephardic language and tradition gradually began to disappear. In these circumstances, Davičo and Laura Papo took steps either to preserve the memory of the Sephardic legacy or to maintain and revitalise this tradition and the Judeo-Spanish language.

This type of literature proliferated after the Holocaust when conservation became even more essential due to the fact that most of the Sephardic communities in Europe were virtually obliterated or else dispersed.[1] This situation heightened consciousness of the precarious condition of the Sephardic heritage and the need to preserve what remained of a once flourishing tradition. The outcome was the emergence of movements for the recovery of Sephardic culture, but mostly in the diaspora (France, Israel and the USA) rather than in the countries or regions that originally contained large Sephardic communities. Some of these efforts were undertaken by individual authors as the result of their own initiative, whereas others form part of an organised effort to revitalise the dying legacy. With a new appreciation for the Sephardic tradition, such as the celebration of holy days, customs and the traditional way of life, folk literature acquired a particular place and emphasis in the works of Sephardic authors.

Nonetheless, unlike before WWII when different practices of using folk material were employed, such as collection, re-creation, imitation, adaptation or even misrepresentation of the tradition, in the second half of the twentieth century one technique dominates. Sephardic authors from the former Yugoslavia concentrate on the collection, conservation and dissemination of the tradition in post-Holocaust Europe. Their main aim is to conserve the memory of what used to be their tradition and, if possible, to reactivate it.

Gina Camhy and Isak Papo, the two Bosnian Sephardic authors examined in this part, perfectly exemplify this change in approach. In spite of their importance in the Sephardic milieu, very little is known about them and their work. Whereas Davičo was a distinguished intellectual in Serbia in his time, and Laura Papo was recognised as an educated woman, a writer and a collector of folklore, both the scope of Camhy's and Isak Papo's work and the lives of the authors themselves remain lacunae.

Two facts are usually associated with Camhy's life and work. First, she was married to Ovadia Camhy, an eminent Sephardic activist and the editor of *Le Judaïsme Sephardi* (hereafter *JS*). Second, she was one of the main contributors to several Sephardic periodicals such as *JS*, *Vidas Largas* (hereafter *Vidas*) and *Aki Yerushalayim* (hereafter *AY*), all published in France and Israel rather than in her native Bosnia. Isak Papo, on the other hand, is known for several articles on Bosnian Judeo-Spanish and for his collection of tales, *Cuentos sobre los sefardíes de Sarajevo*, published just before his death (I. Papo and others 1994). In addition to his own tales, the collection also gathers some by Camhy and Rikica Ovadia (1913–1997), both born in Sarajevo, and Clarisse Nikoïdski (1938–1996), who was born in France into a Sephardic family from Bosnia. The following points summarise the similarities and differences between Camhy and Isak Papo:

— both authors were born in Sarajevo, where they grew up in a Sephardic environment in which Judeo-Spanish was still spoken. However, Camhy created her work as part of a larger movement in Paris, whereas Isak Papo's work was the result of individual initiative in his native community;

— neither created their work within a traditional Sephardic environment. In Paris, Camhy lived in a new, progressive Sephardic community comprising members mostly from different European Sephardic communities. Although Isak Papo remained in Sarajevo, the community there changed after WWII when most of its members had either perished or emigrated. This changed environment led both authors to dedicate their work to recovering the legacy of a particular Sephardic community, the Bosnian one;

— both Camhy and Isak Papo received an education in the Serbian language. However, they wrote their literary work in Judeo-Spanish, the language of their homes. Their aims behind this decision and the choice of Judeo-Spanish for their work is suggestive of their attitude towards their native legacy in the post-Holocaust era;

— the readership of their work was determined by this choice of language. Camhy published all of her work exclusively in Sephardic periodicals and in Ladino, although the language of the area where she was living was French. Thus her texts were written for and about the Sepharadim who not only understood the language but were also familiar with the subjects of her writing. Isak Papo also chose Judeo-Spanish for his literary work, with the aim of preserving some evidence of that language from Bosnia. However, he purposely published his tales with a Serbo-Croatian translation for two reasons: there were scarcely any Sepharadim left in his environment who could understand the language; and, he aimed for the book to reach the general readership in the country. Furthermore, in order to disseminate his work outside of Bosnia, he also published an English translation of his collection;

— the choice of topics was conditioned by the gender of the authors. Camhy's writing reflects a female point of view and deals with topics which within the Sephardic tradition and patriarchy were typically related to women, such as taking care of the children and the home, cooking, celebrating Jewish holy days, the preparation of the marriage trousseau, traditional medicine and beliefs. Isak Papo, by contrast, focuses on describing members of the community or merely collecting folklore (folk tales) that he learned in his community. Being a man, customs related to the home, which are traditionally associated with women, do not constitute his main memories of the community;

— the authors' selection of topics, including folk literature, was aimed at creating a positive image of the Sephardic community. Both Camhy's and Isak Papo's work exemplify acts of memorialisation. They both write from their memory and with the aim of conserving the memory of the past. What is worthy of note is that it is the pleasant things they choose to remember about the community and the past: the celebrations of holy days, ceremonies, family life and food. This applies to the folk literature as well. By choosing what they write about, they are placing a certain value and emphasis on what they consider to be worthy of presentation, thus creating a kind of canon. And this canon, in the words of Stuart Davis, is 'both a memorialisation of the cultural past and also a representation of it for new generations' (2012: 6).

Camhy was the first of the two to start writing and publishing. She began doing so in the 1950s in Paris, whereas Isak Papo's work appeared in the late 1980s, culminating with the publication of his tale collection in 1994. I shall examine each author's use of folk literature with the aim of drawing parallels between their work and the techniques and practices used by Davičo and Laura Papo prior to WWII.

1. Gina Camhy: An Author to Be Discovered

Although Gina Camhy (1909–1990) is one of the most important Sephardic cultural figures of the second half of the twentieth century, very little is known about her.[2] She signed her work with her married name, Camhy, and was of a Yugoslavian, specifically Bosnian, background, as indicated briefly in some of her publications — for example, the following heading of her tale 'Purim' ('Festival of Lots'):

> Tout en maintenant notre orthographe, nous tenons à respecter la prononciation de l'auteur de ces souvenirs, Madame Gina Camhy, originaire, comme notre poétesse Clarisse Nicoïdski, de Yougoslavie. Gina Camhy est l'épouse de celui qui des années durant se consacra au judéo-espagnol en dirigeant notamment la revue *Le Judaïsme Sephardi*, nous voulons dire Ovadia Camhy auquel nous tenons à rendre hommage. (Camhy 1983: 38)[3]

Seemingly, only one article focusing on Camhy's work has been published to date.[4] Bearing in mind this void, the focus here will be on the important role Camhy's work played in the movement to recover the Judeo-Spanish language and culture, her literary work as a reflection of a realm occupied by women and her collection of folk literature. I shall argue that Camhy became a writer in the post-Holocaust era for ideological purposes, to safeguard, preserve, disseminate and revitalise her legacy.[5]

Camhy was born in Sarajevo in 1909 and grew up there during the time the Sarajevan Sephardic community was undergoing significant changes as a result of the disintegration of the Ottoman Empire. One major change concerns education: in 1894 in Bosnia, the Sephardic educational system switched to the Serbian educational system in the Serbian language, and this schooling became mandatory for girls as well as boys (Pinto 1987: 82; Vučina Simović 2016: 122–28). Thus Camhy must have received her education in the Serbian language. The fact that she spoke both Serbian and Judeo-Spanish and yet chose the latter for her work may indicate a conscious decision to revitalise the language in direct contrast to a number of her near contemporaries from the same region such as Davičo and Žak Konfino (1892–1975), both Serbian, or Isak Samokovlija (1889–1955) from Bosnia, who wrote about Sephardic topics using Serbian as their means of communication.

In her attempt to reconstruct the Sephardic past, Camhy writes both about Bosnia generally and about her own youth and family specifically. Hence her narrative represents a source of information about her life in Bosnia. For instance, in her essay, 'El arte culinario de los sepharadim de Bosnia: el guisado de mi madre' ('The Culinary Art of the Sepharadim from Bosnia: My Mother's Cooking'), Camhy talks about her parents, particularly her mother, who was born in Romania as the daughter of a Rabbi, Mose Perera (1958: 736). According to Camhy's account, her mother and father had never met before they were married because, in keeping with the traditional customs of the time, their marriage was arranged by her grandparents.

We know next to nothing about the large family of eleven children into which she was born. The only information we have about her siblings is found in a poem, 'Tres conĝas' ('Three Roses'), written as a kind of homage to three of her sisters who perished in the Holocaust (1966: 32). The fact that her parents' marriage was an arranged one, that her grandfather was a rabbi and that she was born into a large family are all indications that Camhy was exposed to Sephardic traditional values and a family life rooted in that same tradition and Jewish religion.

Camhy spent a good part of her life living in Paris. We do not know exactly when she abandoned her homeland, but it was in France where she met and married Ovadia Camhy, General Secretary for the World Sephardi Federation and the editor of *JS*. At least two facts indicate that her maiden name could have been di Sasson. In one of her tales, 'Mi nona' ('My Grandmother'), she reveals that her paternal grandmother was called Rahelona di Sasson (1981: 45). The second clue is that Camhy sometimes signed her works as Gina Camhy la Sassonica (1956: 496), the latter being her nickname, but which can also indicate that Sassonica (diminutive of Sasson) is a derivation of her maiden surname.

In addition, in an article dedicated to Ovadia Camhy upon his death, Haïm Vidal Sephiha mentions the deceased's wife, whom he calls Angelina (1983–84: 13–15). This could well be her full first name although she always signed her work as Gina. This article also reveals that Camhy spent a period of time in London with her husband when the centre of the World Sephardi Federation moved there. This stay in the British capital is also mentioned in Camhy's tale, 'El sabado en mi civdad' ('Shabbat in my Town'), where in a few lines at the end of the tale Camhy remarks upon similarities in the way Jewish festivities were celebrated in London, in the synagogue which she attended at Holland Park, and in Sarajevo (1955: 311).

While it is clear that there are still many gaps waiting to be filled about Camhy's life, more can be said about her literary work. The next chapter discusses her work and locates it within a larger movement for the recovery of the Sephardic language and tradition. Camhy joined this Sephardic crusade not only as a Sephardic Jew but also as Ovadia's wife who, as stated above, was an eminent Sephardic activist and the editor of *JS*.

Camhy's Activism in Safeguarding and Promoting Sephardic Life and Language

Camhy is an example of a Sephardic author who created her work distanced from her home country and her community, inasmuch as her literary activity began in Paris. Sephardic life in Paris did not resemble Camhy's life in Bosnia. Although she did not stray from Jewish practice, both the religion and Sephardic customs became a remnant of Camhy's childhood and her family origins. The same was true for other Sephardic authors of the second half of the twentieth century who fostered memory works. As Schorsch has highlighted, 'the very prominence of the Sephardic past, though hovering over the authors' lives like a family ghost, or fairy godmother, seems also eternally to dissipate, to become a mere phantom of memory or nostalgia' (2007: 86).

Camhy's work is a perfect example of Schorsch's affirmation. Her stories compare the Sephardic culture from the first half of the twentieth century, as she remembers it, with the situation in which her community found itself after WWII. Schorsch

(2007: 83) notes that many Sephardic authors who composed memory works are not usually writers by profession, and neither was Camhy. In fact, before abandoning Bosnia, probably soon after WWII, Camhy had not published a single work, in spite of the existence of several possible avenues of publication. Before the beginning of WWII, Bosnia was the centre of the Judeo-Spanish and Jewish press in the former Yugoslavia. From the first decade of the twentieth century until 1941, several Sephardic and Jewish newspapers, such as *La Alborada*, *Jevrejski glas* (*The Jewish Voice*) and *Jevrejski život* (*Jewish Life*) were launched.[6] These periodicals invited members of the Bosnian Sephardic community to collect and submit folk material or their own work for the newspaper to publish (Armistead, Silverman and Šljivić-Šimšić 1971: 65–66). For example, in the Jewish newspaper *Židovska Svest* (*Jewish Consciousness*), published in Sarajevo between 1919 and 1924, Dr Moric Levy, Chief Rabbi, issued an announcement asking his fellow Sepharadim to help him collect some of the remaining material of their oral tradition:

> I tim bi htio da svratim pozornost na ove naše stare priče i da zamolim širu javnost, ako tko imade koju staru priču — svakako na španjolskom orginalu — ili ako tko imade još priliku da te priče bilježi, neka nam pomogne pri sakupljanju tako skupocijenog materijala koji se već skoro izgubio. (1919: 2)[7]

> (With this, I would like to draw attention to our old stories and ask the general public, if anyone has an old tale to send — in Spanish of course — or has the opportunity to write down some of these stories, to do so and help us collect this precious material, which is nearly lost.)

Leading Sephardic cultural figures of that time, such as Laura Papo, Abraham Buki Romano (1894–1943) and Abraham Cappon (1853–1930), made significant contributions to these newspapers (Vidaković-Petrov 1990: 64). However, Camhy did not publish any of her work in these periodicals or prior to WWII. Her lack of urgency to write may have been due to two factors: first, she was not a writer by vocation and, second, both the language and tradition were still alive and showed no signs of disappearing in the foreseeable future. However, WWII and the Holocaust changed that situation rapidly and motivated Camhy to start writing for ideological reasons, to safeguard and, if possible, revitalise the tradition and the language of her community.

Camhy found herself in an ideal place to accomplish her goals. From before WWII, Paris had become one of the main centres for the recovery of Sephardic culture. Several societies, such as the Confédération Universelle des Juifs Sepharadim (1925) and the Association Culturelle Sepharadite de Paris (1930), as well as different periodicals were created in this city for this purpose.[8] Camhy's husband was the director and editor of one of these periodicals, *JS*, initially founded in 1932 as a monthly newspaper of the Confédération universelle des Juifs Sépharadim (Abravanel 2013: 113). During its first stage, which ran to 1940, its aims were, as Nicole Abravanel succinctly puts it, 'l'affirmation et la revendication d'une conscience sépharadiste' (2013: 113). The second stage was again launched in Paris but years later, from February 1950 until December 1951, while the third stage was published in London from 1953 until 1966 (Abranavel 2013: 115). Owing to the changed circumstances in the aftermath of WWII, the aims of this third period, in which the periodical was subtitled *la nouvelle série*, also changed, as I explain below.

With the exception of two tales, 'Kuento de Pesah' (1981: 40–41) and 'La tombola' (1987: 79–80), which appeared in *AY*, Camhy published all of her essays, tales, poetry and recipes in *JS*. She made contributions to two further Sephardic periodicals, *Vidas* and *AY*, but most of these works, as seen in the table below, are mere adaptations or complete or partial reworkings of her previous works.

TABLE 2.1. Table of adaptations of Camhy's *JS*'s work in *Vidas* and *AY*

JS	Vidas
'Purim en mi civdad'	Retitled 'Purim'

JS	AY
'Mi nona'	'Medesina popular' (extract from 'Mi nona') 'El prove ke supo enganyar al riko' (a folk tale taken from 'Mi nona') 'El servidor haragan' (a folk tale taken from 'Mi nona') 'Mi nona' (only an extract of 'Mi nona' from JS in spite of having the same title)
'La vida en envierno en Sarajevo'	'Si gritavas komo gritas...' (a folk tale taken from 'La vida...')
'El arte culinario de los sepharadim de Bosnia: el guisado de mi madre'	Retitled 'El gizadu di mi madre'
'El casamiento de la Bukitza IV: consejos de la madre antes de la boda'	Retitled 'Kunsejus de la madre a Bukitsa'
'Tres conĝas'	Retitled 'Tres kondjas a mis ermanas deportadas'
'El casamiento de la Bukiza IV: consejos de la madre antes de la boda'	'Dos kantigas de boda' (one of the wedding songs 'Madre un manseviko' appears in 'El casamiento...')
'El limud de Babu'	'El tio Chuchu' (a folk tale taken from 'El limud de babu')

It is safe to assume that Gina, as Ovadia Camhy's wife, started creating her work to help her husband, a staunch advocate of the collective movement in Paris to safeguard and revitalise the culture of Spanish Jews. This assumption derives from two facts. First, her first published work, 'Purim en mi civdad', appeared in *JS* (1955: 267–69). Prior to this, Camhy had not published anything in France or Bosnia, which means she initiated her work as a writer in the periodical directed by her husband. Second, with the exception of two tales, 'Kuento de Pesah' and 'La Tombola', all of her work was published in *JS*. Indeed, once *JS* ceased to exist, Camhy almost completely abandoned her writing, though she continued to reprint parts of her work in other Sephardic periodicals. She did this in different ways: by adapting some of her works or making minor changes to them, or by dividing one long story or an essay into several parts and then publishing each part separately under a different title (see the table above). Nonetheless, after the closure of *JS* she practically stopped creating new works.

The use of Judeo-Spanish represents one of the main issues in achieving *JS*'s goals and, therefore, those of Camhy as well. As Ruth R. Wisse maintains, a work of great Jewish literature is usually written in a Jewish language; otherwise, the Jewish experience would be difficult, if not impossible, to convey (2000: 322). Wisse's claims are borne out by Camhy's choice to write all of her work in Judeo-Spanish although she was probably educated in the Serbian language and, having lived in Paris, spoke French well. Furthermore, she not only chose Judeo-Spanish as the means of her communication but also promoted the language policy of her husband and *JS*, which sought to modernise Judeo-Spanish by basing it on Spanish. This attitude by *JS* confirms that their Iberian heritage was embedded in the minds of the Sepharadim and was a crucial part of their identity.

However, the language policy of *JS* went through different stages. As described above, there were three phases in the publication of *JS*. During the first period, between 1932 and 1940 — that is, prior to WWII — the periodical was not only published in Paris, but also in French, the common language of all Jews alike living in France, regardless of where they were from. Thus in this first phase, the target readership was local, including both a non-Jewish and Jewish French public. Nonetheless, it is highly probable that the newspaper also targeted Sepharadim living outside of France, in the countries of the former Ottoman Empire and North Africa, where the schools of the Alliance provided an education in French. Those who were educated in these schools spoke fluent French, the language of the classroom.

The aims of the newspaper in this first phase consisted mainly of disseminating information on Sephardic life and current affairs rather than working on the recovery of the language or the legacy. This is because at this time the Sephardic communities in the former Ottoman Empire were still very much alive and their first language was still Judeo-Spanish, which can be seen by the rich literature created in this language at that time.[9] In other words, the heritage was not perceived to be in imminent danger. The beginning of WWII marked the end of this first period in the life of *JS*. The second phase defined itself as a 'revue bilingue' (Abravanel 2013: 314). In addition to French, the newspaper also invited articles in English. However, French remained the dominant language as the newspaper was still being published in Paris.

In the third and final phase, which lasted from 1953 to 1966, the newspaper added a subtitle of *nouvelle série*. The place of publication moved from Paris to London (Abravanel 2013: 115). In keeping with the new aims of the newspaper, an important change regarding the language took place. In addition to articles in French and English, now Spanish, and more importantly, Judeo-Spanish were introduced (Abravanel 2013: 114). This fact indicates an important shift in the aims of the newspaper: *JS* was no longer just a newspaper about the Sepharadim and their culture but it was now a newspaper that intended to recover the Sephardic heritage after the Holocaust and revitalise its language. In fact, the decision of the periodical to publish articles in Judeo-Spanish represents a significant change in its intent:

safeguarding a language on the verge of extinction, even at the risk of one part of the potential readership of the journal not understanding the contributions in Judeo-Spanish. As Abravanel points out, it became 'la revue ambitionne de revitaliser' (2013: 113). Camhy's work and choice of language contributed to this aim.

Once Judeo-Spanish was introduced as one of the languages of the periodical, the issue of the standardisation of Judeo-Spanish arose. There was no standardised orthography for Judeo-Spanish in Latin characters, because for centuries Judeo-Spanish had been written in Hebrew letters.[10] Therefore, the newspaper tried to modernise Judeo-Spanish based on the Spanish language, an act which entailed both morphology and phonetics. As a result, the variations which are found in the Judeo-Spanish spoken by authors from different Sephardic communities did not appear in their original form. The adoption of one transcription system by *JS* rendered it impossible to appreciate all the varieties of the Judeo-Spanish speaking world.

This was also the case with Camhy's writing in *Vidas* and *AY*. Both *Vidas* and *AY* standardised the Judeo-Spanish transcription system in Latin characters according to their own rules (Koén-Sarano 1999: xxx). However, the editors of *Vidas* decided to publish Camhy's essay 'Purim' (1983: 38–43) by adapting it to their spelling rules while at the same time maintaining other phonetic and syntactic traits of her Judeo-Spanish, allowing us to come to some conclusions regarding the language policy of *JS* and Camhy's own Judeo-Spanish.

The society Vidas Largas was founded in 1979 with the idea of uniting the members of the Paris Sephardic community to work on the development, conservation and promotion of Judeo-Spanish culture (anon. 1982: 26–27). In June 1982, the society launched its own periodical, *Vidas largas: Bulletin de l'Association pour le maintien et la promotion de la langue et de la culture judéo-espagnoles*, directed by Guy-Maxime Lizoir and Haïm Vidal Sephiha. The periodical ran for less than seven years (1982–88), during which time seven issues were published containing a number of important articles on Sephardic folklore and tradition.

In 1983, *Vidas* published 'Purim', Camhy's first essay, which had been published in *JS* almost thirty years earlier under the title 'Purim en mi civdad' (1955: 267–69). Camhy's text from *Vidas* is preceded by a note from the editors of the periodical explaining that it is published in accordance with the journal's spelling rules, but 'nous tenons à respecter la prononciation de l'auteur de ces souvenirs, Madame Gina Camhy' (Camhy 1983: 38). Although *Vidas* had its own policy regarding the spelling of Judeo-Spanish, its transcription of Ladino in Latin characters was similar to the spelling practice found in Sephardic authors from Bosnia. The latter wrote Judeo-Spanish influenced by the spelling system of Serbo-Croatian. Thus they used phonemes such as /k/ as in *kriatura* instead of /c/ for *criatura*, which would be Spanish spelling favoured by *JS*; or, /dj/ as in *nostaldjia* instead of /g/ for *nostalgia*. It suffices to look at the literary works of Isak Papo or Rikica Ovadija, both from Bosnia and both Camhy's contemporaries, to comprehend that these traits are typical of Judeo-Spanish from Bosnia.[11] And these phonemes were also used by *Vidas*.

The main features of Camhy's Judeo-Spanish, conserved in *Vidas*, is the use of closed vowels, /i/ for /e/ and /u/ for /o/. This is considered to be a common trait of Bosnian Judeo-Spanish.[12] Compare the following extract from *Vidas* with the *JS* version: 'Un dia *antis* si preparava las roskas finas, una espesya *di* pan *amasadu kun* azeti, *lus fularis pintadus kun bunbunikus...*' (Camhy 1983: 38; [my emphasis]) and 'Un dia *antes* si preparava las roscas finas, una especia *de* pan *amasado con* aceite, *los folares pintados con bonbonicos...*' (Camhy 1955: 267; [my emphasis]). Not only does *JS*'s spelling resemble modern Spanish (*roscas*, *aceite*, *especia* instead of *roskas*, *azeti*, *espesya*), but the opposition of open/closed vowels typical of Bosnian Judeo-Spanish is lost in the *JS* version.

In short, Camhy started writing and publishing her essays, tales, poetry and recipes once away from her Bosnian home and in Paris, in the active Sephardic cultural revival movement which emerged there after WWII. She joined the efforts of her husband to revitalise the Judeo-Spanish language and the culture of Spanish Jews, mainly through the periodical *JS*, of which her husband was the editor and director. In this journal, Camhy published all of her work in Judeo-Spanish.

Furthermore, Camhy continued to fight for the same cause once *JS* shut down. She became a valuable contributor to other Sephardic periodicals, namely *Vidas* and *AY*, which shared the same goals as *JS*. However, Camhy barely wrote anything new after the closure of *JS* but rather re-edited her previously published work, with no or only minor changes. In this way, she continued to disseminate worldwide her own work and, more importantly, the language and tradition of the Sepharadim.

Finally, her decision to publish her work in Judeo-Spanish was essential for her goal of reactivating this endangered language. Unfortunately, the policy of *JS* of modernising Judeo-Spanish to resemble Spanish renders it impossible for us to appreciate the traits of Camhy's own Judeo-Spanish and consequently that of the Bosnian Sepharadim. However, the other periodical, *Vidas*, in which only one of her works was republished, does allow us to see phonetic, morphological and syntactic traits of her Judeo-Spanish. What can be appreciated in her texts wherever they were published is how she highlights different authentic features of her community, a detailed description of Jewish festivities, customs and folklore, points I examine in the following chapter.

Recalling the Past: Jewish Festivities, Food and Poetry in Camhy's Literature

In this chapter, I discuss Camhy's work as a reflection of a realm in which women prevailed. This has been highlighted by Paloma Díaz-Mas, who maintains that Sephardic literature written by women tends to depict the home environment because it was there that women held the leading role (2009b: 72–73). The forms of traditional life that Camhy describes are closely connected to religious practices such as the celebration of Purim, Pesach (Passover) and Rosh Hashanah (Jewish New Year). Celebration of these dates in the Jewish calendar takes place primarily in the home, usually during the course of a family meal, where women are in charge of several key elements, such as the preparation of food in accordance with *Kashrut*, Jewish religious dietary laws.[13] Camhy's literature intends to re-create this lost world while living away from the community that was once hers and is now a memory. In relation to this, another genre must be also examined: the traditional poetry which, according to Camhy, the Sepharadim from Bosnia associated with the celebration of Purim. I intend to highlight the incorporation of these profane songs into this particular festivity, which constitutes a unique trait of the Bosnian Sephardic community.

Camhy's literature as a whole can be defined as memory work. According to Schorsch, this type of literature is relatively recent among the Sepharadim, 'following on the heels of a large number of Ashkenazic memoirs written in Europe, memoirs of immigrants Jews to the United States (overwhelmingly Ashkenazic), and memoirs of experiences in the Holocaust (again, overwhelmingly Ashkenazic)' (2007: 87). This assertion is only partly true as vestiges of this literature in the Sephardic world can be traced back to the end of the nineteenth century, as shown in *Part I*.

These Sephardic authors, including Camhy, usually grew up surrounded by Sephardic tradition but also experienced the cultural, social and political changes which the Sephardic communities underwent in the twentieth century. Camhy, for instance, was raised in the spirit of the Jewish religion and the Sephardic language and tradition. But even while she was growing up, changes were taking place in the life of her community, including the Sepharadim abandoning their traditional education and switching to a secular education in the Serbian language. Consequently, the role of women also changed as they now started to gain an education and speak languages in addition to Judeo-Spanish. Furthermore, after World War I, Bosnia became part of the Kingdom of Serbs, Croatians and Slovenes, which contributed to the Sepharadim's distancing themselves more and more from their roots and assimilating into this new country. However, in spite of these new circumstances, Camhy claims that 'malgrado el viento de modernismo que soplava en la civdad, las tradiciones eran respectadas, la religion observada' ('regardless of the wind of modernisation which was blowing in the city, the traditions were respected, the religion observed') (1955: 310).

The fact that Camhy was a female author determined in many respects the topics of her work. Pilar Romeu Ferré notes that memory works written by women offer a different vision of the world to that of men (2008: 104). This is expressed not only in general terms but also in the details they consider relevant and which depict the world of women as separate from that of men. This female vision entails several general features which appear repeatedly, such as the solidity of a large family, neighbourly friendliness, the importance given to culinary skills which produced tastes and aromas of exquisite fragrances, faithfully continuing to observe traditions, or showing profound respect towards their elders. Therefore, the memoirs, autobiographies and testimonies of Sephardic women offer information about the life of a traditional Sephardic society steeped in ancestral customs which no longer exist. At the same time, this literature allows us to reflect upon how the Sepharadim themselves construct the discourse of their own recent past and their own collective memory.[14]

FIG. 2.1. *Kandil di Shabat* ['Shabbat candle'], Bosnia.
From the private collection of Eliezer Papo

Camhy's work falls in line with the findings of Romeu Ferré and Díaz-Mas, as can be seen by some of her titles: 'Purim en mi civdad' ('The Festival of Lots in My Town'), 'El sabado en mi civdad' ('Shabbat in my Town'), 'Los aparejos de Pesah' ('The Preparations for Passover'), 'El limud de babu' ('The Anniversary of my Grandfather's Death'), and 'El arte culinario de los sepharadim' ('The Culinary Art of the Sepharadim'). A particularly apposite example is her treatment of *Kashrut*.

The significance of food goes far beyond nourishment. As Davis has noted, dietary regulations form part of one's heritage and reflect one's sense of identity: '[the heritage] exists in objects we might use in our daily lives, in the buildings we inhabit at home and at work, the food we eat' (2012: 6). In this way, a community's past is recalled, where it lived and where it ventured, all the while accompanied by its familiar, comforting food habits (Pomeroy 2006: 146). The importance of food is apparent in a number of dishes Camhy cites in her work. Between 1958 and 1965, Camhy published in *JS* numerous articles on food made by the Bosnian Sepharadim.[15] She indicated which dishes were made for Shabbat, which for Passover and which formed part of daily Sephardic cuisine.

In traditional societies, the preservation of this type of heritage belongs to women; it is transmitted among them, usually from mother to daughter. This can be seen in Camhy's essay, 'El guisado de mi madre' ('My Mother's Cooking') (1958: 736–37), in which she recalls how her mother prepared food, what kind of dishes she made for certain occasions and what advice she offered to her daughters related to cooking. The preparation of food, according to Camhy's mother, is a key element of every home and a key duty of every *balabaya* ('housewife'). This highlights the position of women in the Sephardic family: in the home –– and within the home, in the kitchen:

> Un dia antes [de Purim] si preparava las roscas finas (una especia de pan amasado con aceite), los 'folares' pintados con bonbonicos, en forma de corazon, o con los iniciales de las personas a quien se va regalar. Despues si preparava las roskitas de alhashu (con nuezes), il tishpishti, la baklava y diversas tortas para mandar 'platicos de Purim'. (1955: 267)

> (A day before [the Festival of Lots] *roscas finas* (a type of bread prepared with oil), heart-shaped 'folares' covered with chocolate, or with the initials of the people for whom these were meant as gifts, were prepared. Then *roskitas de alhashu* with walnuts, the *tishpishti*, the *baklava* and various other cakes were made to send as 'Purim's gifts'.)

Sephardic cuisine makes ample use of walnuts and almonds, as can be seen in this description of sweets prepared for Purim. According to Claudia Roden, this legacy was most probably brought from Spain: 'Jews specialize in almond pastries, and in marzipan made in the Spanish way, with the ground almonds cooked in sugar syrup to a dry paste' (1999: 261). Olive oil is another extensively used ingredient seen as a legacy of the Jews. During the Middle Ages in the Iberian Peninsula, olive oil was used by Christians, Muslims and Jews alike. However, Christians used lard (pork fat) for cooking meat while the Muslims used clarified butter. Neither of these ingredients could be used by the Jews as the rules of *Kashrut* forbid the consumption of pork as well as the mixture of meat and dairy products and thus the use of butter (Roden 1999: 259; Pomeroy 2006: 143).[16] Camhy's recipes highlight the use of olive oil in Sephardic cuisine, not only for cooking but also for baking (1958: 774–75; 1959: 821; 1960: 874).

Another important ingredient widely used in Sephardic kitchens, including Camhy's, is aubergine. In her article about the Sephardic cuisine in Bosnia, Camhy enumerates no less than twelve dishes made by her mother in which the main ingredient was aubergine: *anchussa, mussaca, dolma, picada, aivar, bocadico, esfongato, insalata, fetas, a la Dalmata, yaprakes* and *turlu* (1960: 874). The association of the use of aubergine with Jews goes back to medieval Spain, when this vegetable was used as a reference to the dietary habits of the Jews or the *conversos* in Christian Spain from the fifteenth to the late nineteenth century (Pomeroy 2006: 138). In fact, several inquisitorial trials referred to aubergine dishes, such as *boronía* or *cazuela de verengenas moxíes*, consumed during Sabbath lunch, as proof of judaising (Gitlitz and Davidson 1999: 144). Spanish Jews adopted aubergine while living in al-Andalus and later took it with them as they moved north to Christian Spain, where its consumption was considered typically Jewish. One such dish, known as *almodrote de berendjena*, consisting of mashed aubergine baked with eggs and cheese, is still one of the most popular dishes among Istanbuli Jews (Roden 1999: 259). Camhy mentions this dish, which she calls *anchussa*; she provides her mother's recipe and explains how to prepare it, thus demonstrating its presence in the Bosnian Sephardic tradition (1960: 874).

Camhy might have been encouraged by her husband to start creating literary works, but the topics of her work and the type of literature she wrote were most certainly inspired by the literature she knew while growing up in her native Bosnia. This conclusion is based on the fact that she herself mentions the kind of Sephardic literature and Sephardic authors to which she was exposed before WWII (1956: 496–500). Laura Papo's name stands out; she undoubtedly influenced Camhy's work with regard to the topics treated and the language used.

Camhy mentions Laura Papo in her tale, 'El casamiento de la Bukiza' ('Bukiza's Wedding').[17] Published in four installments (1956: 496–500; 1956: 533–35; 1957: 597–99; 1957: 644–46), it describes all the preparations for marriage of a Sephardic woman. The protagonist is based on Camhy's cousin, Bukiza. In the first part, Camhy reveals that it was while she was watching a play written by Laura Papo being performed by the group La Matatia that Bukiza met her sweetheart, Davule. This reveals that Camhy most probably frequented Sephardic theatre performances in Sarajevo. As indicated earlier, contemporary Bosnian (Sephardic) theatrical life was very much alive and productive in the first half of the twentieth century. At the same time, by mentioning Laura Papo, Camhy shows that she knew her work and was probably influenced by it.

This can be seen by the fact that Camhy chose to write all of her work in Judeo-Spanish, as did Laura Papo, in addition to fostering similar topics and motifs: the position and the role of a Sephardic woman within her own society, the clash between the old and the new, the presence of folklore in everyday life. Likewise, before the text of 'El casamiento de la Bukiza', a short note reveals that, although the customs of the Sepharadim of Bosnia are described here in the form of a tale, the author — Camhy — also intends to write a play depicting them (1956: 496). Although no plays by Camhy are extant, this paragraph nonetheless indicates that Camhy planned to write one. And since Laura Papo was best known for her plays, which Camhy saw performed in Bosnia, she most likely viewed Laura Papo as a literary role model.

Camhy was also influenced by Laura Papo in her use of folk literature. Camhy frequently used oral poetry and narrative to display the richness and vividness of this tradition in her own home and in the Bosnian Sephardic community. However, her use of folk literature differs from that of Laura Papo, as discussed in the following chapter. Here the focus is on the *coplas de Purim* that Camhy cites as part of Bosnian Purim celebrations.

The *coplas* ('couplets'), a specific type of poetry first documented in the eighteenth century, are the most typical genre of Sephardic literature. The poems are usually narrative or descriptive and contain acrostic stanzas. Although occasionally adopted by oral tradition, they were usually written by known authors rather than being anonymous (Dias-Mas 2006: 160).[18] *Coplas* usually had religious or didactic themes, celebrating stories from the Old Testament, such as the story of the wife of King Ahashverosh, Queen Esther, who saved the Jews from the threats of Haman (*coplas de Purim*), or the story of the exodus in which the Jews were freed from slavery

FIG. 2.2. Purim celebrations.
Jevrejski istorijski muzej, Belgrade, Serbia

in Egypt (*coplas de Pesah*). However, *coplas* can also simply depict Sephardic folk customs and habits, such as cuisine, an example of which is *Koplas del gizado de las berendjenas*, which describes the various ways of preparing aubergine (Díaz-Mas 2006: 163–65).

Camhy's 'Purim en mi civdad' is a reality-based essay describing Purim in Bosnia (1955: 267–69). At the beginning, Camhy indicates that she recalls such celebrations with nostalgia. This is not only because the custom had started to fade away but also because she was no longer in Bosnia, and she found that the celebration of this holiday differed elsewhere (1955: 311). In addition to a very detailed description of the food and customs, such as holding costume parties or playing games, Camhy highlights lyrical songs as one of the most essential elements of these festivities. As Davis points out, 'one's heritage can be located in stories, memories passed down from generation to generation, in the ritual acts of the day, year or lifespan' (2012: 6).

Camhy recalls four songs being performed for this day (1955: 268–69). The first is typical of Purim and marks the end of one year's festivities and the coming of the next holiday, Passover: 'Purim, Purim lanu | Pesah en la mano' ('Purim, for us Purim | Passover is almost here'). Samuel Elazar from Bosnia also recalls this song being performed and explains its historical symbolism: 'Poesía que se cantaba después de Purim, pero antes de la fiesta de Pasha, como recuerdo de que el pueblo de Israel, liberado de la esclavitud egipcia, atravesó el Mar Rojo' (1987: 341). Furthermore, Elazar underlines the occasion and place where it was usually sung in Bosnia: 'se cantaba durante las labores de casa, entre Purim y Pesah' (1987: 210).

We can assume that this song was most likely performed by women, as it was the women who were in charge of the ritual cleaning of the house in preparation for Passover (Camhy 1956: 425; Elazar 1987: 341).[19]

However, the other three songs that Camhy cites are more striking for two reasons: their link to Purim in spite of being purely secular in nature, and their emphasis on heartbreak. This means that they were not originally composed to be performed for Purim but eventually became part of the repertoire of the Bosnian Sepharadim's celebration of this day. All three songs, 'Adio kerida' ('Goodbye, my love'), 'Sekretos kero diskuvrir' ('I want to tell my secrets') and 'Yo hanina, tu hanino' ('I'm beautiful, you're beautiful'), are expressions either of heartbreak or the exaltation of love. Particularly interesting is the song about heartbreak, 'Sekretos kero diskuvrir' (hereafter 'Sekretos'), which, despite its melancholy tone, was associated with Purim, the most cheerful of all Jewish festivals.[20] The first stanza of the poem reads:

> Sekretus keru diskuvrir
> Sekretus di mi vida.
> Los syelus keru pur papel,
> La mar keru por tinta.
> Lus arvolis pur pendula
> Para eskrivir mis dertis (Camhy 1983: 40)[21]

> (I want to tell my secrets
> Secrets of my life.
> The sky will be my paper,
> The sea my ink.
> The trees my pen
> To describe my broken heart)

This stanza immediately reveals that this is a love song expressing broken-heartedness or the longing for the beloved through the use of the Turkish borrowing *dertis*, meaning 'heartache' (Nehama 1977: 121). The lines from 'Los syelos...' to the end adhere to an old rhetorical formula found in Jewish sources such as the Talmud or the Midras Rabbah (Vidaković-Petrov 1986: 144). In the Talmud, the formula appears in a legend about Yehoshua ben Levi, a third-century Rabbi who headed the school of Lydda in the southern land of Palestine (Vidaković-Petrov 1985: 186–87). The legend, told by Johanan Ben Zakai, recounts how Yehoshua was permitted to visit paradise and ends with these words: 'If the sky was paper and all the trees were pens and the whole ocean was ink, these would not suffice to describe my wisdom' (Kivistö 2014: 140). This led Vidaković-Petrov to conclude that there must be a direct line connecting old Jewish sources with the modern variants of the poem.[22] However, these might not be the only source as this motif, according to Ernst Robert Curtius (1984: 1, 231–35), can also be found in Medieval Latin texts across Europe. Furthermore, it has also been recorded in a number of folk songs in Iberia (see, for instance, Rodríguez Marín 2005: 209 n. 2377; 265 n. 3553; Díaz-Mas and Sánchez-Pérez 2013: 97; 203–04 n. 25), thus indicating that this motif has also been absorbed and disseminated by oral literature.

Although examples of the song have been recorded among both the Western and Eastern Sepharadim, the groups performed the poem for different occasions and to convey different meanings. As Vidaković-Petrov explains:

> Among the West Sephardim (Morocco) the formula is contained in the concluding stanza of a long *quiná* [lament] called *La almenara*, where it is interpreted in the context of Tiš'á beab [...] as an expression of the tragic destiny of the people after the destruction of the Temple. (1986: 146)

Among the Eastern Sepharadim, specifically in Salonica, this formula was also sung in the temple for the Ninth of Av:

> Como lo diće de una manera image una de las endechas que se recitan en el día de hoy en las quehilot, si los árboles se trocarían en péndolas, y la mar en tinta, ellos no bastarían para recontar los desterramientos, los pogromos, las calumnias y todos los males donde fue víctima el pueblo judió de cuando él pedrió su morada nacionala. (Díaz-Mas 1982: 181)

> (As it is described in a metaphor of one of the laments which are recited today in synagogues, if trees were to become pens and sea ink, these would not suffice to recount all the expulsions, pogroms, slanders and all the evil to which Jews were exposed once they lost their home.)

However, in spite of this information, all other examples of the song collected from among the Eastern Mediterranean Sepharadim, including the one by Camhy, suggest that this formula had a different role in the Eastern Mediterranean: that of a secular love song (Vidaković-Petrov 1986: 147). The question that arises here is why the Sepharadim in Bosnia would have associated this song with Purim. What connection could there have been between this joyful festivity in the Jewish calendar and a sad love song? The answer to this may lie in the fact that Purim takes place during the month of Adar (February-March), and as Gila Hadar has pointed out:

> The month of Adar was the month when traditionally weddings were held. It was in this month that marriage agreements were signed between families and many wedding celebrations took place, and to this may be traced the origin of the phrase: 'Purim de las novias', 'Sabah di las novias'. (2006: 55)

This custom of wedding arrangements is described in detail in other sources that indicate that wedding ceremonies were held during this particular month and hence many love songs, whether happy or sad, could be linked to this particular holiday.[23] As not all arranged weddings produced happy marriages and not all young couples managed to fulfill their desire to get married, 'Sekretos', with its melancholy content, has its place within this festivity. However, there are no testimonies in other Sephardic communities that cite this particular song as part of Purim celebrations, and therefore it can be considered a unique trait of the Bosnian Sephardic community.

Unlike 'Sekretos' or 'Adio kerida', which also describes an unhappy love situation, the third song, 'Yo hanina, tu hanino', exalts love through a wedding ceremony between two people in love. The song 'refleja la costumbre de enviar a un corridor o casamentero para tramitar el posible matrimonio, concertar las condiciones económicas que se ofrecen para unir así a los dos agraciados (*hanino* y *hanina*, del hebreo: *hen*=gracia)' (Weich-Shahak 2013: 183). This poem represents another unique element of Bosnian Sephardic folklore, because it is from there that the only known versions proceed. In addition to the one by Camhy (1955: 268), three more versions have been recorded, all collected by Susana Weich-Shahak (2013: 183–84). The first two were recorded from Dona Cohen and Clara Kadmón-Cohen, both originally from Sarajevo, but who now live in Israel. The third one was given to Weich-Shahak by Simo Calderón, originally from Macedonia. However, after emigrating to Israel, Calderón lived with people who had come from Sarajevo, and he most likely came to learn this poem from them.

Camhy's essay, 'Purim en mi civdad', was published again in *Vidas* under the title 'Purim' (1983: 38–43). Minor changes to the text indicate that Camhy adapted the tale for its republication. One of the noteworthy changes is the poetry Camhy cites as part of the celebrations of Purim in Bosnia. Unlike the first edition, which included four songs, here only two appear. The first is 'Purim Purim lanu...', and the second is 'Sekretos', thus reinforcing the idea of this secular song being performed as part of the Purim celebrations in Bosnia. The two other songs, 'Adio kerida' and 'Yo hanina, tu hanino', were not included. Camhy may have decided to omit them because they were not part of the usual repertoire for Purim, but it is impossible to know for certain.

Whatever the case, the *coplas de Purim* that Camhy cites indicate the uniqueness of the Sephardic community in Bosnia compared to other Sephardic communities. While 'Yo hanina, tu hanino' was documented exclusively among Bosnian Sepharadim, 'Sekretos' shows how a song underwent a change of performance context, consequently entailing a shift in interpretation. In Bosnia, 'Sekretos' was not a song which describes suffering on a national level and thus was not linked to the Ninth of Av, as it was in Morocco; rather, it was a personal song, expressing feelings of unrequited love. This interpretation enabled its association with Purim celebrations, which traditionally take place during the month of Adar when wedding ceremonies are held. This connection between the song and Purim, according to Camhy's account, occurred in her community and, as stated above, the lack of evidence demonstrating the use of this song for Purim in other communities makes this a unique trait of the Bosnian Sepharadim.

Furthermore, Camhy's literature depicts topics which encompass the world of women. The dominant issues concern the role of women in the traditional Sephardic society and the celebration of the most important Jewish holidays. In her literature, Camhy focuses only on her community, thus revealing valuable information about the Bosnian Sepharadim in times when they were undergoing important historical, social and cultural changes. Another important aspect of her work, which I examine in the next chapter, is the oral narratives that she collected and published within her tales.

Folk tales in Camhy's Work: Collections, Recovery and Dissemination

By turning her eyes to her community and its customs and traditions, Camhy inevitably afforded folklore a special place in her work. Her treatment of folk literature is above all that of a collector. Although Camhy introduces genres of oral literature, such as folk tales and folk poetry, into her work, she does not make the same use of them as Davičo or Laura Papo, who employ them as commentary on the unfolding story or as the basis for their work. Camhy does so merely to record evidence of folk literature in order to safeguard it and disseminate it. This use of folk literature is typical of Sephardic authors from the region during the second half of the twentieth century.

Camhy's work on collecting, safeguarding and disseminating Bosnian Sephardic folk literature, particularly folk narrative, represents one of the fundamental aspects of her work for various reasons. Firstly, barely any examples of Sephardic folk tales have been recorded in Bosnia. Unlike the *romancero* or chapbooks from Bosnia, where a considerable range of examples have been collected and recorded (Armistead 1978: III, 86–99; Elazar 1987), in the field of folk narrative only two examples were known: a tale told by a certain *sinyora* Katan and published by Kalmi Baruh (1930: 140–45), and 'El sadrezán' ('The Grand Vizier'), compiled by Cynthia M. Crews in Sarajevo in 1929 from an anonymous seventy-year-old washerwoman (1979: 168–78). Therefore, Camhy's collection of folk tales enlarges and enriches the relatively small repertoire of Ladino folk narrative already in existence in Bosnia.

Although she had also collected poems and songs, a special bond existed between Camhy and folk tales as they were a connection with her childhood and with her grandmother, who was the main source for diverse folk material: 'Las consejicas de mi nona eran famosas y muy divertientes. Cuando, por enjemplo, ella mos topava haraganas, ella mos contava anecdotas y mosotros la escuchavamos con grande atencion. He aqui una de ellas' ('The folk tales of my granny were famous and very entertaining. When she used to find us idle she told us anecdotes and we listened to her carefully. Here is one of them') (Camhy 1955: 354). In addition to respecting and following Jewish religious principles, as in her descriptions of Shabbat, Purim or Hannukah, we can see that in her home, among family, there was also a tradition of transmitting folk heritage from generation to generation. The home, as highlighted by Reginneta Haboucha, was one of the main places where generations of Sephardic Jews transmitted tales: 'Sephardic Jews inherited a long and varied tradition of storytelling. Like other fellow Jews, they have been telling and retelling their history through weekly Torah readings and holiday celebrations, as well as at family and social gatherings' (1992: 19).

The fact that Camhy's grandmother was her main source for folk material is in keeping with the assumption that, in accordance with the traditional role of Sephardic women, it was the women who were the main guardians and performers of oral literature. The home was at once their realm and one of the key places where folk literature was imparted. This has been corroborated by the fact that when Manuel Manrique de Lara set out to compile ballads from among the Eastern Mediterranean Sepharadim, his informants were mainly Sephardic women, most of whom were illiterate members of the lower classes who nevertheless knew and performed folklore:

> It is significant to verify that most of the people who sang or recited ballads and songs for Manrique de Lara were women. There is a list of almost 120 women as survey informants while there are about 30 men. In some locations, such as Jerusalem or Rhodes, only the women were able to sing or recite ballads to him. Even if the family relationships among the informants only appear occasionally in Manrique's notes, if we take the surnames into account, we can reach the conclusion that on some occasions Manrique interviewed several generations of women belonging to the same family. For example, in Tangier he interviewed Simhá Bennaim, aged 98, Hanna Bennaim, aged 70, and Clara and Estrella Bennaim, aged 24 and 18. (Díaz-Mas 2009a: 84)[24]

Unlike her fellow citizens, Laura Papo and Kalmi Baruh (1930: 113–54; 1933: 272–88), who conducted interviews with the members of the Bosnian community, Camhy never carried out such interviews. This is due to the fact that she only began writing once in Paris. The fact that her collection comes from her own memory, from what she had heard and learned in her home, means that she was simultaneously an informant and a collector. By publishing her work and including folk tales, Camhy contributed both to ensuring that the tradition did not fall into oblivion and to revitalising it.

Although Camhy introduced folk tales into her own work, they are not directly related to the plot of her stories. This technique of using folk material is quite different from that seen in Davičo or Laura Papo. Those authors used elements of folklore to reinforce the ideas of their own stories, often drawing a parallel between the plot of their own work and the plot of the folk material they used. Camhy, by contrast, introduces tales by simply highlighting her grandmother's custom of recounting them and then providing the text of the tale the way that she remembers it. For example, 'Suegra ni de baro buena' is the title of a folk tale introduced in her essay 'La vida en envierno en Sarajevo' ('Winter Life in Sarajevo') (1955: 390–91). The essay itself consists of several parts: the main part is dedicated to the description of winter in Sarajevo and describes the kinds of games that were played then, such as chess, cards, *endivinar los dedos* ('odds and evens') and *la tombola* ('bingo').[25] Camhy includes four stories at the end of the essay. The first is about an annual ball, and the second is about Hanukkah; both are connected to the essay because they are winter events.

Nevertheless, the other two stories are *konsežas*, a term that Camhy herself uses and which in the Sephardic world, as stated earlier, designates a folk tale. One of these two tales is the above-cited 'Suegra ni de baro buena'. This folk tale has no connection to the main subject matter. It makes reference to a well-known Sephardic proverb which indicates that the relationship between a woman and her mother-in-law is a complicated one. Therefore, the purpose of introducing this and the fourth tale, also a folk tale, is just to record them and thus contribute to their safeguarding and dissemination. Likewise, other folk tales Camhy published usually appear within a larger story but have no thematic connection to it.

Camhy published a total of eight folk tales. Sometimes they appear with a title, while at other times they are introduced with a general term, *konseža*, or with no introduction, as the table below shows:

TABLE 2.2. Eight folk tales collected and (re)published by Camhy in *JS* and *AY*, and their ATU or Haboucha's Judeo-Spanish tale-type numbers

JS	AY	ATU tale-type number	Haboucha's tale-type number
No title given; appears as part of 'Mi nona' (1955: 354)	'El servidor haragan' (1982: 44)		★★1950B 'Thirsty Man Too Lazy To Fetch Himself a Drink'
No title given; appears as part of 'Mi nona' (1955: 355)	'El prove ke supo enganyar al riko' (1981: 40–42; 2004: 110–11)	ATU1543 'Not One Penny Less'	
'Suegra ni de baro buena'; appears as part of 'La vida en envierno en Sarajevo' (1955: 390–91)			★★903C 'Not Even in Pictures'
'No gritates'; appears as part of 'La vida en envierno en Sarajevo' (1955: 391)	'Si gritavas komo gritas' (1985: 75)		★★912 'Had You Only Done Then What You Do Now'
No title given; appears as part of 'El limud de babu' (1957: 679)			★★1722 'Close Shop!'
No title given; appears as part of 'El limud de babu' (1957: 679)	'El tio Chuchu' (1986: 65)		★★1216 'So We Can All Live'
No title given; appears as part of 'El limud de babu' (1957: 679)			★★1681C 'Eye Doctor Advised to Become a Dentist'
	'Kuento de Pesah' (1981: 40–41)	ATU1541 'For the Long Winter'	

The table shows several features of the material collected by Camhy and her working methods. It indicates that in order to disseminate her work, she republished her tales in different places. Thus, four out of eight folk tales, which had previously appeared in *JS* as parts of longer tales, were re-edited for *AY*. Due to their self-contained nature, they were easily reprinted independently.

Furthermore, according to the ATU or Haboucha's classification, all eight folk tales fit within two categories: jokes and anecdotes, or numbskull stories. There may be two reasons for this. First, as Camhy acknowledges, her grandmother's purpose in telling these tales was to entertain her grandchildren and make them laugh (1955: 354). Secondly, Camhy aims to present and construct a positive image of her community and the past by choosing to write about symbolic days and festivities of the Sephardic world as well as by introducing folk tales that are enjoyable and entertaining. Camhy's use of humour to create a positive image of the community is a technique also used by Davičo with his *Women's Tricks*.

Another noteworthy feature of these tales is that only two of them, 'El prove ke supo enganyar al riko' ('A Poor Man Who Knew How To Trick a Rich One') and 'Kuento de Pesah' ('A Tale of Pesach'), belong to internationally known tale-types, recorded in ATU catalogue (2004), as indicated by their reference numbers in the table above. Others appear in Haboucha's catalogue of Judeo-Spanish folk tales (1992) and were assigned numbers preceded by two asterisks, meaning that they are oicotypes, i.e., recorded only in the Sephardic or Jewish tradition.

The traditional background of these tales and their Sephardic idiosyncrasy also lies in the use of fixed language forms typical of Sephardic oral tales. *Avia de ser* would be the most usual opening to a tale, while *Eyos tengan bien i mozotros tambien* is a common closing formula. Although these opening or closing formulae are typically found in fairy tales, in the Sephardic tradition they appear in any kind of folk tale, not only indicating its oral character but also suggesting a cultural adaptation of the story to the Judeo-Spanish tradition of storytelling:

> When, because of the changing circumstances surrounding a storytelling event, an audience has little or no understanding of Judeo-Spanish, the storyteller must settle for the incorporation of expressions and proverbs into a narrative performance in the dominant language. When Judeo-Spanish expressions do not lend themselves to translation, they must be replaced by equivalent expressions, such as opening and closing formulae in the fairy tale: 'Avia de ser' (Once upon a time), 'Eyos tengan bien y mozotros tambien' (May it go well for them, and also for us). (Alexander-Frizer 2008: 14–15)

A case in point is the tale 'El prove ke supo enganyar al riko', which opens with 'Avia de ser un servidor muy haragan' ('Once upon a time, there was a lazy servant') and ends with the well-known formula 'Ellos tengan bien y mosotros también' (1955: 354–55). The story can be summarised as follows: with the intention of deceiving his wealthy neighbour, a poor man pretends every morning to plead to God to grant him one hundred gold coins, swearing that he would not accept one coin less. His neighbour, surprised that anyone could refuse gold, regardless of the quantity, throws him a purse containing ninety-nine coins to put him to the test. The poor man thanks God and then, when the miser tries in vain to get his money back, exclaiming that it was he who gave him the coins, the trickster insists that it was God. Wanting to retrieve his money, the wealthy neighbour takes the case to court. Refusing to appear in court dressed in rags, the trickster demands that his neighbour dress him regally and supply him with a donkey on which to ride. The wealthy miser accepts, himself trudging through the mud. When they appear at court, the trickster alludes to his neighbour's unkempt appearance claiming that such a man could not have lent him the money. He argues further that it would have been equally ludicrous for his neighbour to have dressed him in finery and given him a donkey on which to ride to court. When the miser confesses that he has done just so, the judge rules in favour of the trickster (Camhy 1955: 354–55).

The tale is a combination of two different tale-types, ATU1543, 'Not One Penny Less' and ATU1642A, 'The Borrowed Coat' (Uther 2004: II, 282–83 and 349). Several examples of it have been recorded among the Sepharadim. Koén-

Sarano collected a version in 1984 from Ester Malkí Koen, a Sephardic Jew from Izmir, Turkey, which she published twice: in *Kuentos del folklore de la famiya djudeo-espanyola* (1986: 161) and in *Djohá ke dize?: kuentos populares djudeo-espanyoles* (1991: 217). The tale follows the same pattern as Camhy's, with one minor difference: here the main character is called Djohá, whereas in Camhy's version he bears no name.[26] Nevertheless, in various tale-types usually having Djohá as a protagonist, a comic character well known both among the Arabs and the Sepharadim, he is often unnamed:

> El nombre del personaje se ha deformado al pasar de una región a otra, a veces precedido de Sī (por Sīdī), especialmente entre los bereberes, o con el nombre turco, Nasr al-Din, especialmente entre los países de la Europa del Este y Asia, por llegar a ellos a través de la versión turca. Otras veces cambia de nombre o aparece de forma anónima. (Thomas de Antonio 1933: 190)

Numerous examples of this tale-type naming Djohá as protagonist have been recorded among Arabs and Turks. In the Arabic versions, he is called Juhā, whereas in the Turkish versions he is known as Nasr al-Din Khodja (Boratav 1955: n. 19; Hikmet 1959: 115; Wesselski 1911: 1, 220 n. 54).[27] In fact, there is evidence that this tale may have appeared among the Sepharadim in Bosnia as a result of cross-cultural exchange between the Sepharadim and their (Ottoman) environment, a common occurrence throughout the Sephardic history in the Ottoman Empire. As Tamar Alexander-Frizer points out:

> The Sephardic group, like every other Jewish ethnic group, cannot create the borders of the internal group circle without referring to broader reference groups: the stock of Jewish culture common to all Jewish groups; the connection to the land of origin, Spain, that is unique to this group; the relationship to the places they resided in the interim before coming to Israel, particularly the Balkan countries; and, finally, living in a pluralistic Israeli society. (2008: 23)

The tale under discussion was recorded among the Ottomans in Bosnia as early as the eighteenth century and could easily have been passed on to the Sepharadim. It appears in the *Ljetopis* (*Chronicle*) by the Bosnian Muslim author Mula Mustafa Ševki Bašeskija (1731/32–1809). Ševki Bašeskija was born into a poor family in Sarajevo, where he grew up and started working as a public scribe. He spent his entire life in Bosnia, mostly in Sarajevo, although he visited Belgrade, Serbia, briefly on one occasion (Mujezinović 1987: 5–7). At the age of twenty-five, Ševki Bašeskija began his *Ljetopis* to record important events from his environment. In addition to chronicling data and necrology, the book contains various tales and anecdotes, a chapter on dreams and their interpretation, the Hebrew, Serbian and Italian alphabets, folk songs and riddles (Mujezinović 1987: 13–14).

One of the tales (*hićaja*) contained in the book is a Turkish version of the tale-type analysed here in which Nasr al-Dīn Khodja appears as the main character. This tale follows the pattern of Camhy's, combining the same two tale-types where the wealthy neighbour is duped and a trial ensues. However, there is a basic difference regarding ethnicity: here the wealthy neighbour is a Jew (Ševki Bašeskija 1987: 372). As a result of the acculturation of the tale to the Sephardic mentality, the identity of the dupe has been changed in Camhy's version; he naturally loses his Jewish label, although he retains the Jewish stereotypical characteristics. The miser is portrayed as someone who has money and is greedy (he cannot believe that someone would refuse gold or money) and who therefore receives a deserved punishment in the end. Also, the practice of morning prayers in both Camhy's and Koén-Sarano's versions alludes to Jewish religious customs. Morning prayer is called *šajarit* or *tefilá* and is one of the three daily prayers performed in Judaism. The other two are *minhá*, taking place after noon, and *'arbit*, at dusk (Díaz-Mas 2006: 37).

After examining the presence of folk tales in Camhy's work, several points can be made. Firstly, 'El prove ke supo enganyar al riko' is only one of the eight folk tales that Camhy recorded and published, which reveals that the Sephardic narrative tradition from Bosnia consisted of a wider repertoire than was originally believed to be the case. All the tales are either jokes and anecdotes or numbskull stories, and most of them are oicotypes. They were orally transmitted to Camhy in her home. In this chain of oral transmission, Camhy was an important link as it was she who conserved the tales in written form, publishing them in different periodicals and thereby preserving them for posterity. Secondly, the tale 'El prove que supo enganyar al riko' is particularly worthy of note as it represents the oldest known example of this tale-type among the Sepharadim. At the same time, it may very well be the only Djohá tale known from Bosnia. Although the name of the protagonist is not mentioned, Djohá or Nasr al-Dīn Khodja usually appears as the main character in this tale-type not only in the Sephardic tradition but in the Arabic and Turkish ones as well. Moreover, it is highly probable that this tale-type in Bosnia was adopted from the Turkish tradition.

Lastly, Camhy introduces folk tales into her own works but does so without connecting them to her plots. The aim is to collect, safeguard and disseminate the folk legacy from Bosnia, a legacy greatly endangered after the Holocaust. This practice regarding folk literature typifies the Sephardic authors of the region and elsewhere during the second half of the twentieth century. In addition to Camhy, Isak Papo, whose work I analyse in the next section, is another example of this.

2. Isak Papo: The Last Traces of (Original) Ladino Creations in Bosnia

The writings of Isak Papo (1912–1996) from Sarajevo, Bosnia, represent the last traces of Sephardic literature from this region. Although works have been produced in relation to the history, literary criticism and culture of Spanish Jews from Bosnia, original creations in Ladino are no longer being produced there. Isak Papo's most important work, which he also edited, is a collection of tales entitled *Cuentos sobre los sefardíes de Sarajevo* (hereafter *Cuentos*, 1994) which appeared just two years before his death. *Cuentos* was published in Split, Croatia, rather than Bosnia because contemporary Bosnia was being torn apart by the Civil War in the former Yugoslavia (1991–1995). It consists of four parts. The first part encompasses forty tales collected or written by Isak Papo. The other three parts contain the works

TABLE 2.3. The list of Camhy's works published in *JS*, *Vidas* and *AY*

(1) Camhy's contributions to *Le Judaïsme Sephardi*

1. 'Purim en mi civdad', March 1955, 6: 267–69
2. 'El sabado en mi civdad', June 1955, 7: 310–11
3. 'Mi nona', September 1955, 8: 353–55
4. 'La vida en el envierno en Sarajevo', December 1955, 9: 389–91
5. 'Los aparejos de Pesah', March 1956, 10: 425–27
6. 'El casamiento de la Bukiza', June 1956, 11: 496–500
7. 'El casamiento de la Bukiza II: la besadura de mano', October 1956, 12: 533–35
8. 'El casamiento de la Bukitza III: el conocer', January 1957, 13: 597–99
9. 'Hamisha asar o la beraha de las frutas', January 1957, 13: 599–600
10. 'El casamiento de la Bukitza IV: consejos de la madre antes de la boda', May 1957, 14: 644–46
11. 'El limud de Babu', October 1957, 15: 678–79
12. 'El arte culinario de los sepharadim de Bosnia: el guisado de mi madre', March 1958, 16: 736–37
13. 'El arte culinario de los sephardim de Bosnia: el guisado de mi madre II', October 1958, 17: 774–75
14. 'El arte culinario de los sephardim de Bosnia: el guisado de mi madre III', April 1959, 18: 821
15. 'El arte culinario de los sephardim de Bosnia', February 1960, 19: 874
16. 'El arte culinario sephardi', October 1960, 21: 940
17. 'El arte culinario sephardi', August 1961, 22: 983
18. 'El arte culinario de los sefardis: comidas de envierno', December 1961, 23: 1015
19. 'El arte culinario', July 1962, 24: 1064
20. 'El arte culinario', December 1962, 25: 1098
21. 'El arte culinario sephardi: comidas de Pesah', June 1963, 26: 1139
22. 'El arte culinario sephardi: comidas de Pessah', December 1963, 27: 1152
23. 'El arte culinario sephardi', August 1964, 28: 1236
24. 'El arte culinario', January 1965, 29: 1267
25. 'Tres conĝas', January 1966, 31: 32

(2) Camhy's contributions to *Vidas largas*

1. 'Purim', April 1983, 2: 38–43

(3) Camhy's contributions to *Aki Yerushalayim*

1. 'El gizadu di mi madre', June 1980, 6: 31–33
2. 'Dos kantigas de boda', July 1980, 6: 49
3. 'Tres rechetas a baza de berendjena', June 1980, 6: 50–52
4. 'Medesina popular', November 1980, 7: 17–20
5. 'El prove ke supo enganyar al riko', January 1981, 2.8: 40–42
6. 'Kuento de Pesah', April 1981, 3.9: 40–41
7. 'Mi nona', June 1981, 3.10: 45–46
8. 'Kunsejus de la madre a Bukitsa', January 1982, 3.12: 15–17
9. 'El servidor haragan', October 1982, 4.15: 44
10. 'Tres kondjas a mis ermanas deportadas', January–April 1985, 6.24–25: 32
11. 'Si gritavas komo gritas...', December 1985, 7.26–27: 75
12. 'El tio Chuchu', July–December 1986, 8.30–31: 65
13. 'La tombola', September–December 1987, 9.34–35: 79–80
14. 'El prove ke supo enganyar al riko', July 2004, 25.75: 110–11

Fig. 2.3. Isak Papo [sitting in the centre], Bosnia.
Jevrejski istorijski muzej, Belgrade, Serbia

of three Sephardic women authors: Gina Camhy (nine tales) and Rikica Ovadija (eighteen tales), both born and raised in Sarajevo, and Clarisse Nikoïdski (two tales), born in Lyons, France, into a Sephardic family originally from Sarajevo. All of these authors created their work in the aftermath of WWII: Isak Papo and Ovadija in their community of origin, Bosnia, whereas the other two did so separated from it, in France. Although Camhy and Nikoïdski did not create their work in their native Bosnia, both they and their work have roots in their native Sephardic tradition. Isak Papo considered them peers and therefore quite logically included them in his work.

Isak Papo's work can be divided into two streams: research on the Judeo-Spanish language, and his literary work in this language. In each, he focuses only on Bosnia, by either writing papers on the Judeo-Spanish dialect spoken there or writing stories depicting his community. It was the situation in which the Bosnian Sephardic community found itself after the Holocaust, in which most of its members had either been killed or dispersed, that prompted Isak Papo's activities to safeguard, preserve and collect what remained of the community's heritage. Furthermore, his activities were the product of his own initiative in Bosnia and not part of a larger movement to revitalise the Sephardic tradition, as was the case for Camhy in Paris.

Of particular importance is the language of Isak Papo's work. Isak Papo wrote his academic papers in Serbo-Croatian, as the target audience was the academic environment in the former Yugoslavia. However, when writing literature dealing with Sephardic topics, Isak Papo mostly employed Judeo-Spanish. Another issue of relevance concerns the methods Isak Papo used to disseminate his work, both in the region and elsewhere, by providing Serbo-Croatian and English translations of his literature written in Ladino, which enabled his work to reach a wider readership.

Furthermore, an analysis of Isak Papo's use of folk literature shows his work to be mainly that of a collector. As with Camhy, there is no evidence that Isak Papo undertook fieldwork in Bosnia to gather material. The source of his tales was his own memory. Minor differences can be found between his work and Camhy's: in addition to preserving the tales of his community, Isak Papo tends to embellish them with a local flavour by giving the characters Bosnian names and setting them in Bosnia.

Isak Papo's pro-Sephardic Activism

Isak Papo represents an interesting figure in the Sephardic cultural milieu of the second half of the twentieth century as, like Davičo, he is an example of a Sephardic Jew who fully assimilated into the Yugoslavian cultural mainstream. However, unlike Davičo, Isak Papo endeavoured to disseminate elements of the Sephardic tradition in the original language of that tradition.

Isak Papo was born in 1912 in Bosnia into a Sephardic family of which nothing is known (I. Papo and others 1994: 191). In addition to his mother tongue, Judeo-Spanish, he undoubtedly learned Serbian at an early age, as at that time the Sepharadim had already started acquiring an education in the Serbian language. During WWII, Isak Papo was taken along with his mother and sister to a forced-labour camp on the island of Rab in Croatia, an ordeal which led him to join the Resistance. His university degrees were gained in Zagreb, Croatia, and Imperial College, London. After the war, he worked as a civil engineer and a university professor in Sarajevo until retiring (I. Papo and others 1994: 191).

Although his profession was scientific rather than literary, which is why the scope of his literary work is limited, Isak Papo believed in the necessity of preserving and disseminating his native heritage, and this conviction led him to write and collect Sephardic tales. The Sarajevan Sephardic community, as he had known it before WWII, had ceased to exist, and their centuries-old culture was on the verge of disappearing there. As Muhamed Nezirović points out, in 1941 there were some 10,000 Jews living in Sarajevo, the majority of them Sepharadim. Of 9,000 taken to concentration camps, only 1,237 returned to Sarajevo (1992: 43). With this situation in mind, Isak Papo started producing papers on the Judeo-Spanish of Bosnia, highlighting Turkish and Hebrew influences on Bosnian Ladino (I. Papo 1995 and 2010; E. Papo 2013a: 295 n. 4).

Isak Papo's academic papers were written in Serbo-Croatian and directed towards the academic community of his country. His literary works, however, were usually written in both Ladino and Serbo-Croatian, as can be seen with *Cuentos*, initially published as a bilingual Judeo-Spanish/Serbo-Croatian edition.[28] The decision to publish his works in both languages was not random. Unlike Camhy, Isak Papo did not aim to revitalise the Judeo-Spanish language and its heritage. His goal, like that of Davičo, was to collect evidence and preserve the memory of a tradition that once existed in Bosnia. In contrast to Davičo's choosing Serbian to achieve this goal, in order to convey the true Sephardic experience, Isak Papo chose Judeo-Spanish for his works. However, producing works only in Ladino would have reduced his readership to a minimum in Bosnia, as the number of Judeo-Spanish speakers there was insignificant. Thus in order to ensure his work would reach the local readership, encompassing both Jewish and non-Jewish audiences, he himself translated the tales into Serbo-Croatian.

Furthermore, to make sure his work would reach an even wider readership, Isak Papo undertook two more initiatives. Firstly, he looked for the appropriate place in which to publish his works in Ladino for a Sephardic audience who could enjoy them in the original language. Realising that a wider movement to preserve his mother tongue existed in several places, he chose to publish part of his work in *AY* in Israel (1987a and 1987b).[29] Secondly, wanting to disseminate his work beyond the borders of the former Yugoslavia, he had an English translation of *Cuentos* made by Zjena Ćulić and Myrna Svičarević. This also appeared as a bilingual edition.

However, his major success lies in collecting a number of folk tales, showing that the Bosnian Sephardic narrative tradition was as important as that of ballads and proverbs. In the following two chapters, examples of some folk tales collected by Isak Papo and their significance for the Bosnian Sephardic tradition will be examined. I shall include, albeit briefly, Matilda Koén-Sarano's fieldwork among members of different Sephardic communities for the purposes of a comparison method. Her work will be examined in more detail in *Part III*.

Folk Tales in Isak Papo's Collection: Enriching the Tradition

Due to the unprivileged situation of the Sephardic heritage in the second half of the twentieth century, memory became one of the main tools to preserve the tradition and cultural identity of the Sephardic Jews. It was through remembering important events and moments of the Sephardic past that the tradition was preserved. An important part of that past is folklore, with all its enjoyable aspects, and this is precisely what the Sephardic authors of this period chose to remember and collect. Further, this memory of the past is enriched by the addition of elements of the new situations the Sepharadim experienced in the modern era. The two tales discussed in this chapter are examples of this union of tradition, memory and modernity.

These two tales are ATU782, 'Midas and the Donkey's Ears', and ATU775, 'Midas' Short-sighted Wish' (Uther 2004: I, 433–34; 441–42).[30] The example of the former appears in Isak Papo's *Cuentos* under the title 'Il čuflet dil pastor' ('Shepherd's Flute') (1994: 34). It is a well-known folk tale that the Bosnian author most probably wrote down or rewrote from memory. Another example of the second tale-type was collected by Koén-Sarano from an informant from Greece whose family originally came from Turkey (2003: 150). Both of these tales constitute rare examples of these tale-types in the Sephardic world, and both were collected as late as the end of the twentieth century. Their appearance among the Sepharadim is not only due to the influence of the environment but also to a conscious attempt to continue developing the Sephardic oral tradition by introducing new elements hitherto unknown in the recent Sephardic past. The fact that one example comes from Bosnia and the other from Greece shows that this phenomenon surpasses the borders of the former Yugoslavia.

As previously stated, *Cuentos* comprises four sections, each dedicated to a different author. The first section contains the forty tales signed by Isak Papo, some of which are in fact folk tales. There are several facts that indicate their folk background. Firstly, some of the tales ('Il čuflet dil pastor', for example) use typical linguistic formulas found in Sephardic folk tales, such as *avia de ser*. Secondly, some have been recorded either in the ATU catalogue as internationally known oral tales or in Haboucha's catalogue of Judeo-Spanish folk tales ('Il dukadu infurkadu' ['The Suspended Ducat'], or 'La vingansa di lus talmidim' ['The Revenge of the Students']) (I. Papo and others 1994: 34; 40).[31] Lastly, some of these tales do not appear in either catalogue but have been collected and recorded as examples of oral narrative tradition by other Sephardic authors from Bosnia or outside of the former Yugoslavia ('Il mas lindu fižiku' ['The Most Handsome Son'], for example) (I. Papo and others 1994: 76).

The fact that Isak Papo failed to mention any names or sources of the tales he published, but instead signed them with his own name, suggests that he most probably did not carry out any fieldwork. Like Camhy, he is likely to have reproduced these tales from memory, using his home environment as his immediate source: 'Mi nona jemada Tija Rahelona, komu todas las nonas, vinjendu a vižitarmus, ahuera di lus asukritus ki mus trajija sjempri stava pronta di imbevisermus kun kunsižitjas' ('Whenever my grandmother, who was called Tija Rahelona, came to visit us, she, like all other grandmothers, would always bring us sweets and was always ready to tell us an entertaining story') (I. Papo and others 1994: 36). As in the case of Camhy, here too it was the writer's *nona*, a woman, who was the source of folk wisdom.

'Il čuflet dil pastor' (hereafter 'Il čuflet') opens the collection. It belongs to the ATU tale-type known as 'Midas and the Donkey's Ears'. The first testimonies of this tale appear in classical literature. Ovid's version, contained in his *Metamorphoses*, is the oldest known example, which is why the tale-type also became known as Midas's Ears. The fact that Maja Bošković-Stulli (1967) gathered examples deriving from four continents shows the remarkable presence of this tale worldwide.

The story of King Midas can be summarised as follows: King Midas lived in the woods and pastures and worshipped Pan. In a musical contest between Pan and Apollo, Midas preferred Pan's pipes. When it is Apollo with his lyre who is declared the winner, Midas expresses his dissatisfaction, thereby offending Apollo, who punishes him by making his ears grow into ass's ears. From that moment on, Midas attempts to cover his ears with an ample turban. Unfortunately, his ears are noticed by the servant that cuts his hair; bowed down by the weight of this secret, he unburdens himself by confessing this knowledge to a hole that he dug in the ground. After describing his master's ears, he covers the hole and departs feeling relieved. However, some time later a patch of reeds grows where the hole was. When the wind rustles through them it reanimates the words uttered by the servant, and the king's secret becomes common knowledge (Ovidio 2005: 595–99).

Ovid's version contains the following series of folk motifs which constitute the body of the folk tale:

— the king has a secret which he endeavours to hide, killing those who discover it. Usually the secret is a physical defect consisting of a non-human feature typifying some kind of animal, the most frequent one being the ears or horns of an ass or horse (F511.2.2);

— he decides to pardon the life of the person who cuts his hair or shaves his face on the condition that he keeps the secret (N465);

— oppressed by the secret, the barber/servant falls ill and, following another's advice, decides to utter the secret in a deserted place (C420). By doing so, his oppression is alleviated (D2161.4.19.1);

— reeds grow where the barber has revealed the secret which, rustled by the wind, betray the secret (D1316.5); or the said reeds are used to make a musical instrument, which later betrays the secret (D1610.34); and,

— when the secret becomes common knowledge, the king forgives the barber believing that nothing in this world can remain hidden (Bošković-Stulli 1967: 63).

Although these motifs constitute the basis of the story and reappear from one version to the next, throughout the course of time the tale acquired new elements while simultaneously doing away with others, thereby adapting to the different cultures in which it was fostered. This was the case of the version collected by Isak Papo, in which there is also a king who has a loyal servant. The servant spends so much time by the King's side that it is inevitable that he see his master naked. His friends and relatives want to know what the King looks like naked, so they persist in their demand for him to reveal this knowledge. Having sworn he would not say a word, at first the servant keeps his promise. However, before long he begins to feel the pressure of having to remain silent, so he goes to the mountain, digs a hole and buries the following words: 'Jo vidi il kulu dil re blanku i kurladu' ('I saw the King's white rosy bottom'). After a while a tree grows in this place, and one day a shepherd who is passing by takes a branch to make himself a flute. As fate would have it, the only thing to come out of the flute once he starts to play is the secret about the King's buttocks (I. Papo and others 1994: 34).

What makes this Sephardic version unique compared to other versions inter-nationally is what constitutes the secret here -— i.e., the source of the servant's problem. A comparison with the known versions of the tale, both older ones and those compiled throughout the twentieth century, indicates the dominant presence of ass's ears, from Ovid and other Roman authors, such as Gaius Petronius Arbiter (from the first century) and Fabius Planciades Fulgentius (from the late fifth century), to the modern versions of Korea, Tibet, India, Israel, Egypt, Russia, Bulgaria, Macedonia, Serbia, Croatia, Italy, Portugal, Ireland, Chile, Argentina, Cuba and the Dominican Republic (Bošković-Stulli 1967: 119). In fact, it is not uncommon for ass's ears to appear even in areas where another type of animal trait prevails as the secret. For example, in Ireland, Wales or Brittany, a horse's ears or head is the most common defect, and yet we find versions with ass's ears as well. The same can be said for versions collected from Muslims in which, together with the horns that comprise the king's secret, examples of ass's ears are also found (Bošković-Stulli, 1967: 124). Therefore, it can be supposed that 'Midas's ears' is one of the base elements of the tale.

In light of this, the issue arises of the type of secret which spurs all the action in the Sephardic version from Bosnia: 'il kulu blanku i kurladu'. In spite of the fact that ATU classifies tale-type 782 as a religious one, the type of secret here seems to suggest that it is actually a comic one. The white and rosy backside cannot be considered either a physical defect of the King or a secret to be kept. The servant simply sees the King nude and then must not speak about it. Therefore, the secret the servant needs to keep does not fit within the general type of secret found in other examples worldwide. The reason may well be the fact that this part of the tale does not conform to the ATU782 type, but to another type instead.

The motif of seeing the king's bottom appears in tale-type ATU235C★, 'A Bird Had New Clothes Made' (Uther 2004: 1, 149).[32] This is a very rare tale-type of which only a few examples have been recorded internationally. In addition to Middle Eastern and Asian versions (Palestinian, Iranian, Indian, Uzbek), this tale has been collected in Spanish-speaking areas, with examples from Spain (Andalusia, Catalonia) as well as Latin America (Venezuela, Mexico) (Uther 2004: 1, 149). Some of these versions, particularly those from the south of Iberia (Seville, Murcia, Córdoba), were edited and published by José Manuel Pedrosa (2012: 127–52). In the tale, a bird has acquired new woollen clothes and has tricked the tailor in order not to pay him. Then it goes to the court and mocks the Prince, claiming it is more elegant than the Prince himself. After it is caught, the Prince insists on eating it, and after doing so, he gets a stomachache. Upon passing gas, the bird comes flying out, saying: 'Eh, eh, eh... , que le he visto al hijo del rey el culo!' (Pedrosa 2012: 133–34). Several more versions were collected in Andalusia, which indicates that it was precisely in this region where the tale was both known and popular (Pedrosa 2012: 135). Bearing in mind that no example of ATU235C★ has been recorded in the Balkans, it could very well be that the tale was known among the Sepharadim there as part of their Hispanic heritage. By borrowing this new element from a different tale, the Sephardic ATU782 tale-type has changed its nature from a religious to a comic tale.

However, the influence of the Balkan environment can be seen in the second part of the Sephardic tale. The element of revealing the secret by digging a hole from which a tree later grows is a common ending in the ATU782 tale-type in the Balkans, which curiously has not been recorded in Spain (although it is apparent in many regions worldwide). In the indexes and collections of Spanish folk tales (Boggs 1930; Espinosa 1946; Camarena and Chevalier 2003), not a single example of the tale appears, while, on the contrary, versions have been compiled in nearby countries such as France, Portugal, Morocco and Algeria.[33] In the Balkans, nonetheless, numerous examples have been collected. In the former Yugoslavia alone, approximately 150 versions of the tale exist, edited by Bošković-Stulli (1967:

76–282; 297–99). The abundant presence of the tale in the former Yugoslavia, including Bosnia, leads me to conclude that the Sephardic tale collected by Isak Papo was influenced by Serbian and Croatian versions of the ATU782 tale-type.[34] This shows how the Bosnian Sephardic community, and Isak Papo as a transmitter and collector of its folklore, combined various elements, maintaining the old while borrowing the new from other cultures in the local area, thereby enriching the Sephardic heritage. Isak Papo's 'Il čuflet' is but one example.

King Midas is also the protagonist of another tale-type, ATU775, 'Midas's Golden Touch' (Uther 2004: 1, 433–34), the oldest known version of which is again found in Ovid's *Metamorphoses*. In this story, King Midas asks Dionysius to grant him the ability to turn everything he touches into gold. His wish is fulfilled, but he soon realises that, rather than being a blessing, it is actually a curse. In the end, he begs Dionysius to rid him of this power (Ovidio 2005: 595–97). The tale contains a number of universal folk motifs recorded in Thompson's catalogue (1966):

— Absurd short-sightedness (J2050)

— Short-sighted wish: Midas's touch. Everything to turn to gold (J2072.1.)

— Midas's golden touch. Everything touched turns to gold (D565.1.)

— Man given power of wishing (D1720.1.)

— Immoderate request punished (Q338)

— Overweening ambition punished (L420)

This tale-type was barely known in the Sephardic world until 1988, when Sara Yohay told Koén-Sarano the following story that she had heard from her grandfather: one day King Midas, whose kingdom was in Thrace and who was known for his miserly nature and greed for gold, allowed Djohá, a famous magician, to spend the night in his castle. In return, he asked Djohá to give him the power to turn everything he touched into gold. His wish is granted, but as a consequence, he eventually died of hunger (2003: 150).[35]

This tale was published by Koén-Sarano (1996: 118) in the original language, Judeo-Spanish, and subsequently in its translation into English in Koén-Sarano's *Joha: The Jewish Trickster* (2003: 150). According to Koén-Sarano, this tale most probably entered the Sephardic oral tradition from a written source because one of the protagonists, King Midas, originated in Ovid (1996: 116). At the same time, there are number of elements which indicate that the tale went through a process of domestication. Instead of the Dionysius of Ovid's version, the famous comic character of the Sephardic world, Djohá, appears.[36] In Ovid's tale, King Midas comes from Phrygia in Asia Minor. The Sephardic tale, by contrast, takes place in the north of Greece, the informant's native land, and has, hence, been localised.

What is interesting is that Koén-Sarano published this tale in her collection of comic tales dedicated to Djohá, who is well known in the Sephardic world as a trickster and a fool. As Djohá appears only as a protagonist of comic tales, the fact that he is a main character in this tale suggests that we might be dealing with a comic tale. However, this tale, according to ATU, is a religious tale, and recorded international versions of it follow the pattern of Ovid's story in which the main character is punished for his greed. The Sephardic version is in keeping with this philosophy and employs satire to convey its message and impart the intended lesson: the condemnation of greed.[37] Moreover, the moral in the Sephardic version is taken even further, because due to his greedy wish, King Midas ultimately dies, whereas in other internationally known versions, including Ovid's, the King is forgiven after having learned a lesson. This Sephardic tale, thus, cannot be classified as a comic tale in spite of the presence of Djohá as it contains no other comic elements apart from the character. Moreover, Djohá is stripped of his classic role of a trickster and a fool. Here he is identified as a magician, someone who has supernatural powers. The oicotypification of the tale was not enough to change the core of the tale and make it comic.

Worthy of note is the connection that exists between Isak Papo's tale and this one. In each case, according to the ATU classification, we are dealing with religious tales, and in each the oldest known versions are from Ovid and have King Midas as the protagonist. But in each case, the Sephardic versions have undergone an attempt to adapt a religious narrative to a comic one. In Isak Papo's case this was achieved by changing the nature of the secret the servant knows from the king having ass's or horse's ears to having a white and rosy bottom. Here the adaptation to the comic element was achieved successfully. However, in the case of Koén-Sarano's tale, although an emblematic humorous character, Djohá, appears as one of the protagonists, the tale does not contain any comic elements and, thus, fits perfectly within the religious classification of this tale-type. Both of these examples show how the Sephardic tradition was enriched by the introduction of fresh elements.

The examined Sephardic examples clearly show how Ladino tradition continued to develop in the late twentieth century by introducing new material into the lore which came not only from oral but also written sources, thereby expanding the repertoire of oral tales in the Ladino language and culture. Nevertheless, Isak Papo did not only collect tales in which new elements had been introduced. The following chapter examines tales that he collected that have a long tradition among the Sepharadim in Bosnia and elsewhere.

Continuation of the (Bosnian) Sephardic Narrative Tradition in Isak Papo's Work

The previous chapter dealt with the recent appearance of some tale-types in the Sephardic world, both in Bosnia and elsewhere. This chapter examines two more tales collected by Isak Papo which, contrary to what happened in the two examples in the previous chapter, are texts that represent a continuation of the tradition. Two traits can be discerned in relation to these examples. Firstly, they are oicotypes — i.e., they have only been recorded in the Sephardic/Jewish (or Spanish) tradition. And secondly, examples of these tales had either been collected or written down previously by other Sephardic authors in Bosnia. Thus Isak Papo's examples demonstrate that some elements of oral tradition continued to be fostered.

'Suegra ni de barro buena' belongs to Haboucha's ★★903C tale-type, 'Not Even in Pictures' (1992: 379–80). The tale has been widely recorded in the Bosnian

Sephardic tradition, from which most of the known examples come. The oldest extant example dates from the early twentieth century and is found in the work of Laura Papo.[38] However, in her case, it has not been preserved in the form of a tale. Laura Papo used the tale from oral tradition as a starting point to write a play, *Suegra ni de barro buena*, which speaks, as does the tale itself, about the difficult relationship which exists between a woman and her mother-in-law. However, in her play she reverses the plot of the tale: here it is the daughter-in-law who is the source of the bad relationship, and not the mother-in-law. This is in keeping with Laura Papo's practice of not only recording samples of oral tradition from her environment but also of re-creating them and producing something new and different.

Other Bosnian examples of this tale come from the second half of the twentieth century. Camhy published a version as part of her essay 'La vida en envierno en Sarajevo' (1955: 390–91). She transmits the most common content of the story in its traditional form: a recently married young woman listens to her girlfriends talking about their mothers-in-law but cannot participate in the conversation as hers is dead. Therefore she asks her husband to make a clay statue of his mother. However, whenever she cleans the house she has to move the statue from one place to another until one day, weary of this constant obstacle, she throws the statue on the floor, breaking it to pieces. The characters here bear no names, and no location is mentioned.

Isak Papo's tale differs in both its content and the innovation of giving the characters names which bestow upon them a certain familiarity for his readers: Aron and Mazalta have a son named Alberto. Mazalta dies at the age of forty-five and, needing a woman to see to the household chores, Aron advises his son to marry his girlfriend, Renika. Realising that Aron misses his late wife deeply, his daughter-in-law, Renika, suggests that a statue of his late wife should be made in order to comfort him. Thus the reason behind Renika's request for the statue to be made does not correspond to that of Camhy's or other known versions of the tale. When Renika begins the Passover preparations, she tires of looking after the house, the two men and the children, and in a moment of anger throws the statue out the window, thereby corroborating the proverb 'Suegra ni de barro buena' (I. Papo and others 1994: 64–66).

Isak Papo's re-creation of the story does not lie merely in setting the action around Passover, an important Jewish holiday characterised by a spring cleaning of the house preceding the holiday; he also re-creates the story by giving a local flavour to the tale through the usage of names which sound familiar and by placing the tale in his native town of Sarajevo. This is a common technique employed by Isak Papo. Another example is his 'La vingansa di lus talmidim' ('The Revenge of the Students') (I. Papo and others 1994: 40). This tale belongs to the tale-type 1832*R, 'Clever Repartee of Pupil to his Teacher', which, together with other examples of it collected in the Sephardic tradition, is another oicotype (Haboucha 1992: 703–04). The story is about students who, weary of the bad treatment they constantly receive from their teacher, decide to take revenge. To do so, they choose the biblical episode of Ruth and Boaz, and just before coming to the end of the first stanza they stop, awaiting their teacher's well-known response. The angry teacher as usual shouts 'Mamzirim, kupilim, il gverku vus jevi' ('You scoundrels. You are all scoundrels. May the devil take you!'), to which the students reply, 'A el i su mužer i dos sus fižus' ('And him and his wife and his two children') (I. Papo and others 1994: 40). The domesticated nature of the tale to the local environment can be seen by Isak Papo's describing at the beginning of the tale how one hundred years earlier Sephardic students in Sarajevo were educated in the Torah in religious schools (*meldares*) while at the same time being taught the local language, i.e. Serbian.

This local character of the tales is evident in another oicotype collected by Isak Papo that also represents a continuation of the tradition. The tale is called 'Il mas lindu fiziku' ('The Most Handsome Son') and does not have any ATU or Haboucha tale-type number. Nevertheless, it was quite popular in the Bosnian tradition. The oldest known example was recorded by Laura Papo in *La mužer sefardi de Bosna* (Nezirović 1992: 218 n. 28). It tells of a mother who asks her neighbour to take food to her son in school. As the neighbour does not know what the son looks like, his mother describes him as the loveliest boy in the school. The neighbour goes to the school looking for the loveliest boy, but she cannot find any boy lovelier than her own so she gives the food to him.

While there is no specific location in Laura Papo's text, Isak Papo wrote down another version of this same tale which follows the pattern of Laura Papo's tale, with the difference that the school is located on Lagubina Street in Sarajevo, very close to the Sephardic neighbourhood (I. Papo and others 1994: 76). This shows that Isak Papo does not re-create the oral narrative the same way Laura Papo does. Instead, he tends to set the tales in Sarajevo in order to make them sound Bosnian rather than merely Sephardic.

3. Conclusion to Part II

In *Part II*, the works of two Sephardic authors from the former Yugoslavia from the second half of the twentieth century, Gina Camhy and Isak Papo, were analysed. Written in Judeo-Spanish and focusing entirely on their native community of Bosnia as the backdrop, their work represents the last traces of the Sephardic community of Bosnia and aims to recover aspects of Bosnian Judeo-Spanish culture.

However, their work not only emerges in different places but also with different goals. Camhy creates her work in Paris, where she settled after abandoning Bosnia. The French capital became the centre of the pro-Sephardic movement in the aftermath of WWII, where several societies and periodicals were launched to collect, safeguard and revitalise the language and the culture of the Spanish Jews. Thus, her work in Judeo-Spanish forms part of this movement and shares the same goals. Isak Papo, by contrast, remained in Bosnia and began creating his work with the aim of preserving the memory of a once flourishing culture: the culture of his home. He endeavoured to collect and safeguard the legacy of the Sephardic community in Bosnia, which was largely destroyed by the Holocaust.

Both of these authors collect evidence of oral literature, particularly oral narrative. Camhy usually introduces folk tales as part of her stories and essays, whereas Isak Papo limits himself to recording and publishing them in their own right. It is interesting to note that most of the examples of folk tales they collected are oicotypes. Another dominant trait of this material is that all the tales are comic, which forms part of both Camhy's and Isak Papo's attempt to create a positive image of the community, their past and tradition.

Unlike Davičo or Laura Papo, who both employ various techniques to re-create oral literature and whose own original pieces are rooted in the tradition, Camhy and Isak Papo focus on collecting and safeguarding evidence of folk tradition. They do not create new works that derive from oral tradition, nor do they use examples of oral tradition to illustrate or comment on their own stories. Isak Papo often gives Sephardic names to the protagonists of these narratives and places them in Sarajevo, thus giving them a local flavour, but this practice is far from the earnest and complex re-creations seen in Davičo or Laura Papo. The reason for this may well be the fact that neither Camhy nor Isak Papo were writers by profession.

The fact that comic tales dominate their work indicates the importance of this genre in the Sephardic world, and, where Sephardic comic tales are concerned, the unavoidably fundamental element is Djohá, the best-known trickster or fool of the Sephardic world. This endearing figure will be the subject of *Part III*.

Notes to Part II

1. On Sephardic memory works, see Lévy Zumwalt and Lévy 2001; Schorsch 2007; Díaz-Mas 2009b; Romeu Ferré 2008; 2012; 2014; 2016 and 2019.
2. Although the author's name in *AY* appears as Djina Kamhi, here I shall apply the spelling used in *JS*, Gina Camhy, as it is here where Camhy published most of her work.
3. I provide the full list of Camhy's publications (in *JS*, *Vidas* and *AY*) at the end of this section.
4. See Ž. Jovanović 2016.
5. On the concept of ideology as a set of conscious and unconscious ideas which make up one's goals, expectations and motivations, see Eagleton 2007.
6. On the Sephardic press in the former Yugoslavia, see Vidaković-Petrov 1990: 54–72 and 2013: 69–96; Tauber 2011: 39–89.
7. Levy was a passionate collector of the Sephardic cultural heritage. He was preparing an extensive collection of Sephardic folklore for publication when WWII broke out. He was imprisoned in a concentration camp in 1942, where he was killed. His collection was destroyed in 1941 during the destruction of the Great Temple (*Kal Grande*) in Sarajevo. See Nezirović 1992: 230–31.
8. For more information on Paris as a centre for revitalisation of Sephardic culture, see Abravanel 1996.
9. On this, see Romero 1992: 177–218.
10. I deal with this issue in more detail in *Part III*.
11. For Isak Papo's and Ovadija's literary work, see Isak Papo and others 1994. These traits can also be seen in the works of Laura Papo and Buki Romano of Bosnia from the first half of the twentieth century. See L. Papo 2012 and Baruh 1930: 113–54. Also, see Stulic 2018.
12. For an account of Bosnian dialect of Judeo-Spanish, see Quintana Rodríguez 1997: 47–65 and 1998: 593–602; Štulić, Vučina and Zečević 2003: 380–96; Stulic 2018: 23–48.
13. For more information on this, see Díaz-Mas and De la Puente 2007: 85–160.
14. On this, see Varol 2003–04: 231–60 and Romeu Ferré 2012: 9–23.
15. See the list of her works at the end of this section.
16. On Jewish dietary laws, see Kraemer 2007.
17. Although Camhy uses here Bukiza as a proper name, it is actually a nickname. Bukiza derives from Buka, 'older sister', the same as Bohora.

18. Also, see Romero 1992: 141–72.
19. For more information on *coplas* sung for *Purim*, see Hassán 2010 and Romero 2011.
20. For more information on the nature of Purim, see Danon 1996: 63–67; Díaz-Mas 2006: 47–48; and, Díaz-Mas and De la Puente 2007: 143–45.
21. I am following the spelling of *Vidas*, from which these lines were taken, because this periodical kept the phonetic traits of Camhy's Judeo-Spanish. The song also appears in *JS* (1955: 268–69).
22. For a detailed analysis of the song, see Vidaković-Petrov 1985 and 1986.
23. For more information on the custom of wedding arrangements and ceremonies during Purim, see Molho 1950: 342–43 and Romero 2011: 412–13.
24. For some remarks on women as performers of oral literature among Sephardic Jews, see J. Cohen 1995: 182–200; Seroussi 2003: 195–214; Díaz-Mas 2007: 187–200 and 2008: 255–66.
25. For more information on the game *endivinar los dedos*, or *pares y nones* as it was called in Salonica, see Molho 1950: 131–32.
26. Djohá also appears as the protagonist of another Sephardic version of the tale, also recorded by Koén-Sarano (2003: 284).
27. For more information on Djohá, see the introduction to *Part III*.
28. Also, see <http://elmundosefarad.wikidot.com/papo-isak-prof-dr-ing> [accessed 23 April 2019].
29. *Aki Yerushalayim: revista kulturala Djudeo-espanyola* began to be published in 1979 in Israel with the goal of disseminating the Judeo-Spanish language and culture. Its publication in printed form came to a halt in 2016 with numbers 99 and 100, mostly due to financial problems. The editors expressed their intention of continuing to publish the periodical in electronic form, as stated in the following online article: <https://esefarad.com/?p=76248> [accessed 29 April 2019].
30. This chapter is derived from my article published in *Boletín de literatura oral*. See Ž. Jovanović 2018b: 9–20.
31. See also Haboucha 1992: 622; 703–04.
32. I would like to thank Dr José Manuel Pedrosa (Universidad de Alcalá, Spain) for drawing my attention to this fact.
33. Curiously, Ovid's version of the tale was known in Spain from medieval times through either translations or adaptations. A summary of it appears in the work of the great Alfonso X the Learned, *La General Estoria* (Brancaforte, 1990: 263). It also appears in an unpublished manuscript, *Los morales de Ovidio* (BNE, MS 10144), from the first half of the fifteenth century, a Castilian translation of *Ovidius moralizatus* by Pierre Bersuire (c. 1290–1362). The translation, commonly attributed to Alfonso Zamorensis (Alfonso Gómez de Zamora?), was probably commissioned by the Marquis of Santillana (Marqués de Santillana) (Carr 2005: 194). This shows that Ovid's version of the tale was known in written sources in Spain from the Middle Ages. However, the ATU782 tale-type, according to available sources, is unknown in Spanish oral tradition.
34. For more detail on this, see Ž. Jovanović 2014a.
35. Haboucha also recorded a version of this tale-type in 1975 in Israel from a seventy-five-year-old storyteller, Mazal Tov Lazar, which, however, differs considerably from the one here. On this, see Haboucha 1995: 323–40.
36. In yet another Sephardic version of this tale, instead of Djohá the prophet Elijah appears. This shows another level of domestication, or in Von Sydow's term (1965: 219–20) oicotypification, of the story to Sephardic mentality by using a Jewish prophet as one of the characters. See Koén-Sarano 1996: 120–21.
37. An exemplary satire, according to Haboucha (1995: 336), is particularly alive in Jewish tales.
38. On this, see *Part I*.

PART III

Djohá Tales in the Sephardic World: Tradition, Identity and Memory

Thus far, the efforts made by the Sepharadim of the former Yugoslavia to collect, preserve, revitalise and disseminate their own culture have been examined. Here, it will be seen that in spite of all the events that have had devastating effects on Judeo-Spanish culture, examples of spontaneous survivals continue against all odds to endure in great abundance.

A case in point are the comic tales involving a character called Djohá, a trickster and fool, whose origins among the Spanish Jews are to be found in the Middle Ages in al-Andalus. Djohá's presence in the everyday life of the Sepharadim is of an intrinsic nature and shows a remarkable continuity as a centuries-long tradition. In order to show the endurance of this character among the Sepharadim it is necessary to go back to al-Andalus and early examples of Juhā tales among Arabs (from the tenth to thirteenth centuries).[1] It was the Iberian Muslims who transmitted this figure to the Jews. From there during the late Middle Ages when the Sepharadim arrived in the Ottoman Empire the tales of Djohá were enriched and enlarged upon with tales about a similar character in Turkish tradition.

Furthermore, in addition to dealing with this character in Sephardic historical tradition, its continued presence to date will be made evident. The focus of this section will be on examples of Djohá tales collected in the former Yugoslavia from the end of the nineteenth century onwards, and Koén-Sarano's collection of Djohá tales from the late twentieth century. Koén-Sarano's tales, however, were collected from both the Sepharadim of the former Yugoslavia and also those living in other countries in which they settled.

Some of these tales were compiled in languages other than Judeo-Spanish, such as Serbian, Italian or Hebrew. Regardless of this, they confirm an uninterrupted tradition around this character beginning in the Middle Ages, while also providing insight into how the particular communities and the collectors viewed their identities, elucidating the purpose and interest of collecting the tales.

1. Medieval Roots of the Character: Juhā in Al-Andalus

Different opinions have been expressed regarding al-Andalus as the point of origin of Djohá among the Sepharadim. While some scholars claim that Juhā was unknown in al-Andalus among Iberian Muslims, who therefore could not have introduced him to the Jews (Vivas Bailo 1989: 21), others maintain that it was at the time of the co-existence of Muslims and Jews in medieval Spain that this character was transmitted to the Jews as a result of significant cultural contact and exchange between these two ethnic groups (Bornes-Varol 1995: 64; Corriente 1999: 72; Alexander-Frizer 2008: 432–33). The opinion of these scholars is based on the fact that Juhā is originally an Arabic character that, according to them, was most likely known and fostered in al-Andalus. However, they fail to provide any example of this character in al-Andalus in either the works of an Arabic or Jewish author.

This chapter will demonstrate that Juhā was indeed known in al-Andalus by highlighting two different Arabic sources in which this character appears: one from the tenth century and the other from the thirteenth. Both of these formerly unknown sources prove beyond doubt that Juhā was known in al-Andalus and that it is, therefore, safe to assume that the process of acculturation and domestication of the Arabic character to the Jewish environment first took place prior to the expulsion of the Jews from Spain and their subsequent settling in the Ottoman Empire.[2]

Juhā is an ideal example of how a single character with the same or slightly different name and similar traits — those of trickster and fool — can appear in various cultures, regions and ethnic groups as a result of cultural contact. It is within the Islamic (Arabic) world that this figure was originally created and developed. However, Juhā captured the imagination of other ethnic groups that came into contact with Islamic culture:

> Todo el mundo lo [Juhā] conoce en Iraq, Siria, Líbano, Yemen, Arabia, Egipto, Túnez, Argelia, Marruecos o Mauritania, y también fuera del mundo árabe: es famoso en Turquía, y conocido en Samarcanda, Armenia, Afganistán, Turquestán, El Cáucaso, Rumanía, Bulgaria, Yugoslavia, Crimea, Ucrania, Rusia, Nubia, Sudán, Senegal, Grecia, Albania, Malta, Sicilia, Calabria, Cerdeña o al-Andalus. (Thomas de Antonio 1993: 189)

In this enumeration of countries and regions, there is one that stands out due to its place and time: al-Andalus. Al-Andalus refers to territories of the Iberian Peninsula governed by Muslims at various times between 711 and 1492.[3] Clara María Thomas de Antonio proposes al-Andalus as one of the regions where Juhā was known but does not provide any evidence of his existence in this area. Yet, this potential evidence is precisely what is of most interest given that prior to their expulsion from Spain in 1492 the Jews had lived alongside Muslims. The contact between the two ethnic groups was so vigorous and intense that Rina Drory maintains that 'the entire body of Jewish literature [in the Middle Ages] is, in fact, a product of cultural contacts with Arabic [literature]' (1998: 282).[4]

Bearing in mind the continuous cultural contact throughout the Middle Ages between Arabs and Jews, and the Arabic origins of Juhā, the question arises as to whether the Jews adopted this character while they were living in al-Andalus or whether they drew from more than one source. The answer to this question cannot be found in extant Sephardic texts because all the examples of Djohá tales among the Sepharadim were recorded in the nineteenth and twentieth centuries and merely confirm the fact of a long-lasting tradition related to this character.[5] They do not reveal when or where the Spanish Jews learned about him. We therefore need to resort to indirect proof in Arabic sources during the Middle Ages, particularly those of al-Andalus, in order to hypothesise about possible cultural contact and influence. This information confirms that the centuries-long tradition of Djohá among the Sepharadim represents part of their Iberian heritage, a heritage which they continued to foster ever since.

One thing is clear: it was in the Middle East and not in al-Andalus that Juhā originally appeared. Both the oldest mention of Juhā in written sources and an anecdote about him appear in the first half of the ninth century in the work of Abū 'Uthmān 'Amr ibn Bahr (*c.*776/77–868/69) from Basra, known by his nickname, al-Jāhiz (Richards 1998: 408).[6] Already by the end of the tenth century, Juhā enjoyed such widespread popularity among Arabs that he became the central figure of a number of stories which were to form an anonymous miscellany, *Kitāb Nawādir Juhā* (*The Book of Juhā's Anecdotes*). Although not extant, we know of the book's existence through Abū al-Faraj Muhammad ibn Ishāq al-Nadīm (930–990/98), a Baghdadi bookseller and the author of the *Al-Fihrist* (*The Catalogue*), a work of unique importance for the history of Arabic literature (Rosenthal 1956: 6–11; Kimber 1998: 355–56).[7]

These examples of Juhā in written sources clearly show that he was well known and popular among Arabs in the Middle East from the early Middle Ages. As regards the presence of Juhā in al-Andalus, on the one hand, José Luis Vivas Bailo maintains that this comic figure was unknown (1989: 21). He bases his views mostly on historical circumstances, arguing that the politics of al-Andalus in its initial stages was rather independent from other Muslim centres, Baghdad in particular. This is why Juhā did not reach al-Andalus at the beginning of the Muslim rule there. Although contact with the Muslim East later increased, and literary and scientific sources from these areas started circulating throughout al-Andalus, these works, in Vivas Bailo's view, barely contained any folk elements (1989: 20–21). Thus he concludes that Juhā never reached al-Andalus, not even at a later stage.

On the other hand, Fernando de la Granja (1971: 236), Bornes-Varol (1995: 64) and Alexander-Frizer (2008: 432–33) maintain that Juhā was known in al-Andalus among Muslims (and Jews). To support their claim, they cite medieval examples of certain tale-types in the Arabic world in which Juhā usually appears as the protagonist. Although they fail to offer any concrete examples with Juhā from al-Andalus, they nevertheless assume that these tales must have existed there. Furthermore, in his analysis of the modern Judeo-Spanish of Thessaloniki, Federico Corriente finds words of Arabic origin, one of which is *Ǧoja* (Juhā), and states:

> La preservación, en una serie de dichos, del recuerdo de este personaje mítico del folclore árabe, el famoso 'tonto listo' Juhā, es una prueba más de la mayor duración del biculturalismo entre los judíos de la Península Ibérica, con respecto a los cristianos, que olvidaron mucho antes esta herencia. (1999: 72)

Deriving from the twentieth-century Judeo-Spanish, this example does not, however, constitute solid proof of Sephardic Djohá's medieval Andalusi origin. Significantly, I have found references to Juhā and tales about him that have gone unnoticed in the works of two Arabic authors from al-Andalus: one from the late tenth century and the other from the twelfth.[8] This confirms the fact that Juhā existed in al-Andalus before the expulsion of the Jews.

The oldest known reference to Juhā in al-Andalus appears in the work of Abū l-Walīd 'Abd Allāh b. Muhhamad b. Yūsuf b. Nasr al-Azdī al-Qurtubī, known as Ibn al-Faradī.[9] Ibn al-Faradī was born in Cordoba in 962 and died there in 1013. He spent part of his childhood in Toledo with his father, where he received his first education in Muslim law and philosophy. After his father's death, he returned to Córdoba, the main intellectual centre of the time. There he studied law, tradition, literature and history, and worked with scholars both from al-Andalus and from the Middle East who had migrated to al-Andalus.

A significant event for Ibn al-Faradī's intellectual development was his pilgrimage to the Middle East, which enabled him to establish contact with erudite people from this region and thus expand his knowledge of Arabic culture and literature, which he later disseminated in al-Andalus. He studied in Cairo, Mecca and Medina. It is thus probable that the author became familiar with Juhā tales during this pilgrimage. As stated above, it was in the Middle East where Juhā emerged among Arabs and where he already enjoyed great popularity in Ibn al-Faradī's time.

Ibn al-Faradī mentions Juhā in his *Kitāb al-Alqāb* (*The Book of Nicknames*), which is a kind of dictionary of nicknames. The common practice in the book is either to offer information known to the author about the person behind a particular nickname or to explain the nicknames by recounting anecdotes about them. Thus, under Juhā, Ibn al-Faradī reveals that his true name was Isaac Aba El Ghusn, and he was known for being absentminded. The sources used by the author apparently derive from oral tradition. We know this because Ibn al-Faradī offers six short anecdotes that had been told to him about Juhā.

One of those anecdotes says that Juhā was dragged before a judge on the accusation of beating up a man. The judge asks the accusers for proof, but Jūha says that there is no need for proof because he confesses to the offence. The judge finds this funny and lets him go (Ibn al-Faradī 1992: 38–39). Another anecdote, which reveals that Juhā was a simpleton, deals with the cause of his death. Too dumb to drink water from the river, Juhā died of thirst while on a riverboat and was buried in Sūq al-Amīr on the bank of the Euphrates (Ibn al-Faradī 1992: 38–39). The intended humorous tone of these anecdotes shows that Juhā was associated with comic situations.

Further, Abū l-Haŷŷaŷ Yūsuf b. Muhammad b. 'Abd Allāh b. Galib b. Muhammad b. 'Abd al-'Azīz al-Balawī al-Mālaqī, known as ibn al-Šayj, includes two Juhā tales in his *Kitāb alif bā*. Ibn al-Šayj, nicknamed Benaxeij (Son of the Sheikh), was born into a wealthy and very religious family in Málaga in 1132/33 and died in his native town in 1208 (Asín Palacios 1932: 195–96; Peña Martín 2007: 274–75). He made his first educational forays in Málaga in the field of philology: phonetics, lexicography, semantics, grammar, versification and literary history.

Although Ibn al-Šayj continued his education in Seville and Ceuta, it was a two-year pilgrimage to the Middle East that enriched his knowledge in different fields (Peña Martín 2007: 275–76). It could very well be that Ibn al-Šayj learned about Juhā during his pilgrimage to the Middle East, just as Ibn al-Faradī had during his own sacred journey.

Ibn al-Šayj wrote works in both prose and verse. Unfortunately, most of his works have not survived. It is in his major piece, *Kitāb alif bā*, that he makes reference to some of his works which have thus far not been found (Asín Palacios 1932: 208–09). It is also here that the two Juhā tales appear.

Kitāb alif bā was written in 1206–07, just a year before his death.[10] This work represents a type of *alphabetaria* that the author composed for the purpose of educating his youngest son, which is why he made frequent use of *exempla*, which entertain while serving a didactic purpose. The segment of the book of interest here is the one on philology, which includes tales and legends. Miguel Asín Palacios provides a list of titles in Spanish of all the tales and legends corresponding to this part (1932: 218). There we find 'Los cuentos del tonto Chehá'.[11] Emilio García Gómez includes these tales in his *Antología árabe para principiantes* and entitles them 'Dos historias del tonto Ŷehā' (1969: 10).[12] Both anecdotes are very short, and although *exempla* were most commonly used for didactic purposes, these two Juhā tales lack any teaching value as they contain no moral message. Apparently, their main purpose was merely to provide entertainment via the comic situations in which Juhā finds himself.

In the first tale, Juhā goes to the mill where the wheat for the townspeople is kept and starts putting some in his basket. When he is asked why he is doing this, he replies that he is crazy. Subsequently, when he is then asked to share some of his wheat with the townspeople he replies that he would then be twice as crazy (García Gómez 1969: 10). I have not been able to find another example of this tale-type, nor a specific number in ATU catalogue referring to this particular plot other than ATU1525Z★, 'Other Tales of Thefts', which is a generic reference to all tales dealing with unusual theft situations (Uther 2004: II, 254).

In the second tale, however, Juhā appears under his full name, Abu 'l-Ghusn, rather than his nickname. Several sources seem to confirm that Juhā's name was Abu 'l-Ghusn. Both Ibn al-Faradī and al-Maydānī (twelfth century) cite this name as indicating the person who lies behind the nickname Juhā (Freytag 1838: 403). In addition to this, Charles Pellat maintains that Juhā was a historical figure who might have been called Abu 'l-Ghusn Nūh al-Fazārī (1965: 591). The tale describes a situation in which Abu 'l-Ghusn is digging a hole in the desert and a passerby asks him to explain the deed. Abu 'l-Ghusn says that he has buried some money in the desert but cannot find it now. The man suggests that Abu 'l-Ghusn should have used a sign to indicate the location to himself, and the latter replies that he had done so by noticing a cloud in the sky which was no longer there when he returned (García Gómez 1969: 10). This reply is an example of folk motif J1922.2.1, 'Fool seeks the ears of grain in the direction of the cloud toward which he has sowed them' and appears in the tale-type ATU1278, 'Marking the Place on the Boat' (Uther 2004: II, 97), of which Ibn al-Šayj's anecdote is an example.

Both Ibn al-Faradī's reference to Juhā and the anecdotes about him, and the two tales by Ibn al-Šayj show beyond any doubt that this character was known in al-Andalus as early as the tenth century. In addition to these, eight more Juhā tales appear in the work *El libro de los huertos en flor (Ḥadāʾiq al-azāhir)* of an Andalusi author Abū Bakr ibn ʿĀṣim (1359–1426), translated to Spanish by Desirée López Bernal (see Ibn ʿĀṣim 2019: 177 n.435; 178 n.439; 182 n.457; 187 n.480; 188 n.481; 188 n.482; 188 n.484; 212 n.592). Although the corpus of Juhā tales in al-Andalus is not abundant — which does not exclude the possibility that future research may discover further material — it is sufficient to claim that the Jews had probably learned about this character from the Iberian Muslims prior to their expulsion from the Peninsula. The Jews in Spain spoke fluent Arabic and had used this knowledge to convey elements of Arabic culture and philosophy not only to the Jews of Western Europe but also to Christians, both in Spain and elsewhere. They accomplished this by translating scientific, philosophical and literary works in Arabic to Hebrew, Latin or the vernacular language (G. Menéndez Pidal 1951: 363–80; Gil 1985; Romano 1988: 955–78). Upon their arrival in the Ottoman Empire in the late Middle Ages, the Spanish Jews encountered a rich cycle of comic tales from the Turkish narrative tradition, whose protagonist is called Nasr al-Dīn Khodja (Turkish *Nasreddin Hoca*). Khodja is an honorific title in Turkish for a teacher or a man of distinction (Nehama 1977: 256). Both the character and the tales about him intertwined with the Judeo-Spanish narrative about Djohá.

Djohá and Nasr al-Dīn Khodja in the Ottoman Empire

The Turkish narrative tradition indicates that there was indeed a man by the name of Nasr al-Dīn Khodja whose tombstone can be found in the Turkish town of Ak Shehr (Marzolph 1993: 1018). Alija Isaković mentions the existence of certain documents which suggest that Nasr al-Dīn Khodja was born in the small village of Horto, Greece, in 1206 as the son of the imam ʾAbd Allāh Efendi, that he received an education in Konya, today's Turkey, and that he died around 1284/85 (1984: 8). According to Vladimir Gordlevski', there is an entire cult around this character in Ak Shehr, where he was allegedly buried (1957: 255). For example, young couples who are about to be married go to his grave and invite him to their wedding so as to avoid an unhappy marriage; or, those suffering from eye diseases go to his grave to be cured by pressing some earth from his grave to their eyes.

   The earliest anecdotes about Nasr al-Dīn in the Turkish language are quoted in Ebu 'l-Khayr-i Rūmī's (d. 1480) *Saltuk-name* and Lāmiʿī Čelebi's (d. 1531) *Letāʾif* (Marzolph 1993: 1018). Although Nasr al-Dīn Khodja emerged in the Turkish tradition independently of any other similar character or tradition (Braginskli' 1957: 12–13; Marzolph 1993: 1019), the narrative about him was enriched in the process of cultural interaction with the Muslim population of the Middle East. For instance, according to Pellat, the tales of Nasr al-Dīn Khodja formed an independent collection into which were incorporated the stories of the Arabic Juhā, which had been handed down orally (1965: 591). This assumption by Pellat can only be a matter of speculation as no solid proof has been found thus far which can confirm this hypothesis beyond doubt. We can only claim with certainty that from the nineteenth century there are examples of tales in which the two characters are intertwined due to the existence of printed collections which show this (Marzolph 1993: 1019).

This mixture of tales can also be seen in the case of the Judeo-Spanish Djohá. Koén-Sarano believes that 'la figura de Djohá está atada a la figura de Nasreddin Hodja' (1991: xiv). Alexander-Frizer maintains that 'in Turkey the Jewish and Turkish characters fused together into a character with the name: Nassar-a-din Effendi Joha', thus claiming the mixture not only of the tales but also of the characters' names (2008: 433). Proof of this is the collection of Djohá tales published by an anonymous author in 1911 in Thessaloniki (Bornes-Varol 1995: 62–63). The tales were printed in Judeo-Spanish Rashi script, and Djohá appears as the main character of these tales. However it is not Djohá that appears in the title of the collection but the Turkish character, *La Vida de Nasrudin Hodja*, thus indicating the fusion of these two characters. Likewise, Koén-Sarano collected a tale, 'Ke koman los vistidos' ('Let Them Eat Clothes'), in which the protagonist is called Nasaraddín Hodja: Djohá (1991: 331). Here Djohá is depicted as being the nickname of Nasr al-Dīn Khodja.

In summary, in these two chapters, the presence of Juhā is clearly seen in the Muslim tradition of al-Andalus from at least the tenth century, the date of the oldest known reference to this character in that region, found in the work of Ibn al-Faradī. Juhā also appears at the beginning of the thirteenth century in the *alphabetaria* of Ibn al-Šayj, another author from al-Andalus. Thus it can be concluded that the tales about him were passed down among the Iberian Muslims, and in the process of cultural exchange between them and the Jews, the latter most probably adopted the character and made him their own.

This cultural contact and influence continued to form part of the Sepharadim's everyday life after they abandoned Spain. When they arrived in the Ottoman Empire, they enriched the corpus of tales on Djohá by appropriating jokes and anecdotes about a similar character from the Turkish tradition called Nasr al-Dīn Khodja. However, they did not relinquish the legacy brought from Spain and continued to foster comic tales, jokes and anecdotes featuring a character they perceived as their own: Djohá. The following chapters show how this tradition regarding Djohá endures to this day.

2. 'Our' Character: Sephardic Identity in Djohá Tales from the Former Yugoslavia

Examples of Djohá tales in the former Yugoslavia have been collected from the end of the nineteenth century. However, prior to WWII, the efforts made by those who collected the tales, namely Haim Davičo and Tihomir Djordjević (1868–1944) did not aim to ensure the continuation and revitalisation of the Sephardic tradition. Thus the material was collected and published in Serbian rather than Judeo-Spanish as little to no importance was given to the original language of these tales.

However, in the second half of the twentieth century, Djohá material was collected and published in Judeo-Spanish as a result of the different attitude taken by post-war Sephardic authors or collectors towards their Sephardic heritage. After WWII and the Holocaust, the efforts were focused on re-activating the tradition, which included the revitalisation of the Ladino language. Hence the preservation of the original language in which the tales had been passed down for centuries became of upmost importance. The work of the two Sephardic Jews to be examined here are Žamila Kolonomos (1922–2012) and Eliezer Papo (1969–), the former from Macedonia and the latter from Bosnia, whose work regarding Djohá tales and other Judeo-Spanish oral material reflects these changes in attitudes and aims. I also analyse the work of Žak Konfino (1892–1975). As Konfino's work entails both periods under consideration and hence his Djohá tales reflect both of the aforementioned attitudes, particularly with regard to the language issue, his work serves as a suitable conclusion to the entire chapter.

The corpus of Djohá tales in the former Yugoslavia is unfortunately rather limited. Yet, it is sufficient to demonstrate an impressive endurance of Djohá among the Sepharadim in the region —— a tradition which, as shown earlier, goes back to the Middle Ages and the Iberian Peninsula. The corpus from the first half of the twentieth century consists of one anecdote introduced by Davičo in his tale 'Luna' (1888) and nine tales collected and published in Serbian in 1939 by Djordjević.

Djohá also appears in the collection of an American linguist Max A. Luria (1891–1966). In 1927 in Bitola (formerly known as Monastir), Macedonia, Luria collected eighteen konsežas, one of which has Djohá as a protagonist (Luria 1930: 29–30). However, his work will not be studied here because my focus is on authors and collectors from the former Yugoslavia, most of them of Sephardic origin, and their attitudes towards their own heritage.[13]

The corpus covering the second half of the twentieth century includes one Djohá tale published in 1978 by Kolonomos and twenty tales told by Eliezer Papo and published by Koén-Sarano in 2003. Eliezer Papo's tales will additionally be discussed in the chapter on Koén-Sarano's work, including details about her fieldwork and her *Folktales of Joha: Jewish Trickster* (hereafter *Folktales of Joha*, 2003), which includes tales told by Eliezer Papo.

Bearing in mind that the assimilation process of the Sephardic communities in the former Yugoslavia was well advanced in the first half of the twentieth century and particularly the fact that most Sephardic communities perished in the Holocaust, all the examples of Djohá tales from the region serve as proof that, in spite of all the adversities already mentioned, the narrative tradition regarding this character managed to endure to the present day.[14] An additional point highlighted here concerns the perception of Djohá among the Sepharadim in the former Yugoslavia and how their cultural identity is embodied in this figure.

The Sephardic Hero in the Serbian Language Prior to WWII

The oldest reference to Djohá in the former Yugoslavia is to be found in Serbia in the work of Haim S. Davičo, who made frequent use of oral literature to reinforce the main idea of his own works. 'Luna' (1888) is a case in point. The main plot of 'Luna' revolves around a love story between young Sephardic couples who are faced with a variety of difficulties in their courtship. However, parallel to the love story is an allusion to the conflict that exists within the community between those who blindly follow tradition and those who progressively embrace more open-minded ideas. The story is set during the time when the Sephardic community in Belgrade was transitioning from an Ottoman lifestyle to a more liberal western-European one.

Davičo uses these conflicts to construct his characters, some of whom support these ideas and some of whom oppose them. One of the characters that defends traditional values is Ćir ('Sir') Čelebon who organises a *tajfa* in his home. A *tajfa*, according to Davičo's account, is a winter Sunday-evening gathering (2000: 49). The guests discuss the situation in their community, and Ćir Čelebon insists on the preservation of the old way of life. To counteract Čelabon's perspective, another character, Moreno Katalan, tells a short anecdote whose aim is to explain that change is inevitable and cannot be forestalled. The protagonist of that anecdote is none other than Djohá.

The story goes as follows: Djohá was convinced that he would be able to save an old wall that was falling down by putting his back against it to support it. However, as soon as the wind blew, the wall collapsed, burying Djohá among the rubble (Davičo 2000: 51). The moral of the anecdote is explicit: opposing what is inevitable can do no good. The anecdote here illustrates the overall idea of Davičo's work: that the life of the Sepharadim will be affected by change, and they should welcome and accept what is unavoidable. To reinforce this idea, Davičo uses traditional wisdom condensed in this Djohá anecdote. In addition, he illustrates here what Koén-Sarano claims: that adults often make use of Djohá tales to 'dizir a otros kozas ke no tinían la ozadía de dizirles derechamente' ('to tell someone something you do not dare tell him openly') (Koén-Sarano 1991: xiv).

A curious response accompanies this anecdote: someone says out loud *pishkado* ('fish'), and everyone switches to another topic. Davičo offers an explanation of the meaning of the word and the context in which it was used among the Belgrade Sepharadim: to put an end to an unpleasant argument or depressing conversation, it was sufficient for someone to say *pishkado* out loud for everyone to immediately change the topic (Davičo 2000: 51).

As part of his strategy, Davičo integrates into the text additional information to explain culture-specific references. He does this by offering an explanation either in the main text or in brackets. The examples of *tajfa* and *pishkado* illustrate this practice. Even more interesting for us here is how Davičo explains to his target audience just who Djohá is: 'neka vrsta jalijskog Nasradin-hodže' ('a kind of Nasr al-Dīn Khodja from Yalia') (Davičo 2000: 51).[15]

The introduction of *glosas*, such as this explanation, was not exclusive to Davičo but constitutes a widespread phenomenon in the Judeo-Spanish literary world from the middle of the nineteenth century (García Moreno 2010: 76). Sephardic authors or translators commonly introduce clarification for specific words, expressions or terms they use, usually in brackets.[16] Introducing explanatory glosses entails a 'carácter subjetivo, pues es el glosador el que decide tanto *a*) qué pasajes necesitan glosa, como *b*) cuál haya de ser la aclaración introducida' (García Moreno 2010: 76).

This is evident from the elements Davičo chooses to clarify, Djohá being one of them. Readers in Serbia were not familiar with Djohá, since he forms part of the Sephardic (or Arabic) culture, but they did know the character of Nasr al-Dīn Khodja well. Under the rule of the Ottomans, the Serbs adopted the Turkish character and made him part of their folklore in the same way that the Sepharadim adopted Djohá from the Arabs.[17] To give the Serbian readers an idea of the nature of Djohá, Davičo deploys a procedure which consists of finding rough cultural equivalents for a specific source-language term or name. Thus he compares a Sephardic character, Djohá, with a similar character known to the target audience. Both of these procedures — providing additional information and finding rough cultural equivalents — represent forms of cultural transposition.[18] Although these *glosas* can be coloured with subjective nuances, this parallel between the Sephardic Djohá and the Turkish or Serbian Nasr al-Dīn Khodja is drawn in other testimonies collected from among the Sepharadim from the former Yugoslavia, namely in the collection of Djohá tales by Djordjević.

Serbian ethnographer Tihomir R. Djordjević (1868–1944) recorded among Serbian Sepharadim from Belgrade nine Djohá tales which he published in 1939 in the *Glasnik Etnografskog muzeja u Beogradu* (*Journal of the Ethnographic Museum in Belgrade*). Each tale bears a title given by Djordjević himself, as shown in the table below.

TABLE 3.1. Djohá tales collected by Tihomir Djordjević in Belgrade, Serbia (1939)

Title of the tale as given by Djordjević	Brief summary of the tale	ATU and/ or Haboucha's tale-type number (where applicable)	Other Sephardic Versions
'Džuha i Ukradeno Magare' ('Djuhá and the Missing Ass')	A poor man's sole possession is his donkey. One day, someone steals the donkey from him. As Djohá is very clever, the poor man asks Djohá to help him find the thief. One Friday, as everyone is coming out of the mosque, Djohá poses the question: is there anyone here who has never committed a sin in his life? One man raises his hand and Djohá rightly signals him out as the thief.	Haboucha **1217 'The Missing Ass'	Levy 1944: I, 85 Koén-Sarano 1991: 275

'Džuha i Seme od Kamila' ('Djuhá and the Camel Seeds')	Heedless of his wife's laughter, Djohá plants seeds from which he is convinced camels will grow. After a time, some merchants with camels arrive and settle close to Djohá's field, where they let their camels graze on Djohá's pasture. Djohá sees the camels and takes them home, convinced that they have grown from his seeds, thus proving his wife wrong.		Koén-Sarano 1991: 87; 2003: 224–27
'Čuće Se Sutra' ('You'll Hear All About It Tomorrow')	Djohá needs boards of wood to finish building his house. Knowing that kadí keeps some boards in his attic, he climbs up on kadí's roof and starts taking down the tiles in order to enter the attic. A passerby asks him what he is doing up there, to which Djohá replies that he is playing an instrument. The passerby says he can't hear anything, and Djohá replies: 'Never mind, you'll hear tomorrow'.	ATU1525Z★ 'Other Tales of Thefts' Haboucha ★★1340 'The Musical Saw'	Levy 1944: II, 86
'Džuha i Nove Papuče' ('Djuhá and the New Slippers')	Djohá buys himself new slippers, but annoyed by everyone questioning him about the price, he decides to pretend that he has died. Everyone goes to pay their respects, and just before being put in the coffin, Djohá jumps up and reveals the price of his slippers, hoping that now people will stop bothering him about the price he paid.	ATU1551★ 'How Much the Donkey Cost'	
'Umro Bakrač' ('The Cauldron Has Died')	Djohá is so poor that he has to borrow a cauldron from his neighbour to heat water. One day, he returns the cauldron and gives the neighbour a kettle, claiming that the cauldron has given birth to it. The neighbour gladly accepts the kettle. The next time Djohá borrows the cauldron, he goes to the neighbour and says that the cauldron has died. Puzzled, the neighbour asks him how that is possible, to which Djohá replies that if the cauldron is capable of giving birth to a kettle, it can also die.	ATU1592B 'The Pot Has a Child and Dies'	Molho 1960: 131 Koén-Sarano 1986: 143; 1991: 213
'Džuha kao Trgovac' ('Djuhá the Merchant')	Tired of suffering poverty, Djohá decides to take dry excrement, grind it and sell it as a means with which one can predict the future. The only man who decides to buy this product puts it in his mouth and screams that it is excrement. Djohá answers: 'See, you can already guess what something is'	Haboucha ★★1690 'The Bug Killer'	Koén-Sarano 1986: 137; 1991: 79

'Džuha Traži Sam Sebe' ('Djohá Can't Find Himself')	Before going to bed, Djohá makes a list of where he has placed all his items of clothing. In the morning, he starts checking to see if everything is in its place and realises that the only thing that is missing is Djohá in the bed. He goes out to the street looking for himself until a man he encounters tells him that he is Djohá.	Haboucha ★★1288B 'Numbskull Can't Find Himself'	Confino 1957: 642–43 Konfino 1994: 96–97 Koén-Sarano 1991: 59
'Džuhino Magare' ('Djohá's Ass')	Djohá was asked by a friend to lend him his donkey. Djohá tells the neighbour that he has lent his donkey to someone else. At that moment, the donkey brays behind the house and the neighbour, now knowing that the donkey is behind the house, asks Djohá how he can say he lent his donkey to someone else when it is behind his house. Djohá replies, 'What kind of man are you that you believe a donkey over me!'	ATU1594 'The Donkey is Not at Home' Haboucha ★★1592C 'The Ass Is Not at Home'	Molho 1960: 132 Koén-Sarano 1986: 145; 1991: 207; 2003: 83
'Džuha kao Ludak' ('Djuhá, the Madman')	Djohá is taken to a mental institution. There he asks to be fed kosher food because he is a Jew. One Saturday, he starts smoking and the guard asks him how he can smoke on Saturday if he is a Jew. Djohá replies that he is crazy, and therefore he is allowed to do whatever he wants		Koén-Sarano 2003: 205

Djordjević was the leading figure in the field of ethnology in Serbia at the turn of the twentieth century. He was born in 1868 in Knjaževac, Serbia, and as a son of an Orthodox priest he spent his youth in several Serbian villages where his father was serving; there he became familiar with local folk customs and traditions (Antonijević 1969: 140). In 1887, he enrolled in the Velika Škola (School for Higher Education) in Belgrade in the Department of History and Philology, where he graduated in 1891. Djordjević continued his studies abroad, receiving part of his education in Vienna and afterwards in Munich where he defended his doctoral dissertation (Popović 2010: 3). During World War I, he spent some time in England, which he used to expand and deepen his knowledge of contemporary ethnographic practices. Upon his return to Serbia, he lectured at the Faculty of Philosophy in Belgrade and was elected a member of the Srpska kraljevska akademija (Serbian Royal Academy). He died in Belgrade in 1944 (Antonijević 1994: 18).[19]

Djordjević was interested in studying different aspects of folk tradition, particularly oral literature. This prompted him to begin collecting evidence of folk literature not only from Serbs but also from ethnic minorities living in Serbia, such as the Romani people, Turks, Albanians, Romanians, Vlachs and Jews (Antonijević 1994: 15; Popović 2010: 25). The Balkan region is known for its ethnic variety, represented by several South Slavic peoples (Serbs, Croatians, Macedonians,

Bulgarians, Slovenes), Greeks, Romanians, Turks, Albanians and Jews. This ethnic variety is reflected in the number of different languages spoken by these peoples and the different religions they profess (Vidaković-Petrov 1994: 285).

Because of his dedication to the study of minorities, Djordjević started collecting material from different ethnic groups. The result of this enterprise was his doctoral dissertation, *Die Zigeuner in Serbien*, which dealt with the folk heritage of the Romani people. Djordjević defended his thesis in Munich and published it in two parts, in 1903 and in 1906, in Budapest (Popović 2010: 197). This work proved to be of great importance for his career as it accorded him a good reputation among ethnologists and folklorists both in Serbia and abroad (Antonijević 1994: 12).

There is a disparity in the documentation of his fieldwork. Djordjević himself left several testimonies about his work among the Romani people, whereas for the Spanish Jews barely any information remains.[20] Nevertheless, there are reasons to believe that he used the same or similar methods for his work among the Spanish Jews as with the Romani people, particularly his collection and editorial practices.

Djordjević was known to employ two different procedures when collecting oral data *in situ*. The first consisted of the technique of observation with direct participation, which he used in the case of the Romani people and Vlachs. Djordjević integrated himself into the ethnic group he was researching and took part in their activities and celebrations (Antonijević 1968: 227).

The second procedure included the use of questionnaires created by Djordjević himself. He calls them *uputstva* ('instructions') which were aimed at getting broader information about the evolution of the material collected through a series of questions posed to the interviewees (Popović 2010: 24). As the information accords with the kind we know he elicited from other questionnaires, it therefore seems likely that in the case of Spanish Jews, Djordević used a questionnaire of this type.[21] The information he gives in the prologue to his edition of the Djohá tales indicates that, instead of merely recording the tales, a series of questions were asked during the interview and the storytelling process, such as: 'Kad god sam kog Jevrejina pitao o Džuhi, odmah mi je odgovorio: "Pitate o Džuhi? To je naš Nasredin Hodža"' ('Whenever I would ask any Jew about Djohá, he would immediately reply: "You want to know who Djohá is? He's our Nasr al-Dīn Khodja"') (Djordjević 1939a: 15).

In addition to his direct participation and his use of questionnaires, Djordjević's work is characterised by another contemporary ethnographic practice, that of not always providing information about his informants, such as their names, age, sex, date and place of recording. He was not the only collector of folk material to do this. Cynthia M. Crews, for example, collected folk material from Bosnian Sepharadim in 1929 that included one folk tale and a number of ballads and poems. Yet, as she herself confesses, she never planned on publishing this material and had thus, on occasions such as this one, neglected to write down the names of her informants or any other information related to them (1979: 168). When, years later, she changed her mind and decided to publish the material, all she could remember was that the tale was told to her by a seventy-year-old washerwoman and that the poetry was told to her by two elderly ladies (Crews 1979: 168).

With regard to Djordjević's work, the details concerning informants are sometimes included, but on other occasions he merely specifies 'I heard', 'I was told' or 'People told me' (Popović 2010: 198). This practice of not providing much information regarding his sources was particularly typical during the early stage of his work. For instance, when he started collecting material from the Romani people from Aleksinac, Serbia, between 1901 and 1903, he merely listed them as 'Cigani iz Aleksinca' ('gypsies from Aleksinac') without giving any more specific information (Popović 2010: 202). Later in his work, he started to provide full data that included the first and last names of the source, the time and place of recording and similar information.

In the case of his fieldwork among Sephardic Jews, such information about the informants is missing. This might suggest that his fieldwork was carried out long before its publication in 1939. It could well be that he collected this material in the early stages of his work when he did not consider this data to be relevant and when it was customary for him to omit this type of information.

However, based on the comments he makes in the prologue, it is safe to assume that Djordjević interviewed a large number of people. This is evident from Djordjević's words: 'Mnogi ne znaju gotovo ništa [o Djohi], samo *kažu* da *su slušali* da se o njemu priča, ali *se* više *ne sećaju* šta' [my emphasis] ('Barely anyone knows anything [about Djohá]; *they* just *claim* that *they had heard* people talking about him but *they do not remember* what was being said about him') (Djordjević 1939a: 15). The plural verbs ('they claim', 'they had heard', 'they do not remember') suggest that more than one informant was taken into account. Likewise, the testimonies of Djordjević's informants indicate not only that Djohá tales were now in decline, but also that they were told in all Sephardic communities in the former Yugoslavia, particularly Macedonia (Djordjević 1939a: 15–16).

Although Djordjević does not give precise data regarding the names and ages of his interviewees, he comments in the prologue that it was only the elderly who knew a tale or a proverb about Djohá. This remark shows that oral tradition regarding this figure had started to fade away among younger generations. That is the same conclusion that Djordjević came to while collecting material from other ethnic groups (Popović 2010: 203).[22]

The language in which Djohá material was collected from Spanish Jews is also a relevant issue. Djordjević was a polyglot. He spoke several languages, including French, English and German, and could read Greek, Latin, Romanian and Albanian. He also had a fair knowledge of the Romani language (Antonijević 1994: 16). This indicates that he was able to collect material from some groups in their native language rather than in Serbian. However, in spite of being able to use and understand the languages of some of the ethnic groups from which he collected the material, Djordjević was unsure of his command of these languages and insisted that his informants speak in the Serbian language so as to avoid any misunderstanding on his part:

> Ima već 30 godina od kako sam i ja [...] započeo i proučavanje Cigana u našoj zemlji i beleženje tekstova njihovih pripovedaka. Nažalost ja nikada nisam uspeo da potpuno savladam ciganski jezik. Zbog toga sam uvek tražio da mi

Cigani kazuju svoje pripovetke na srpskom jeziku. Ja sam uvek bio svestan da takav posao ne zadovoljava interes i ispitivača ciganskog jezika, ali mi nije bio moguće činiti drugojače bez štete po tačno beleženje na ciganskom jeziku. (Djordjević 1933: iv)

(It has been thirty years since [...] I started doing research among gypsies in our country and writing down texts of their tales. Unfortunately I have never managed to completely master the language of gypsies. For that reason I have always asked gypsies to tell me their tales in the Serbian language. I have always been aware that this working method is of little benefit for those who do research on the language of gypsies but there was no other way of doing this without the risk of being inaccurate when recording in the language of gypsies.)

Djordjević was aware that this decision to write the tales in Serbian would lead not only to the loss of linguistic record, but also to the loss of part of the uniqueness and authenticity of the tales once they were told in a different language (Djordjević 1933: iv). However, preserving the content of these tales, albeit in a different language, seemed equally important to him (Djordjević 1933: iv). Djordjević's view leads me to conclude that Djohá tales were told to him in the Serbian language. Djordjević was not a Sephardic Jew, and he most certainly did not speak Judeo-Spanish. Apart from French, there is no information of his speaking any other romance language, including Spanish.

Nonetheless, there is one particular practice in his work related to the language that is worthy of mention here. During his fieldwork among non-Serbian ethnic groups, Djordjević occasionally made a note of key points or concepts of a certain tale in the original language, which he placed next to their Serbian translation. We know this from his work with Romani people from Serbia. For example, on one occasion, he recorded a tale about how a virgin gave birth to a bear. After the Serbian word for bear, *mečka*, he writes between brackets the gypsy word for the animal, *aruša*, and next to the word for virgin in Serbian, *nevina devojka*, he writes its equivalent in the Romani language, *datarbjandi* (Popović 2010: 198).

This practice was also applied by Djordjević in his work with the Spanish Jews. For example, the sixth tale in the collection, 'Djohá, the Merchant', tells the story of an impoverished Djohá who decides one day to start cheating people to earn money. He takes dried excrement and grinds it, then announces that he is selling a means with which you can foretell the future. Most people do not believe him, and they refuse to buy this product from him. One person does buy it, but upon putting it in his mouth he starts shouting that it is excrement. Djohá replies that this confirms his claim that his product enables you to immediately start foretelling correctly (Djordjević 1939a: 18).

Djordjević tried to maintain and conserve some concepts of the tale in the original language. This can be seen at the end of the tale, where Djordjević adds in brackets, 'španski: *hapes de indivinar*' ('in Spanish: *hapes de indivinar*'). *Hap*, which etymologically comes from Turkish, means 'pill' in Judeo-Spanish (Nehama 1977: 251). Thus Djordjević makes it clear that Djohá was selling pills for divining the future (*hapes de indivinar*).

With regard to his editing practice, Djordjević intervened in the stylising process of the tales to a great extent. This was a consequence of his collection technique of merely writing down parts of the tale in notes and short sentences during the storytelling process. The tale in its entirety was not written until later, relying partly on the notes taken and partly on his memory (Popović 2010: 203). This means that the narrative was influenced not only by his memory but also by his own language, which fundamentally affects the authentic oral tale. As a result, the language of the tales as published is literary, free of any dialect, obscene words or expressions, and the sentences are clear and concise (Popović 2010: 204). The language of the nine tales Djordjević collected from the Spanish Jews contains all of these features.

The Djohá tales that Djordjević collected were published with the title of 'Džuha u predanju španskih Jevreja u Beogradu' ('Djuhá in the Tradition of the Spanish Jews of Belgrade'). The title itself indicates that the collection work was carried out only in the Serbian capital, although there were other communities of Spanish Jews living in Serbia, namely in Priština, Leskovac and Šabac. The title also highlights that the collection focused only on the tales involving Djohá.

Djordjević's choice to focus only on collecting Djohá tales, and not on any other Judeo-Spanish oral material also in decline, was in all probability influenced by his own interest in the type of narrative that characterises these tales: jokes and anecdotes about a fool and a trickster. On several occasions, Djordjević collected and published tales of Nasr al-Dīn Khodja which he complied from among Serbs, Muslims, Turks and Albanians in the region (Djordjević 1937; 1939b). The figure of Nasr al-Dīn Khodja was brought to the Balkans by the Ottomans and eventually became part of the local folklore as a result of cultural interaction. The presence of Nasr al-Dīn Khodja has, thus, been recorded in the folk narrative of Serbs, Croatians, Bosnians and Macedonians. Djordjević was familiar with this rich tradition in the region and, as he succinctly puts it, 'Džuha i Nasredin hodža su krv jedne krvi, to jest da su isto i da je ono što se priča o jednome isto sa onim što se priča o drugome' ('Djuhá and Nasr al-Dīn Khodja are of the same blood, that is they are the same and what is said about one is true of the other') (Djordjević 1939a: 16). Thus this interest in the character of Nasr al-Dīn Khodja most probably prompted Djordjević to collect tales of similar content from the Spanish Jews whose character had a different name inherited from the Arabic tradition but who Djordjević considered to be one and the same.

It is not only Djordjević who defends this idea of Djohá and Nasr al-Dīn Khodja being identical in nature. It is also expressed by Djordjević's informants in answer to specific questions posed to them about Djohá. For example, one of the questions Djordjević asked was: 'Pitate o Džuhi?' ('Who is Djohá?'). The common response of the informants was: 'To je naš Nasredin hodža' ('He is our Nasr al-Dīn Khodja') (Djordjević 1939a: 15). This general comment indicates that the Spanish Jews in Serbia perceived the Turkish character to be the equivalent of their Djohá. The only difference that they perceived to exist lies in their names: 'Nasredin hodža je tursko ime, a Džuha je špansko' ('Nasr al-Dīn Khodja is a Turkish name and Djohá is a Spanish name') (Djordjević 1939a: 15). This explanation demonstrates that

Djordjević's informants were familiar with the Turkish character and aware of the similarities that existed between it and their own character; it also shows that they perceived Djohá to be part of their Iberian heritage by indicating that the name derives from Spanish.

However, no one among those interviewed was able to give any further information or say anything more about these two characters except that they were both known as fools (Djordjević 1939a: 15). This perception by the Sepharadim in Serbia of Djohá's simple nature rather than his being a conniving trickster is a surprisingly accurate one. As Harriet Goldberg highlights: 'The Eastern Johá is a careless simpleton, less inclined to manipulate his environment than is his North African brother' (1993: 112).

The prologue contains further information of relevance here. After highlighting the conclusion that Djohá tales can scarcely be heard anymore among the Sepharadim from Serbia, Djordjević adds the following: 'Samo još po koji stariji čovek zna da kaže poneku pripovetku ili *poslovicu* o njemu' ('It is only the elderly who know a tale or *a proverb* about him' [my emphasis]) (Djordjević 1939a: 15). This statement reveals Djohá's presence not only in the narrative but also in proverbs and sayings. Djohá's remarks in dialogues have gone through a process of fossilisation up to the point of becoming proverbial or epigrammatic, being representative of what Koén-Sarano calls *kuentos en chiko* ('tales in miniature') (1991: xv).[23] Without being familiar with the original narrative from which a particular proverb or saying emerged, the latter may be incomprehensible as a result:

> Many tale-based proverbs function in discourse as markers that call attention to the speaker's cultural identity. Because hearers who share that identity recognize not only the communal folk wisdom of these sayings but also the details of familiar narratives, they respond to such proverbs more strongly than to less colourful, sentential ones. [...] Certainly these specialized sayings are almost meaningless if their narratives are not known to both speaker and hearer. (Goldberg 1993: 106)

A case in point is the proverb 'Ayre, yévate esta arina' ('Wind, take this flour'), as it stems directly from a well-known tale about Djohá, 'Solución para haraganes' ('Solution for the Lazy'). This title was given by Koén-Sarano, who recorded the tale from Diana Sarano, born and raised in Turkey and Italy.[24] It was first published under the title 'Djohá i l'arina' (Koén-Sarano 1986: 133) and later reprinted as 'Solución para haraganes' (Koén-Sarano 1991: 59). The tale corresponds to the ATU1291D tale-type, 'Other Objects or Animals Sent to Go by Themselves' (Uther 2004: II, 107).

The content of the tale is as follows: Djoha's mother sends him to the mill with a sack of wheat to be ground, but it is so heavy that, by the time he reaches the mill, Djohá is exhausted. Thus when the flour is ready, he is too tired to carry it back. Emptying the bag on the ground, he instructs the wind to take the flour home. Upon arriving home Djohá, expecting the flour to be there before him, is surprised to find that it has not yet arrived (Haboucha 1992: 543). The end of the tale explains the meaning of the proverb: 'I ansí kedó la dicha: "Ayre, yévate esta arina!", ke se uza asta agora, kuando se da a azer una koza a alguno, saviendo muy bien ke no la va azer' ('And this is how the proverb came to be remembered: "Wind, take this flour!", which is used even nowadays when you give someone a task which you know he is not going to carry out') (Koén-Sarano 1991: 59). The proverb is widely used among the Sepharadim (Danon 1903: 81 n. 122 and Benazeraf 1978: 89 n. 273).

Shorn of the story, a saying can be used in different contexts, especially if it encompasses a commonplace lesson and depends no longer on its source for meaning: 'Some tales leave paroemiological trails that later turn up in discourse and either become associated with other stories or just enter into the general stock of folk wisdom as proverbs, proverbial sayings, or even lost metaphors' (Goldberg 1993: 107). However, their link to Djohá usually remains clear, since the tales themselves are widely disseminated and well known among the Sepharadim, so much so that his name is quite often omitted from the proverb as the connection to him seems unambiguous (Alexander-Frizer 2008: 442).

Djordjević did not collect examples of this type of proverb. As stated earlier, his focus was merely on Djohá tales, and it seems that he did not want to stray from that task by collecting any other folk material, even that which included Djohá in a different folk genre. Nevertheless, an abundance of such examples exists and, based on the testimonies of Djordjević's informants, were used in Serbia as well (1939a: 15).

Some of the tales collected by Djordjević depict Djohá as a true Sephardic character whose actions and way of reasoning reflect aspects of Jewish culture and religion. An example of this is 'Djuhá, the Madman': Djohá is taken to a mental institution. There he asks to be fed kosher food because he is a Jew. One Saturday, he starts smoking and the guard asks him how he can smoke on Saturday if he is a Jew. Djohá replies that he is crazy and therefore he is allowed to do whatever he pleases (Djordjević 1939a: 18). The tale has evidently gone through the process of domestication to its environment. Djohá asks to eat kosher food. Hence he is a true Jew who follows the regulations of *Kashrut*. However, what confuses the guard is the fact that Djohá starts smoking on Shabbat, when it is forbidden to kindle or extinguish a fire.[25] However, Djohá gets out of the situation with his wit by claiming that being crazy justifies all of his illogical actions.

While some examples show the Jewish/Sephardic side of Djohá, other examples demonstrate contact with other cultures. 'Djuhá and the Missing Ass' is a case in point. A poor man's sole possession is his donkey. One day, someone steals it from him. As Djohá is very clever, the victim asks Djohá to help find the thief. One Friday, as everyone is coming out of the mosque, Djohá asks if there is anyone among them who has never committed a sin in his life; when one man raises his hand, Djohá rightly singles him out as the thief (Djordjević 1939a: 16–17).

Although the Sepharadim perceive Djohá as their character, in this tale, he goes to the mosque rather than to a synagogue. This indicates that the tale was probably taken from the Turkish tradition and that it went through a partial adaptation to the environment. This is evident in the fact that the actions are attributed to Djohá, the Sephardic figure, and not to Nasr al-Dīn Khodja, the Turkish hero, which is a sign of the acculturation of the tale. But this judaisation is limited merely to the name of the protagonist, since other elements were not adapted to the Jewish culture. Thus Djohá goes to the mosque on Friday as if he were a character from the Islamic world.

This proves the point that the corpus of Djohá tales among the Sepharadim was enlarged upon with comic tales from the Turkish tradition in which a similar character appears as a protagonist.[26] In this process of cultural exchange between the two ethnic groups, some tales went through the process of cultural adaptation to their environment, whereas others were borrowed, maintained and transmitted in their original form.

In summary, Djordjević was able to collect nine Djohá tales in Serbian and publish them just before the beginning of WWII. However, he was not the first to publish Djohá tales in Serbian: in 1888, Davičo introduced an anecdote about Djohá in Serbian in his tale 'Luna'. These publications indicate that in spite of the assimilation process and the language shift, the tradition regarding this character, which had been in existence for centuries, was still alive prior to WWII not only among the Sepharadim in Serbia but also throughout the entire region. This fact is corroborated by the comment made by Djordjević's informants, which appears in the prologue, that Djohá tales existed among all Sephardic groups living in the former Yugoslavia, particularly among those from Macedonia (Djordjević 1939a: 15–16). This may have been true, but regretfully only one Djohá tale was collected in Macedonia prior to the catastrophe of the Holocaust (Luria 1930: 29–30).

The examples presented in this chapter show Djohá's relevance for the Sepharadim themselves. It is clear from the testimonies of Djordjević's informants that he was perceived as their character versus other similar characters of the region, particularly the Turkish Nasr al-Dīn Khodja. Although they were familiar with Nasr al-Dīn Khodja, the Sepharadim were loyal to Djohá, as it is he with whom they identify. They marked this differentiation by calling Djohá 'ours', while Nasr al-Dīn was 'theirs'.

Although humour is the main ingredient of the Djohá tales, serving to make the Sepharadim laugh, they also played a didactic role (Koén-Sarano 1991: xiv). Davičo relates Djohá to Nasr al-Dīn Khodja, and *khodja* means teacher in Turkish. The Sephardic community deployed certain Djohá anecdotes to convey a moral message. He was their *haham* (wise man/teacher). This combination of humour and didacticism in Djohá tales has formed part of their legacy and cultural identity for centuries and impelled the Sepharadim in the region and elsewhere to foster this character despite the changes they were forced to undergo.

However, the testimonies of Djordjević's sources reveal that this tradition was starting to fade, and eventually it was only the older members of the community who continued to embrace it. The chain of oral transmission weakened with the ongoing changes in the Sephardic community, which was turning to a new language (Serbian) and a modern lifestyle, to the detriment of Judeo-Spanish and the old way of life. WWII further contributed to the decline of oral literature in general, including Djohá tales. Yet, in spite of this, defying time and circumstance, some traces of the character can still be found among the remaining members of the Sephardic communities in the former Yugoslavia.

Revival of the Djohá Tradition in the Original Language post-Holocaust

The number of Djohá tales collected in the former Yugoslavia in the second half of the twentieth century is as limited as those collected in the first half for two reasons: the assimilation of the Sephardic communities into wider Yugoslav society, and the annihilation of the vast majority of the Sepharadim from the region in the Holocaust. Owing to these circumstances, the corpus of Djohá narratives from this period is reduced to one Djohá tale collected and published in 1978 by Žamila Kolonomos, a Sephardic Jew from Bitola (Macedonia), and twenty tales told by Bosnian-born Eliezer Papo to Matilda Koén-Sarano, which she published in 2003. This material has two main traits which differ from the pre-WWII material. The first concerns the provenance of the extant corpora. Whereas during the first half of the twentieth century Djohá tales were collected in Serbia, the examples in this chapter come from Macedonia and Bosnia.

The second trait concerns the linguistic aspect of the corpus. Whereas the examples of the first half of the twentieth century were all collected and published in Serbian, the tales from the second half, by contrast, were collected in Judeo-Spanish. Furthermore, although compiled in Judeo-Spanish, Eliezer Papo's tales were published in English. Koén-Sarano's choice to publish Eliezer Papo's tales in English in spite of their having been collected in Judeo-Spanish is a point discussed in detail in the chapter on Koén-Sarano's work. Although the number of examples from this period is small, they demonstrate both that the Djohá tradition managed to endure among the drastically reduced Sephardic communities in the former Yugoslavia and the attempt made to preserve them in their original language.

Žamila Kolonomos was born in 1922 in Bitola, Macedonia, formerly known by its Turkish name, Monastir. She was one of the few Sephardic Jews from this city who survived the Holocaust due to the fact that she joined the Liberation Army.[27] She studied Romance Philology in Skoplje, where her main interest was Judeo-Spanish language and culture (Kolonomos 1978: 39). Her work included collecting folk material *in situ* as well as analysing different aspects of the Ladino language from Macedonia and the oral tradition of the Spanish Jews.[28]

The result of her Macedonian fieldwork is her *Proverbs, Sayings and Tales of the Sephardic Jews of Macedonia* (hereafter *Proverbs, Sayings and Tales*) of 1978. This work, as underscored by the collector herself, is of immense value as it represents the last remnants of the Sephardic culture in Macedonia: 'The proverbs and the short stories were recorded after the great catastrophe of European Jewry by the few surviving members of the former Jewish communities of Bitola and Skoplje who had nothing to rely upon but their memory' (Kolonomos 1978: 82). Most of the material published was given to her by four informants, which points to the fact that there were very few people left to be interviewed.[29]

'Džuhá se kižu kazar' ('Djohá Wanted to Get Married') opens the chapter of *konsežas* in her publication. In this tale, Djohá is an orphan living with his

FIG. 3.1. Žamila Kolonomos, portrait

grandmother. When he is old enough to get married, his grandmother finds a young girl for him, and they become engaged. The grandmother then gives Djohá advice as to how to woo her. She tells him to 'cast an eye at her', meaning to pay attention to her. However, as Djohá is naïve, he understands everything literally, so he goes to the butcher's, buys sheep eyes and throws them at his fiancée. After showing his obtuseness several times in a similar fashion, Djohá's fiancée breaks off the engagement, and consequently Djohá remains single (Kolonomos 1978: 133–35).

This story belongs to the ATU1696 tale-type, 'What Should I Have Said (Done)' (Uther 2003: II, 382–83; Haboucha 1992: 668–70). The motif of casting eyes of cows and sheep after someone belongs to a different tale-type: ATU1685, 'The Foolish Bridegroom' (Uther 2003: II, 371–72; Haboucha 1992: 663–64). The existence of other Sephardic versions of both tale-types among different Sephardic communities confirms that the tale was well known and widely disseminated in the Judeo-Spanish tradition.[30]

It is important to underscore that *Proverbs, Sayings and Tales* does not gather all the material that Kolonomos managed to collect. According to her account, she compiled more material which was lost after the earthquake in Skoplje in 1963 (1978: 35). This seems evident when she broaches the subject of tales and claims that: 'Many of the stories are about a fictitious person called Djuhá (Djooha), a good-natured honest man who takes every word at face value and as a result finds himself often in an unpleasant situation and exposed to ridicule' (1978: 81), thus confirming the previously mentioned statement by Goldberg about the simplicity of Djohá (1993: 112). Kolonomos' view that Djohá was a well-known figure in Macedonia is confirmed by at least two facts. Although Kolonomos only succeeded in publishing one Djohá tale, she highlights Djohá's existence in a considerable number of proverbs, thus underscoring his persistence in the everyday Sephardic life

FIG. 3.2. Eliezer Papo, portrait. From the private collection of Eliezer Papo

through different forms of oral literature albeit without providing further examples (1978: 81). Furthermore, Djordjević's Serbian informants prior to WWII claimed that, although Djohá was known among all Sephardic communities in the former Yugoslavia, he was fostered particularly in Macedonia (Djordjević 1939a: 15–16).

It is interesting to note the way in which Kolonomos describes Djohá, as seen in the quotation above. First, she depicts Djohá as a fictitious character without considering that he might have been based on a true figure which oral tradition later embellished. Second, as one of his main traits, she points out that Djohá was a good-natured and honest man who, due to his simplicity, often gets into awkward situations. It could very well be that the tales Kolonomos knew about him depicted him in such a light. However, in many stories, Djohá also appears as a trickster who tries to cheat others or steal, although his actions are looked upon with sympathy and never judged.

A perception of Djohá similar to that of Kolonomos may be found in the examples given by Eliezer Papo. Eliezer Papo was born in 1969 in Sarajevo, Bosnia, where he grew up and received his primary, secondary and university education (obtaining a Law degree), all in Serbian within the Yugoslav education system. In 1992, while the civil war was tearing Yugoslavia apart, he decided to emigrate to Israel, where he became a rabbi (at which time he changed his name from Ranko, a typical Serbian name, to the Biblical name, Eliezer). He started to teach Ladino at the Ben Gurion University of the Negev (Koén-Sarano 2003: 288). Eliezer Papo is, therefore, an example of a scholar who works on the revitalisation of the Ladino language and Sephardic history, culture and literature, but who has at the same time served as an informant on Bosnian Sephardic tradition, owing to his Bosnian Sephardic background.

In Israel, Eliezer Papo was interviewed by Koén-Sarano, who started collecting evidence of oral literature from members of various Sephardic communities. Eliezer Papo told Koén-Sarano twenty Djohá tales. Although they have their basis in traditional folk motifs, a good part of them are characterised by a contemporary setting, resembling modern jokes and anecdotes. An example of Djohá in a more contemporary situation is the tale called 'Foreign Work'. Djohá goes to Germany to look for work. He shares a house with a Chinese man and a black man. The black man goes to the workplace in search of a job but he is told by the boss that he does not want black people working for him. Then the Chinese man goes and gets a similar reply: the boss does not want 'yellow' people working for him. Being white, Djohá is convinced that he will get the job. But the Chinese man is jealous of him and paints Djohá's face black while he is sleeping. Then he wakes Djohá up and rushes him off to work before he can look at himself in the mirror. When Djohá shows up at work, the boss again says he does not want black people working for him. When Djohá claims that he is white he is given a mirror and when he sees a black face in the mirror he concludes that the Chinese man is a fool because, instead of waking him up, he woke up the black man again (Koén-Sarano 2003: 63).

In its core, this is a traditional tale which uses the motifs from the ATU1284A tale-type, 'White Man Made to Believe He is Black' (Uther 2004: II, 100–01). However, various elements in the Ladino tale indicate that we are probably dealing with a joke re-created in more recent times and associated with Djohá in the Sephardic world. Eliezer Papo's tale is, in fact, the earliest example of this tale-type in the Judeo-Spanish tradition.

One of the elements that indicates that the story is a reflection of modern times is the multi-ethnic setting of modern urban Germany with its migrant labour force. Here Djohá shares a flat with a Chinese man and a black man. All three of them are immigrants who have come to Germany to find work. This setting of the tale differs greatly from that of the Turkish and Balkan surroundings of the Ottoman Empire, where the Sepharadim lived together with other ethnic groups and the majority of the other tales take place. Another element is the characterisation of the German as racist by emphasising the contrasting skin colours of the protagonists. This element describes the experience of migrants in the new context. Djohá is the ideal character for a joke such as this one. His enduring ability to make us laugh renders him transferable to any context or situation.

Similar examples of Djohá tales with contemporary settings are: 'The Mortgage' (64–65), 'Nonexistent Banknotes' (66–67), 'Without Yogurt' (133), 'Noblesse Oblige' (181) and 'General Culture' (189). Eliezer Papo told all these tales in Judeo-Spanish, but they were published by Koén-Sarano (2003) in English, rather than their original language. The Judeo-Spanish manuscripts are kept in Koén-Sarano's personal library.[31]

Prior to Eliezer Papo, no examples of Djohá tales had been collected in Bosnia. However, there are indications that Djohá was known there. Muhamed Nezirović merely mentions the existence of proverbs from Bosnia with Djohá as the protagonist but does not provide the texts themselves (1992: 202).[32] He also cites the testimony of Isak Papo, who claims that only fragments now remain of the Djohá tales that were once told in Bosnia. In the light of this, it is difficult to ascertain whether Eliezer Papo learned all these tales while growing up in Bosnia or whether he heard some (or all) of them after settling in Israel, where he met members of other Sephardic communities.

In summary, Kolonomos published only one Djohá tale, but, according to her account, the tales about this comic figure were highly popular among Macedonian Jewry. She also adds that Djohá was fostered in the tradition of the Sepharadim from Macedonia not only as a narrative hero but also as a protagonist of many proverbs. The available testimonies from Serbia (Djordjević 1939a: 15) and Bosnia (Nezirović 1992: 202) also confirm this statement. In Kolonomos's view, Djohá represents an honest, naïve person who constantly lands himself in trouble and is consequently ridiculed and mocked. Her description of Djoha's simple nature coincides with how he is perceived in other examples collected from Eastern Mediterranean Sepharadim.

Eliezer Papo's examples, by contrast, demonstrate how Djohá has been adapted to new environments. In many of Eliezer Papo's tales, Djohá appears as a contemporary hero who finds himself in all sorts of circumstances typical of our time. This shows how easily the character is transferable to any time, place and situation, a phenomenon which dates back to Medieval Iberia. This character was first adapted to the Jewish environment from the Muslims of al-Andalus and soon became a Jewish (specifically Sephardic) character while maintaining the same name as in Arabic tradition. Later, when the Sepharadim lived in the Eastern Mediterranean under the Ottomans, they encountered a similar character with a different name, Nasr al-Dīn Khodja. They adopted stories about him, but it was 'their' Djohá who was the protagonist.

As will be demonstrated in the chapter on Koén-Sarano's work, after WWII, in the newly created Balkan states, as well as in modern Israel or in the new diasporas (the USA, South America or Europe), Djohá also survived by being adapted to the new circumstances. He recorded the numerous changes and experiences that affected the life of the Sepharadim, depicting all the situations in which they found themselves, such as emigrating to a foreign country and the hardships this entails. Djohá made the Sepharadim laugh, but they not only laughed at him, they laughed with him as they recognised their own personal experiences reflected in his actions.

Although limited, this corpus shows that the tradition regarding Djohá has endured among members of the Sephardic community in the region. The continuity of the character is even more astonishing if we take into account the situation in which the Sepharadim found themselves after the Holocaust. The ongoing presence of Djohá, regardless of where they reside nowadays, will become even more evident in the chapter on Koén-Sarano's fieldwork.

FIG. 3.3. Žak Konfino, portrait.
Jevrejski istorijski muzej, Belgrade, Serbia

Žak Konfino's Tales of Djohá: Two Sides of the Coin

Žak Konfino, a Sephardic Jew from Serbia, published two Djohá tales. Both texts illustrate the two opposing attitudes towards the Sephardic heritage which existed before and after WWII.[33] The first tale, written in Serbian, was published in 1934 in the Serbian daily *Politika* (*Politics*). *Politika* is one of the oldest newspapers in Serbia, published entirely in Serbian and dealing with current affairs. The second, written in Judeo-Spanish, came out in 1957 in *JS* in Paris. In 1994, the latter appeared again in Judeo-Spanish in an Israeli Sephardic periodical, *Aki Yerushalayim* (*AY*), which claimed that the text was translated from Serbo-Croatian to Hebrew and then from Hebrew to Judeo-Spanish.

Žak Konfino (1892–1975) was born into a Sephardic family in Leskovac, a little town in Serbia, which had a small Sephardic community, to Buhor and Klara, neé Koen (Radovanović 2011: 120). He studied medicine in Vienna and spent his life working as a doctor in Serbia. However, the fact that he was a doctor did not deter him from dedicating himself to writing as well. During WWII, he spent three years in a prison camp in Italy. His personal suffering, as well as the suffering of the Sephardic community as a whole, inspired him to write about the tragedy of the Holocaust and how it affected the Sepharadim (Mirković 1953: 239). His writings mainly focus on the life of the Sepharadim in Leskovac and Belgrade. In addition, Konfino was also known in literary circles as a humorist (Vidaković-Petrov 1990:

FIG. 3.4. Konfino's tale published in *Politika*.
Narodna biblioteka Srbije (National Library of Serbia)

91). Thus, writing about a comic character such as Djohá fits perfectly within his literary interests.

In 1934, Konfino published a tale in *Politika* entitled 'Djuhá'. Its narrator, who lives near Djohá's house, tells a story about his neighbour, Djohá. Djohá could not find himself a wife because he had one flaw: he was constantly sneezing. He consults a doctor, who recommends surgery. Djohá agrees, and the surgery is successful. Consequently Djohá finds a wife and gets married. Six months into his marriage, Djohá starts sneezing again. His wife insists that he undergo surgery again, but Djohá refuses. The purpose of the surgery was to find a wife and now that he is married there is no need to undergo surgery. One day, Djohá goes to see his neighbour, the narrator, and starts complaining about his sneezing problem. During the night, he sneezes uncontrollably because he cannot find a handkerchief, the only thing that stops him from sneezing. Wishing to be of assistance, the narrator directs a petition to the readers of the story: anyone knowing how to prevent Djohá from losing his handkerchief at night should let the former know. This will prevent Djohá from having to go through surgery again (Konfino 1934: 14).

This tale of Konfino's has not been recorded in the Sephardic tradition or any other, nor is there a reference to it neither in ATU nor in Haboucha's catalogue. Although the tale contains various folk motifs related to sneezing (A1537.1 'Sneezer Wished Long Life'; D1372 'Magic Object Causes Continued Sneezing'; D1812 'Omens from Sneezing') as well as a traditional character such as Djohá, the way the story unfolds and the fact that it contains the contemporary element of surgery leads me to believe that Konfino wrote the tale himself, drawing from Sephardic traditional sources rather than having collected it.[34]

The strong presence of the narrator's voice is what makes this story peculiar. On several occasions, the narrator interrupts the main story about Djohá to express his own points of view about the situation: that he finds it sweet and innocent that someone sneezes from time to time, or that it is not good to marry a woman who places conditions on a marriage. The narrator's role is not only that of telling the story; he also participates actively in it as someone who personally knows Djohá. His addressing the audience at the end by seeking their help is a typical device used in folk literature and common in storytelling performance. Bearing all this in mind, I suggest that this is a re-creation by Konfino, who uses a number of traditional elements to create a story of his own making.

Similar to Davičo, Konfino places a *glosa* next to the title (in the form of a footnote) in which he explains that in the oral tradition of the Sepharadim, Djohá represents a figure similar to that of Nasr al-Dīn Khodja from the Turkish tradition. Konfino's perception of the character coincides with that of Davičo, Djordjević and Djordjević's informants, all of whom pointed out this similarity between the two characters. Thus, all the Serbian sources about Djohá concur with this portrayal of the Sephardic hero. The aim of this act of cultural transposition was to find an adequate cultural equivalent in the target language; it was logically directed towards the Serbian readers who had probably never heard of Djohá or what he represented. They were, however, familiar with the nature of Nasr al-Dīn Khodja. The latter, as stated earlier, formed part of their folklore, too.

Thus, it is clear that Konfino's main aim was to introduce Djohá to the wider readership in Serbia, which justifies his choosing Serbian as the means of communication and *Politika* as the place of publication, as opposed to Judeo-Spanish and the Sephardic press. Various Jewish newspapers existed in the region at that time, namely in Bosnia, where he could have published the story mainly for the Sepharadim either in Judeo-Spanish or in Serbian, given that some of these periodicals were bilingual. In fact, Konfino was a valuable contributor to the Jewish periodical *Jevrejski glas* where he published some of his works, mostly in Serbian but also in Judeo-Spanish (Vidaković-Petrov 1990: 91). By abandoning the Judeo-Spanish language while at the same time choosing to write about Sephardic topics, Konfino's work contributed to preserving the memory of a heritage that once existed, as opposed to attempting to recover and revive it. This Djohá tale, which appears prior to WWII, fulfils this goal.

However, this character in Konfino's work takes on another role after WWII. In 1957, in the Sephardic periodical from Paris, *JS*, Konfino published a tale entitled 'Djuha, pasha de la madre! ('Djuha, the Apple of Your Mother's Eye'). Unlike the first tale from 1934, which is a more original work, this Djohá story fits perfectly within Haboucha's **1288B tale-type, 'Numbskull Can't Find Himself' (1992: 542–43).

The story depicts Djohá as a schoolboy who, due to his untidiness and inability to find his clothes in the morning, is constantly late for school. His teacher advises him that before going to bed at night he should write down exactly where his things are. Djohá follows his teacher's advice and writes everything down, including that he is in bed. In the morning, Djohá is able to find all of his items of clothing except himself in bed. So once again he is late for school (Confino 1957: 642–43).

This tale of Konfino's was reprinted nearly twenty years after his death, in Israel in 1994, in another Sephardic periodical, *AY* (Konfino 1994: 96–97). It is published under Konfino's name, but doubts arise as to the original language of the tale. In *JS*, the tale appears in Judeo-Spanish under the title 'Djuha, pasha de la madre!' and is signed by Jacques Confino, giving the impression that the latter not only wrote the text but that he did so in the language in which it was published. However, in 1994, the tale appeared as 'I Djoha onde esta?' ('And Where is Djoha?'). Next to the title, there is a footnote which states: 'Este kuento, publikado por Doktor Jak Konfino, mediko y eskritor ke nasio en Leskovach en Serbia, mos fue enbiado, en su traduksion del serbo-kroato al ebreo, por el investigador del djudaizmo yugoslavo Zvi Loker' ('This tale, published by Dr Jak Konfino, a doctor and a writer born in Leskovac, Serbia, was sent to us translated from Serbo-Croatian to Hebrew by the researcher of Yugoslavian Jewish culture, Zvi Loker') (Konfino 1994: 97).

The information reveals several relevant facts. First, it is evident that the version of Konfino's tale in *AY* is a translation of a translation. The periodical claims that the tale was first translated from Serbo-Croatian to Hebrew and then from Hebrew to Judeo-Spanish. The Hebrew translation is not offered, as *AY* is published entirely in Judeo-Spanish. Furthermore, although the translation from Serbo-Croatian to Hebrew was carried out by Zvi Loker, the name of the translator from Hebrew to Judeo-Spanish is not given. It could have been the editor of the journal, Moshe

НАРОДНИ МУЗЕЈ ЛЕСКОВАЦ
САВЕЗ ЈЕВРЕЈСКИХ ОПШТИНА ЈУГОСЛАВИЈЕ
БЕОГРАД
КУЛТУРНО ПРОСВЕТНА ЗАЈЕДНИЦА
ЛЕСКОВАЦ

КОНФИНОВИ
ДАНИ ХУМОРА

25-26. јуна 1991.
Лесковац

FIG. 3.5. Leaflet of a festival *'Konfino's Days of Humour'*.
Jevrejski istorijski muzej, Belgrade, Serbia

Shaul, or one of his close collaborators. Likewise, it is safe to assume that the title of the 1994 version was given by either Zvi Loker or the editor of *AY*. Clearly, it could not have been Konfino, as he had passed away in 1975. The 1957 title of the tale, 'Djoha, pasha de la madre!', could have been Konfino's, but we cannot rule out the possibility that the editors of *JS* may have contributed to the title. What, then, was the original language of the tale?

When the tale came out for the first time in 1957, it was merely signed by Konfino (here spelled Jacques Confino), and no indication of its having been translated from another language is given. Nevertheless, the comment published in *AY* maintains that there was a Serbo-Croatian version of the tale that I have not been able to locate which was used as a source for the Judeo-Spanish version published in this periodical. Consequently, I cannot make a solid affirmation as to whether Konfino initially wrote the tale in Serbo-Croatian and then translated it into Judeo-Spanish for *JS* or whether it was someone else who translated the tale from Serbo-Croatian. The editor of *JS*, Ovadia Camhy, was married to Gina Camhy, who was originally from Bosnia and was fluent in Serbo-Croatian. She was one of the regular contributors to the periodical and might very well have translated Konfino's tale.

Konfino's decision to publish his Djohá tale in *JS* comes as no surprise, given that in the first decades after WWII, one of the main centres of the recovery movement of Sephardic heritage was Paris, where several Sephardic periodicals were launched, such as *JS* and *Vidas*. Konfino's choice of publication venue represents his modest contribution to the efforts undertaken by these periodicals and their contributors to collect, preserve and revitalise the Judeo-Spanish language and culture. This decision was a conscious one, as had been his choice to publish his first Djohá tale prior to WWII in Serbian in *Politika*. The difference in his choice of language and periodicals, and thus the intended readership, attests to the opposing aims of his work.

Whatever the case concerning his aims, 'Djoha, pasha de la madre!' is an example of a true folktale, probably written down from memory by the author rather than collected by him *in situ*. Apart from being recorded in Haboucha's catalogue of Judeo-Spanish folk tales, there is evidence that this tale was popular among the Sepharadim in Belgrade, as Djordjević collected another version of it which precedes Konfino's tale chronologically (1939a: 18).[35]

More proof of the oral nature of the tale is the language of the narration, which is characterised by the use of expressions such as '¡Ay, triste de mi!' or '¡Ay, guay de mi!', both meaning 'Poor me!' and both typical of the colourful language of folk tales; it is also characterised by the moral given in a proverbial saying such as 'Adónde vayas, cualquier cosa que hagas, primero echa una mirada para ver donde te hallas y quien eres' ('Wherever you go, whatever you do, first look to see where and who you are') (Konfino 1957: 642–43). It is very difficult to say more about Konfino's language usage, owing to the language policy of both periodicals in which this tale was published. Both periodicals were published entirely in Judeo-Spanish. However, their policy towards the language differed.

As stated earlier, *JS* aimed to adapt Judeo-Spanish to modern Spanish, whereas *AY* had a different approach. This difference can be observed on various linguistic levels. One of them is the graphic representation of phonemes as seen in these examples taken from Konfino's tale from 1957 versus that of 1994: 'Señor haham, me dolío [*sic*] la cabeza...' (*JS*) / 'Sinyor haham, es ke esta manyana tenia dolor de kavesa...' (*AY*) ('Teacher, sir, I had a headache...'/ 'Teacher, sir, I had a headache this morning...'). Not only is the spelling different, but *AY* as part of its language policy does not include the use of diacritics or the inverted question/exclamation marks. *JS*, by contrast, complying with the rules of modern Spanish, uses both graphic accent and inverted question/exclamation marks, as seen in the following example: '¿No estamos un poco tarde, pasha de la madre, eh?' ('Aren't we a little bit late, the apple of your mother's eye?'). Another difference can be seen in the vocabulary. For example, *JS* uses words such as *calcetines* and *rincón* for 'socks' and 'corner' respectively, whereas in *AY* we find *chorapes/churapes* and *kanton* for the same words, the former borrowed from Turkish (Nehama 1977: 109) and the latter from a romance language, probably Portuguese *canto* or even Catalan *cantonada*.

In summary, Konfino published two tales about Djohá, a character he knew well from the tradition of his family and the Sephardic context in which he grew up.

As someone who supported the idea of assimilation of the Sepharadim in Serbia, he wrote most of his work in Serbian. The first Djohá tale came out before WWII in 1934, and it represented his first attempt to introduce the character to a wider readership in Serbia. To achieve that, he not only published the tale in Serbian but also in an important daily, and made sure that he gave his readers an idea of Djohá's nature by comparing him to Nasr al-Dīn Khodja, who is known in Serbian folklore.

Konfino's second tale about Djohá, by contrast, appeared after the Holocaust and outside Serbia. It was published in 1957 in Paris in *JS*. The tale came out in Judeo-Spanish, and thus it would be logical to assume that Konfino wrote it in Judeo-Spanish were it not for the reprinted version of this tale which came out in *AY* in 1994. *AY* claims that the tale had been translated from Serbo-Croatian to Hebrew and then from Hebrew to Judeo-Spanish.

Regardless of this, Konfino must have been aware of the tale having been published in *JS*, and by choosing this periodical and having his tale published in Judeo-Spanish, he took part in the effort to revitalise the Sephardic language and tradition which took place after the tragedies of WWII. These acts show more commitment by the members of the Sephardic community to maintain and foster their native heritage, particularly the language, which found itself in danger of extinction.

The examples from the former Yugoslavia that we have seen in this chapter show that Djohá was known and fostered in the former Yugoslavia. The testimonies of the members of the Sephardic community, which began to be collected at the end of the nineteenth century, reveal that Djohá was perceived as being authentically Sephardic, the folk character who made them laugh while teaching them a lesson.

The pre-WWII examples were all collected in Serbian with the aim of providing a record of the Sephardic legacy rather than trying to secure its continuation. The post-WWII examples, by contrast, were collected in Judeo-Spanish with the intention of contributing to the revitalisation of the tradition and the language. Taken as a whole, they prove that this centuries-long tradition managed to endure the difficulties with which the history of the Sepharadim is replete. This idea of continuity and revitalisation of the tradition in relation to Djohá tales is further developed in the next chapter on Koén-Sarano's work.

3. Matilda Koén-Sarano's Fieldwork and Editorial Strategies: The Case of Djohá Tales

The first Judeo-Spanish collection of tales entirely dedicated to Djohá, *Djohá ke dize? Kuentos populares djudeo-espanyoles* (hereafter *Djohá ke dize?*) by Koén-Sarano appeared in Jerusalem in 1991.[36] In the opening lines of the introduction, the compiler and the editor of the collection, Matilda Koén-Sarano (1939–), explains the reasons behind her decision to publish a collection of tales dealing with only one character, Djohá: 'I kualos eran los kuentos mas amados, los kuentos ke no mos kansávamos nunca de sintir? Los kuentos de Djohá, naturalmente!' ('And which were the most cherished tales, those that we never tired of listening to? The tales of Djohá, of course!') (1991: xiv). As a Sephardic Jew herself, Koén-Sarano recollects hearing stories about this comic figure in her home while she was growing up. Their main role, according to her account, was both to entertain and to instruct: 'La figura de Djohá akompanyó muestra chikés i está atada a eya. "Sirvía" a muestros padres para darmos exemplos, para eksplikarmos kozas ke no estávamos entendiendo o ke no kiríamos entender, i sovre todo para azermos riyir' ('The Djohá character accompanied our childhood and formed part of it. He "served" our parents by teaching us, by explaining things to us that we did not understand. And, above all, he made us laugh') (1991: xiv). Koén-Sarano's belief regarding the dual function of Djohá tales is, thus, drawn from her own experience as a member of the Sephardic community.

The outcome of Koén-Sarano's fieldwork, which thus far has resulted in two collections of Djohá tales (1991; 2003) and various chapters in other of her works (1986; 2004a; 2004b), confirms the remarkable endurance of Djohá in the Sephardic world. Furthermore, rather than approaching this task of gathering oral data from the standpoint of a paid fieldworker, Koén-Sarano views herself as an ideological emissary with a mission to save the heritage of the Sepharadim, i.e., her own heritage which shaped her cultural identity.

Born in Italy, Koén-Sarano emigrated to Israel in 1962. It was there, in this Hebrew-speaking society, that Koén-Sarano realised the significance of her mother tongue, Judeo-Spanish, and her Sephardic heritage. A familiar song in Judeo-Spanish heard on the radio, 'simbolizó mi nostaljía i me reveló mi verdadera identidad' ('symbolised my nostalgia and revealed to me my true identity') (1986: xvii). This clearly shows that Koén-Sarano considers that her true (Jewish) identity is Sephardic.

Moreover, in order to accomplish her goals of collecting, safeguarding and disseminating the Judeo-Spanish tradition, Koén-Sarano has employed various methods in her work which differ from those of the other collectors studied. Firstly, Koén-Sarano not only interviewed members of the Sephardic community in Israel, who originally came from the territories of the former Ottoman Empire or North Africa, but also those who emigrated to the USA, Canada and South America. The diversity of her informants, as well as their number (over eighty), surpasses that of Davičo, Laura Papo, Djordjević or Kolonomos who, by contrast, limited their fieldwork exclusively to members of their respective communities in Serbia, Bosnia and Macedonia. Thus Koén-Sarano's work, rather than giving a picture of a particular Sephardic group which had settled in a specific area, encompasses the Sephardic world as a whole.

Secondly, Koén-Sarano's work method consisted in systematically recording Djohá tales primarily from women. This decision by the collector was a conscious form of expressing cultural identity. It serves to support Koén-Sarano's belief that a single-sex group of storytellers who meet periodically to tell tales or sing ballads and songs provides the best results for the collector. However, her working with mainly female informants does not suggest that Djohá tales are more popular among women than men. It merely attests to Koén-Sarano's work methods (Alexander-Frizer 2008: 432).

FIG. 3.6. Matilda Koén-Sarano, portrait
From the private collection of Karen Gerson Sarhon

Thirdly, her attitude towards Judeo-Spanish is suggestive of her intentions to propagate and disseminate Sephardic culture. On the one hand, Koén-Sarano reveals that part of the material she collected was told to her in languages other than Judeo-Spanish, such as Italian or Hebrew (1991: xvii). In order to accomplish her goal of revitalising the language, she translated these tales into Judeo-Spanish. On the other hand, on several occasions, Koén-Sarano did exactly the opposite and published part of the Judeo-Spanish material in other languages, namely in Hebrew, which was clearly targeting a general Jewish audience, and also in English, for a wider readership. Her decisions regarding the language she used for publication represents the clear goal of revitalising the Sephardic heritage and disseminating it.

Another fundamental point concerns Koén-Sarano's editorial work. Initially, she embellished and polished the original tales, whereas in the more recent stages of her work she has kept the editing to a minimum. This change in the approach allowed her to pay scrupulous attention to the spoken language and conserve the original tone of the tales as well as to include matters dealing with sex and scatology, elements which, according to Alexander-Frizer, she had earlier censored (2008: 35).

Some collections are dedicated entirely to Djohá, whereas others contain a number of tales about him along with other types of tales and characters from the Sephardic world. I shall base my discussion mainly on these primary sources and testimonies by Koén-Sarano.

Koén-Sarano's Djohá Tales in Judeo-Spanish

As part of the wider movement in Israel for the recovery of the Sephardic language and tradition, Koén-Sarano's first two publications of Djohá tales appeared in Judeo-Spanish. The first book was entitled *Kuentos del folklore de la famiya djudeo-espanyola*, 1986 (hereafter *Kuentos*), and the second *Djohá ke dize?*, 1991. Considering that the latter publication contains only tales about Djohá, it is of more relevance than the former. Comprising 232 Djohá tales, it shows the incredible endurance of this character in the Sephardic world. *Kuentos*, on the other hand, is an anthology of Judeo-Spanish folk tales in which only one chapter (Chapter 3) is dedicated to Djohá, containing a total of thirty-six Djohá tales.[37] Both volumes were published in Israel.

Koén-Sarano has been living and working in Israel since 1962. Yet, she was born and raised in Milan, into a traditional Sephardic family originally from Turkey (Koén-Sarano 1986: xvi). Although she learned Italian outside, at home she only spoke Judeo-Spanish, and her entire upbringing was rooted in Sephardic culture:

> En aviendo resivido una formasión kultural enteramente italiana, me fue dada una edukasión fondamentalmente sefaradía, porké kresí en una famiya sefaradía en su esensia i en todas sus manifestasiones eksteriores: en la lingua avlada en kaza, en la edukasión bazada en la tradisión djudía, [...] en el gusto por el kontar konsejas. [...] Toda mi edukasión fue enfluensada de esta mentalidad djudeo-espanyola, ke me izo lo ke sé. (Koén-Sarano 1986: xvi)

> (Although my cultural education was purely Italian, my upbringing was fundamentally Sephardic, because I grew up in a true Sephardic family with all its external features: the language spoken at home, the upbringing based on Jewish tradition, [...] the pleasure in storytelling. [...] My entire upbringing was influenced by this Judeo-Spanish mentality, which made me what I am today.)

Not only the language spoken in her home, but also the customs, celebrations, songs and cuisine were different from other people in her environment. This generated a sense of ethnic awareness in Koén-Sarano. Even after integrating into Hebrew-speaking Israeli society, Koén-Sarano has continued to foster the language and customs of her home and has dedicated all her efforts to maintaining and disseminating the Judeo-Spanish language and culture. These efforts include her participating in radio programmes and festivals dedicated to the Judeo-Spanish language, culture and tradition; writing tales and poems in Judeo-Spanish; writing a Ladino textbook and a dictionary; and delivering courses in Ladino at Ben Gurion University in Israel. Perhaps her most important contribution, however, lies in her fieldwork, which has resulted in numerous publications.[38]

Koén-Sarano's work in collecting, safeguarding and revitalising the language and culture of the Sepharadim forms part of a larger movement in Israel dedicated to the same goals. An example of such efforts is the work of Kol Israel (The Voice of Israel) which, in addition to broadcasting radio programmes in Ladino, launched a Ladino periodical in 1979, *AY*, with the aim of propagating and conserving the Judeo-Spanish culture and its language. The periodical is published entirely in Judeo-Spanish and includes articles on Sephardic history, literature and folklore.[39] Koén-Sarano has been one of the main contributors to the periodical from its beginning, not only publishing the results of her fieldwork but also her own work (Koén-Sarano 2013a; 2013b). These efforts led to the foundation in Israel in 1997 of the Autoridad Nasionala de Ladino (hereafter the ANL) whose goals are:

— to propagate the knowledge and awareness of the Judeo-Spanish culture;

— to provide assistance to existing Judeo-Spanish cultural institutions and help create new ones;

— to promote, encourage and help the gathering, documentation and cataloguing of Judeo-Spanish literature;

— to publish works by contemporary authors who write about Judeo-Spanish topics, either in their original language or in Hebrew; and

— to organise and promote activities that can disseminate information about Sephardic communities exterminated in the Holocaust.[40]

Koén-Sarano's fieldwork, which fulfils most of the goals of the ANL, is a perfect example of its purpose. Her gathering of oral data started in the late 1970s among the members of the Sephardic community in Israel. She interviewed people from Judeo-Spanish families who, prior to settling in Israel, had lived in the Sephardic diaspora (the former Ottoman Empire and North Africa). She later expanded her activity to include members of the Sephardic community living in Europe, the USA, Canada and South America. Koén-Sarano's role, according to Itshak Navón, was not merely that of a collector of tales (1986: xiii). She herself was also a storyteller, setting down in writing various tales she had heard at home in her family environment.

Her intention to start collecting, revitalising and disseminating the Sephardic language and culture has its origin in Koén-Sarrano's participation in a seminar for writers of radio programmes in Judeo-Spanish organised by the radio station Kol Israel in 1979. According to her account, this was the moment that inspired her to initiate the work which was to become the focal point of her life:

> I agora, aún ke yo sea enteramente integrada en la vida i en la sosiedad de Israel, i tenga i otros enteresos i okupasiones, me parese ke sólo eskriviendo i okupándome de esta lingua i de esta kultura, yo vo a poder, no sólo ayudar a salvar lo ke se puede de muestra kultura i tradisión, ma vo i a poder enrekeser a mí mizma, konservando en mí este patrimonio, ke me va a tener por siempre atada a mis padres, porké una parte de eyos va a kedar en mí por siempre. (1986: xvii)

> (And today, although I am fully integrated into the life and society of Israel and I have other interests and occupations, it seems to me that only by writing and dedicating myself to this language and this culture I will be able not only to help save what's left of our culture and tradition but also enrich myself,

Fig. 3.7. Front and back cover of Koén-Sarano's *Djohá ke dize?*
Courtesy of Karen Gerson Sarhon

safeguarding this heritage which ties me to my parents for good, because a part
of them will remain with me forever.)

Koén-Sarano's 'muestra kultura i tradisión' ('our culture and tradition') refers to
the Sephardic legacy only. The meaning it embodies is that she is a Sephardic Jew,
which entails the use of a specific language, songs, ballads, tales, food and customs
unique to this group and which members of the Sephardic community perceive as
authentically theirs. As this is the culture of her parents and her ancestors, Koén-
Sarano logically identifies herself with this heritage.

Djohá ke dize? was published in 1991 and comprises 232 Djohá tales arranged
in chapters according to Djohá's life cycle: from childhood, through marriage, to
his death. According to Alexander-Frizer, the tales were recorded and published
as narrated in the original language, Ladino, with the corresponding Hebrew
translation (2008: 432). However, Koén-Sarano indicates that some tales were told
to her in Hebrew or Italian by informants who came from Judeo-Spanish families
but who had lost their linguistic ability to communicate in Judeo-Spanish (1991:
xvii). The translation of these tales to Judeo-Spanish was done by the collector
herself, who was also responsible for translating all the tales to Hebrew and giving
them titles (Koén-Sarano 1991: xvii).

Koén-Sarano's choice to publish all the tales in Judeo-Spanish, although some of
them were originally told to her in other languages, suggests a conscious decision
on her part to help revitalise the language. This is supported by the fact that she
does not indicate which tales or how many of them were told to her in Judeo-

Spanish, Hebrew or Italian but simply presents all of them as if they were originally told in Judeo-Spanish. However, in order to disseminate the tales among non-Ladino speakers in Israel, she includes their Hebrew translations, too. Both of these linguistic practices applied by Koén-Sarano are in keeping with the goals of the ANL: to revitalise the Judeo-Spanish language, and to disseminate the Sephardic tradition.

Furthermore, the Judeo-Spanish tales were published in Latin script rather than in the Hebrew alphabet. Almost as late as WWII, Sephardic works had been written/published in Rashi and/or square Hebrew script, thus maintaining what had been their tradition for centuries. During the Middle Ages, the Jews of the Iberian Peninsula used the Hebrew alphabet when writing Romance languages, namely Castilian and Catalan. After the expulsion, this graphic system continued to be used by the Sepharadim in the diaspora and, hence, from the eighteenth century onwards, texts published in Judeo-Spanish deployed this system. However, in the first half of the twentieth century, either as a result of the secular education that the Sepharadim began acquiring in non-Jewish schools, or due to laws imposed by in some countries (such as Turkey in 1928), Latin script replaced what had been the standardised system until then. Consequently, Sephardic authors increasingly started to use Latin script when writing in Judeo-Spanish, and Koén-Sarano was no exception.

There were, however, no rules governing textual editing in Latin script. At the time when Koén-Sarano was preparing the publication of *Djohá ke dize?* several different writing systems for Judeo-Spanish were in use in Latin script, such as 'el sistema turko, el sistema fransés, el sistema del diksionario de J. Nehama' ('the Turkish system, the French system, the system of J. Nehama's dictionary'), but in practice 'kada uno eskrive komo kere, sigún su grado de estudios, el lugar de su orijín o onde bive' ('everyone writes the way they want, depending on their level of education, their place of birth or the place where they live') (Koén-Sarano 1999: ix).[41]

Koén-Sarano opted to use as a basis the rules established in 1979 by Moshe Shaul, the editor of *AY*, which uses this system to the present day (Koén-Sarano 1999: ix). She then modified the system by introducing the rules for accentuation from the Spanish language so as to indicate the correct pronunciation. Koén-Sarano's choice of Latin script for editing the texts in Judeo-Spanish also confirms her intention to make her work accessible to those who do not read Judeo-Spanish in the Hebrew alphabet.

Although most of the informants with whom Koén-Sarano worked had already settled in Israel, a significant number of them came from different parts of the world where the Sepharadim have resided, such as Turkey, the former Yugoslavia, Greece, Bulgaria, Italy, France, Spain, Egypt, Morocco, Algeria and Libya (Koén-Sarano 1991: xxx–xl). The mere fact that the informants Koén-Sarano interviewed came from different regions of the Sephardic diaspora, and yet all fostered the tradition regarding Djohá, is indisputable proof of his endurance. Djohá formed part of their lives in their original settlements, and he continued to do so after they immigrated to Israel. The large number of tales in *Djohá ke dize?* (232) demonstrates the immense popularity Djohá continues to enjoy in the Sephardic world to this day. Furthermore, based on the varied backgrounds of Koén-Sarano's informants, we can confirm that this figure was known in the Sephardic world as a whole rather than being limited to specific areas.

One of the main traits of Koén-Sarano's fieldwork is that the circle of her informants is mainly composed of women, known as The Ladies of Ladino: 'From week to week the group grew, with Levana Sasson, Malka Shabetay, Lea Basson, Lea Cohen, Renée Arochas, Malka Simha, Ester Ventura, Ester Ben-Yosef, Susy Salem... each one of them from a different origin but all of them Ladino-speaking' (Koén-Sarano 2003: 280). These women have two main points in common: they all originally came from different places in the former Ottoman Empire or North Africa and eventually settled in Israel; and they are all Sephardic Jews who continued to speak Judeo-Spanish, their native tongue.[42]

The activities of this group of women were launched in Jerusalem, but it was not long before the news of their meetings spread and a group of women from Tel-Aviv joined the circle, which came to number more than fifty members (Koén-Sarano 2003: 280). The group met once a month, usually in the home of one of the members, and for these occasions, typical Sephardic dishes were prepared and served to uphold their traditions (Koén-Sarano 2003: 281). This kind of environment represents, according to Kenneth Goldstein, the natural context for performing and collecting folklore (1964: 80–81). Several Sephardic testimonies exist, such as the one by Isaac Jack Lévy, which illustrate this: 'I recall that on wintry rainy evenings, men and women gathered in a neighbor's house, shared a meal, and told one story after another until they had to retire for the night' (1989: 69).[43]

The State of Israel supported this activity by giving Koén-Sarano's group permission to hold their meetings on the premises of the ANL, whose secretary, Dolly Burda, was a member of the circle (Koén-Sarano 2003: 281). In addition, the State organised the Festival of Narrators of Tales, held each year during the Sukkot (the Feast of Booths), in which the members of Koén-Sarano's circle of Ladino Ladies participated in telling tales (Koén-Sarano 2003: 281).

This working method of Koén-Sarano's, which included interviewing mainly women, was conducted in keeping with her belief that 'the best results, of course, derive from the recreation of a natural setting, that is, with a circle of habitual tellers, preferably of the same sex, so they can feel free to say what they wish without censoring the tales that come to mind' (2004b: xiii). By 'natural setting', Koén-Sarano refers to the habit of getting together periodically to tell tales or sing ballads and songs as a form of social interaction of the members of the same community linked by the same language, customs, tradition and food. Thus Koén-Sarano's perception of Sephardic folk life sets cultural markers defining its nature: it is oral, it is habitual and it is feminine; the latter being emphasised by making mainly women the storytellers. Although fieldwork carried out from the end of the nineteenth century shows that among the Sepharadim women were the main performers of oral literature, Levy's testimony cited above is just one of several that indicates that this was not always the case.[44] As I have shown in this book, the contribution of men in preserving, transmitting and collecting oral literature should be acknowledged, as well.

Furthermore, instead of a spontaneous gathering of women hearing the stories being told at their homes by their family members or neighbours, the meetings of the group are planned and organised beforehand, the women repeating the stories that they have heard at previous meetings. The result is that they exchange the same stories among themselves, which not only limits the scope of their narrative repertoire, but renders it circular with regard to the text: as a consequence, the tales have less variation than tales transmitted in a natural setting. This repetition of tales, illustrated here by means of tables (see below), is the key artifice of Koén-Sarano's work.

In terms of the text, at the beginning of her work Koén-Sarano viewed herself as an 'ideological emissary with a mission to save the heritage of the Sephardim through the "embellishment" and "polishing" of the original tales' (Alexander-Frizer 2008: 34). First she recorded a tale, then she transcribed it word by word, preserving the tone of the original narration through punctuation, and finally she edited the story to make it readily comprehensible: 'i después traerla [la konseja] a la luz, "lustrándola", komo lustrí el tas de kovre, ke salió afuera entero i briyante del shavón' ('and then to show it off [the tale] by polishing it, just as I polished a copper bowl with soap which then became shiny') (Koén-Sarano 1986: xviii). Her own words make it clear that her intervention was not limited to clarifying narrative elements which thanks to mimicry and gestures were clear in oral form but not so in written form. Her amendments were also intended 'ke les diera una veste literaria' ('to give them [the tales] a literary style') (Koén-Sarano 1991: xvii). This implied significant changes in the style, language and the tone of the narration.

Her act of 'polishing' the tales also resulted in censoring some words and expressions related to sex and scatology. This particularly refers to the type of tales known as *kuentos salados* or *suzios* (obscene tales), which, in Koén-Sarano's own words, 'superavan los límites permitidos por la edukasión' ('surpassed the limits of good manners') (2004b: 17). Koén-Sarano's 2004 collection *Kuentos del bel para abasho* ('Tales from the Waist Down'; hereafter *Del bel para abasho*), published in Istanbul, Turkey, comprises 230 *kuentos salados*, fifty of which are Djohá tales (Chapter 10). Of these fifty tales, twenty-four appear for the first time, while twenty-six had already been published in Koén-Sarano's previous works (see the table below).

TABLE 3.2. Djohá tales from *Del bel para abasho* previously published in *Djohá ke dize?*, *Kuentos salados* or *Folkates of Joha*

Djohá ke dize? (1991)	Kuentos salados (2000)	Folktales of Joha (2003)	Del bel para abasho (2004)	INFORMANT
'Kuanto abasta?' (p. 155)			'Kuanto abasta?' (p. 297)	Yosef (de Habatón) Cohen (1987)
'La primera noche' (p. 135)			'La primera noche' (p. 291)	Sara Yohay (1988)
		'The Paper Shoes' (pp. 32-33)	'Los kalsados de papel' (p. 282)	Maria Bahbout (1988)

		'Stamp of Servitude' (pp. 215-17)	'Los kuarenta ladrones' (pp. 320-21)	Rebeka Cohen-Ariel (1989)
	'Rekuesta lejítima' (p. 59)	'A Legitimate Request' (pp. 114-15)	'Rekuesta lejítima' (p. 296)	Eli Gratsiani (1992)
		'Out of the Mouths of Fools and Babes...' (p. 131)	'Del loko i de la kriatura sale la verdad' (p. 308)	Tsahi Hasday (1999)
		'What an Excuse!' (p. 118)	'Ke eskuza!' (p. 306)	Alex Korfiatis (2000)
		'The Vinegar' (p. 140)	'El vinagre' (p. 316)	Alex Korfiatis (1998)
		'He is Different' (p. 24)	'El es diferente' (p. 277)	Ester Levy (2000)
		'A Strange Bathhouse' (p. 169)	'El banyo de Djohá' (p. 287)	Malka Levy (1991)
		'A Simple Calculation' (p. 103)	'Kuento fasil' (p. 305)	Rashel Perera (1987)
		'A Cheeky Question' (p. 181)	'Demanda en su lugar' (p. 324)	Rashel Perera (1987)
		'When the Apology is Worse than the Fault' (p. 147)	'Kuando la diskulpa es mas negra ke la kulpa' (p. 314)	Kohava Pivis (1999)
		'He Didn't Know' (p. 102)	'El no savía' (p. 290)	Aliza Tsarum (1996)
	'La kara de Djohá' (pp. 30-31)	'Face to Face' (p. 148)	'La kara de Djohá' (p. 315)	Valentina Tsoref (1987)
		'Giraffe Love' (p. 82)	'La jirafa' (p. 298)	Eliezer Papo (1999)
		'The Wishes' (pp. 86-89)	'Los augurios' (pp. 278-80)	Eliezer Papo (1994)
		'Noblesse Oblige!' (p. 181)	'Era Djohá' (p. 325)	Eliezer Papo (1999)
		'To Everything There is a Solution' (pp. 31-32)	'Para todo ay una solusión' (pp. 283-84)	Matilda Koén-Sarano (1994)
		'After the Wedding' (pp. 95-96)	'Después de la boda' (pp. 292-93)	Matilda Koén-Sarano (1997)
		'Joha's Half' (pp. 106-07)	'La meta de Djohá' (pp. 302-03)	Matilda Koén-Sarano (1999)

		'A Costly Trip' (pp. 107-08)	'Viaje danyoso' (p. 304)	Matilda Koén-Sarano (1992)
		'Semantics' (p. 116)	'Semantika' (p. 300)	Matilda Koén-Sarano (1992)
'La lójika de Djohá' (p. 75)			'La lójika de Djohá' (p. 323)	Matilda Koén-Sarano 1998
'Djohá ande el doktor' (p. 85)			'Ande el doktor' (p. 319)	Matilda Koén-Sarano 1990
'Depende de ken murió' (p. 101)			'Depende de ken murió' (p. 333)	Eli Graziani 1992

The type of tales contained within the collection are quite appropriately described by the title. *Bel* is a Judeo-Spanish word that comes from Turkish meaning 'waist'. 'Del bel para abasho', therefore, literally means 'from the waist down'. Related to this is the expression 'avlar del bel par' abasho', which means 'to say nonsense or rude things' (Perez and Pimienta 2007: 60). These tales tend to infringe upon different social taboos related to sex, sexual organs or scatology, and as a result, the members of the Sephardic community, including Koén-Sarano herself, have adopted different attitudes towards them compared to other types of tales.

On the one hand, there are those who argue that 'esto no es kultura: es sub-kultura i no vale la pena de akodrarlo. Kale konservado sólo las kozas ermozas i pozitivas!' ('this is not culture: it is a subculture and therefore it is not worth remembering it. What should be saved are only the beautiful and positive things') (Koén-Sarano 2000: 12). Despite the fact that these tales continue to live in the tradition and they enjoy great popularity, judging from the number of tales collected by Koén-Sarano (230), certain members of the community are of the opinion that these tales give the wrong impression of Sephardic culture and should, therefore, be ignored.

On the other hand, some members of the Sephardic community maintain that these tales should be collected and published, as they form part of Sephardic culture and reflect some aspects of it: 'I esto aze parte de muestro folklor i kale dado un kuadro kompleto' ('This also forms part of our folklore and a full picture [of the culture] should be given') (Koén-Sarano 2000: 12). Koén-Sarano admits that she felt reluctant to collect this type of tales: 'Es emportante notar ke yo no fui nunka a bushkar este djénero de kuento, i ke él me vino a la mano de suyo, entre los otros' ('It is important to point out that I have never looked for this type of tale; it came to me on its own, among the rest') (Koén-Sarano 2000: 14). It is clear from Koén-Sarano's words that she is trying to detach herself from these tales and, thus, it can be surmised that she adopts the first of these two attitudes.

This attitude of Koén-Sarano's influenced her selection of tales and her editorial method once she decided to publish them. With regard to the choice of tales she states that she was guided by literary and comic criteria, making sure to exclude any vulgar elements that the tales might contain: 'Espero de aver reushido, porké mi djudisio es totalmente subjektivo' ('I hope that I have succeeded in this, because my judgment is purely subjective') (Koén-Sarano 2004b: 20–21). In order to make the tales sound less crude, in some cases Koén-Sarano has softened the language, censoring certain words and expressions pertaining to sex and bodily functions. By doing so, she has altered the original tone of the tales. This has been pointed out by Alexander-Frizer (2008: 35) and Yoel Shalom Perez (2004: xv), both of whom collaborated with Koén-Sarano and are, thus, familiar with her practices. In her later works, however, she has favoured a precise rendering of the spoken language over an overly bowdlerised or edited version: 'Keeping the styling to a minimum, she has paid scrupulous attention to the spoken language, without resorting to censorship of matters dealing with sexual intimacy or expressions pertaining to bodily functions' (Alexander-Frizer 2008: 35).

With regard to Koén-Sarano's collections, some of the tales from *Djohá ke dize?* were previously published in her first work, *Kuentos*. Unlike *Djohá ke dize?*, which deals exclusively with tales of Djohá, *Kuentos* is a collection of Judeo-Spanish folk tales dealing with different types of tales and characters. One of its chapters (Chapter 3) is dedicated to Djohá and includes thirty-seven tales (Koén-Sarano 1986: 127–71). The fact that Koén-Sarano reserves a separate chapter for this character shows his unique significance for the Sepharadim. All the tales in the collection were published with their corresponding Hebrew translation, as was the case with *Djohá ke dize?*. After comparing the two collections, *Kuentos* and *Djohá ke dize?*, some changes in the editing of Djohá tales can be seen. Firstly, there are a number of Djohá tales in *Kuentos* which were reprinted in the same form, with the same title, in *Djohá ke dize?* (see the table below).

TABLE 3.3. Djohá tales from *Kuentos* reprinted in *Djohá ke dize?* without any changes to the text, title or informant

TALE	*Kuentos del folklore...* (1986)	*Djohá ke dize?...* (1991)	*Informant and the year when the tale was told*
'Komo enterró Djohá a su padre?'	p. 129	p. 339	Nisim Avigdor (1984)
'Djohá eskrivano'	p. 135	p. 83	Yaakov Elazar (1985)
'Los echos de Djohá'	p. 137	p. 79	Salvo Amado (1985)
'Djohá i el azno del vizino'	p. 145	p. 207	Salvo Amado (1983)
'Djohá i los sesh aznos'	p. 149	p. 189	Miriam Raymond (1984)
'Djohá i los ladrones'	p. 157	p. 251	Roza Salinas (1984)
'La kamiza de Djohá'	p. 159	p. 113	Hana Sharabani (1985)
'Djohá i los sien dukados'	p. 161	p. 217	Ester Koén (1984)
'Oté, hodja'	p. 165	p. 307	Matilda Koén-Sarano (1984)

| 'La fuersa de Djohá' | p. 169 | p. 309 | Miriam Raymond (1984) |
| 'La muerte de Djohá' | p. 171 | p. 351 | Ester Koén-Yohananov (1985) |

Secondly, some were reprinted in *Djohá ke dize?* but with a different title. This means that both the text and the informant of these tales remained the same, but the titles were either completely different or slightly modified. This could lead us to believe mistakenly that we are dealing with two different tales, which is clearly not the case. An example of this is 'Djohá i l'arina' ('Djohá and the Flour') from *Kuentos* (1986: 133), reprinted in *Djohá ke dize?* as 'Solución para haraganes' ('Solution for the Lazy') (1991: 59). Both titles were given by Koén-Sarano who recorded the tale in 1983 from Diana Sarano, born and raised in Turkey and Italy before emmigrating to Israel in 1969. Koén-Sarano reprinted some of the tales from *Kuentos* in *Djohá ke dize?*, but she changed the titles of some of them, most likely because she felt that the titles in *Kuentos* did not properly describe their content or were not catchy enough. Whatever the case, it is clear that we are dealing here with the same text, regardless of different titles (see the table below).

TABLE 3.4. Identical tales that appear under a different title in *Kuentos* and in *Djohá ke dize?*

Kuentos del folklore... (1986)	*Djohá ke dize?...* (1991)	*Informant and the year when the tale was told*
'Djohá i las keiftés' (p. 129)	'Kozas redondas' (p. 43)	Ester Levy (1984)
'Djohá i el gato' (p. 133)	'Djohá lava el gato' (p. 191)	Viktoria Eskenazi (1984)
'Djohá i l'arina' (p. 133)	'Solución para haraganes' (p. 59)	Diana Sarano (1983)
'Djohá i la kuedra del lavado' (p. 141)	'La kuedra del lavado' (p. 203)	Rashel Perera (1984)
'Djohá, la mujer i la puerta' (p. 143)	'Komo evitar pletos' (p. 147)	Rashel Perera (1984)
'Djohá i el berber' (p. 151)	'Djohá ande el berber' (p. 109)	Yaakov Kastro (1984)
'Djohá i la boka de la reyna' (p. 153)	'Un mundo entero' (p. 117)	Levana Sasson (1985)
'Djohá i las hamapolas' (p. 153)	'Kolor atraktiva' (p. 253)	Diana Sarano (1983)
'Djohá i el muerto' (p. 155)	'Resureksión' (p. 341)	Moshe Eskenazi (1984)
'Djohá i la devda' (p. 155)	'La devda de Djohá' (p. 99)	Samy Yohay-Merter (1984)
'Djohá i el korbán' (p. 157)	'El korbán de Djohá' (p. 313)	Viktoria Eskenazi (1984)
'El ijo de Djohá' (p. 163)	'Buen ijo' (p. 177)	Miriam Raymond (1984)

Lastly, in some cases, Koén-Sarano either maintains the same title or gives a similar one for what are actually two different versions of the same tale-type. This means that the tales were told by different informants at different times, which can imply not only changes to the text but also to the plot of the story. Just by looking at the titles, it is hard to conclude whether they are repeated or different versions of the same tale-type. An example of this is ATU1696 tale-type, 'What Should I Have Said (Done)' (Uther 2004: II, 382–83), which in both of Koén-Sarano's collections appears as 'El ojo de Djohá' (1986: 139; 1991: 129). The version that appears in *Kuentos* was told in 1984 by Renée Arochas and Alfredo Sarano. The former was born in Jerusalem into a Judeo-Spanish family originally from Rhodes, Greece, whilst the latter was born in Turkey but lived in Rhodes and Milan before emigrating to Israel (1986: xxiv; xxviii). In 1987, a year after *Kuentos* came out, Koén-Sarano interviewed Pinhás Tokatly, a Sephardic Jew from Jerusalem (Koén-Sarano 1991: xxxviii). On that occasion, Tokatly told Koén-Sarano another Judeo-Spanish version of ATU1696 tale-type, which she published in *Djohá ke dize?* also under the same title 'El ojo de Djohá' (1991: 129).

The differences in the plot between these two versions are apparent at first sight. Arochas's and Sarano's 1986 version is shorter than that of Tokatly and hence contains less plot detail. It recounts how Djohá's grandmother gives Djohá advice to 'va echando d'en vez en kuando un ojo a tu novia' ('go from time to time and cast an eye on your bride'), which meant that he should glance at her fondly. Djohá understands the advice literally, and during the ceremony he throws cows' eyes at his fiancée, leaving everyone confused. In spite of this, he still gets married at the end.

Tokatly's version, by contrast, is localised. The tale takes place in the streets of Jerusalem. Djohá is unable to find a wife for himself, and his mother advises him to 'echar ojadikas' ('cast an eye around'). Djohá buys cows' eyes and goes to Ben Yehuda and Jaffa Streets in Jerusalem and throws cows' eyes at every girl that passes by. Eventually, the police come and arrest him, convinced that he has gone mad. That is why in this version Djohá remains a bachelor.

The comparison of the two tales shows clear differences in the plot between these two versions of the same tale-type, yet maintaining the same title for both of them makes us believe that 'El ojo de Djohá' from *Djohá ke dize?* is nothing more than the same tale, with the same title, as in *Kuentos*. Indicating the difference between variants of the same tale-type is fundamental as it shows the polygenesis of Koén-Sarano's material. (For more examples, see the table below).

TABLE 3.5. Tales in both collections with the same or slightly different title but which are actually two different versions of the same tale-type, told at different times by different informants

Kuentos del folklore... (1986)	Informant and the year when the tale was told	Djohá ke dize?... (1991)	Informant and the year when the tale was told
'Djohá i las berendjenas' (p. 129)	Itshak Sarfaty (1983)	'Berendjenas specials' (p. 61)	Moshe (Chiko) Elazar (1989)
'Djohá i la puerta' (p. 131)	Mayer Koén (1984)	'Djohá, ten kargo de la puerta' (p. 51)	Rashel Perera (1987)
'El ojo de Djohá' (p. 139)	Renée Arochas and Alfredo Sarano (1984)	'El ojo de Djohá' (p. 129)	Pinhás Tokatly (1987)
'El bas de Djohá' (p. 141)	Ester Koén (1984)	'El bas de Djohá' (p. 145)	Itshak Simha (1988)
'El azno de Djohá' (p. 147)	Rejine Israel (1984)	'Djohá i su azno' (p. 193)	Itshak Simha (1988)
'El shamar de Djohá' (p. 147)	Jeannette Ben-Nae (1980)	'Haftoná preventive' (p. 177)	Sara Yohay (1988)
'Djohá i el azno que se ambezó a no komer' (p. 163)	Matilda Koén-Sarano (1985)	'El azno ke se akostumbró a no komer' (p. 193)	Sara Yohay (1988)
'Djohá i el sistem de su padre' (p. 139)	Tilly Alphandery (1982)	'Tal padre, ma kual ijo!' (p. 69) 'Filozofía', p. 249	Charlie Perets (1987) Strea Koén (1989)

Both of the collections discussed are of great significance regarding Djohá for various reasons. Firstly, they demonstrate that the tales about him continue to capture the imagination of the Sepharadim, showing that the tradition regarding this figure is still alive and productive in the Judeo-Spanish speaking world. Secondly, the informants Koén-Sarano interviewed for these two collections come from different places where the Sepharadim have resided, which indicates that Djohá formed part of the everyday life of the Sephardic community as a whole rather than being limited to specific areas or Sephardic groups.

Finally, most of the tales included here were narrated in their original language, Judeo-Spanish. In addition to being published in Ladino, they have also been translated to Hebrew, thus disseminating the Djohá narrative tradition among other Jewish groups. The once exclusively Judeo-Spanish Djohá has now come alive in the Hebrew language and its tradition, as well, and will also appear in the English-speaking world, a point which will be analysed in the next chapter.

Koén-Sarano's Djohá Tales in English

Koén-Sarano's *Kuentos* and *Djohá ke dize?* are not the only works by this collector and author to contain Djohá tales. Following these two works, Koén-Sarano published two more collections worthy of mention: *Folktales of Joha: Jewish Trickster* (hereafter *Folktales of Joha*, 2003) and *King Solomon and the Golden Fish* (hereafter

King Solomon, 2004a). The former resembles *Djohá ke dize?* in that it is a collection entirely dedicated to Djohá tales. The latter resembles *Kuentos* as an anthology of Judeo-Spanish folktales in which only one chapter (Chapter 6) contains Djohá tales. Unlike the previous two collections, which were bilingual (Judeo-Spanish/Hebrew), these two works were published only in English and in the USA rather than in Israel. The choice of publishers and language indicate Koén-Sarano's intention to disseminate Djohá tales outside Israel and suggest the type of audience at which these collections are aimed.

In 2003, Koén-Sarano's *Folktales of Joha* appeared in the USA. These tales were the fruit of the compiler's fieldwork undertaken between 1979 and 2000 (Koén-Sarano 2003: 4). Koén-Sarano's collection method had not changed considerably. The eighty-two informants encompass the traditional geographical distribution of the Sephardic communities: Lebanon, Tunisia, Egypt, Morocco, Turkey, Greece, Bulgaria, the former Yugoslavia, Italy, France, Spain and Israel. However, the inclusion of informants from new places such as the USA and Argentina represents a novelty in this volume. Koén-Sarano continues to employ her preferred method of working mainly with women: women informants outnumber the men, fifty-one compared to thirty-one.

The anthology is structured similarly to her *Djohá ke dize?*, comprising 267 stories which range from Djohá's childhood (Chapter 1), to his relationships with his mother and his teachers at school (Chapter 2), through marriage and his relationship with his wife (Chapters 5 and 6), to fatherhood (Chapter 7), his old age and death (Chapter 15). Other chapters are dedicated to prominent traits, such as 'Joha, the Glutton' (Chapter 13), or different life situations, as in 'Joha in the Hospital' (Chapter 14) and 'Joha and the Law' (Chapter 12), or his roles in society, as in 'Joha and Work' (Chapter 3) and 'Joha and the King' (Chapter 8) (Alexander 2003: 6).

The tales from *Folktales of Joha* were not published in the previous collections by Koén-Sarano (1986; 1991). There are, however, examples of some tales which were told by the same informant on several occasions and then published in different collections. Miriam Raymond, for example, told the story entitled 'Espanto Djustificado' ('A Warranted Fright') in 1984, an ATU1346 tale-type, 'The House without Food or Drink' (Uther 2004: II, 146), which Koén-Sarano published in *Djohá ke dize?* (1991: 345). However, the same informant repeated this very story ten years later, in 1994, which Koén-Sarano then published in *Folktales of Joha* under the translated title of 'Something to Be Afraid of' (2003: 271). Raymond's case illustrates Koén-Sarano's belief that the collector gets the best results when working with a regular circle of informants, men or women, who meet periodically to retell the tales they remember (Koén-Sarano 2003: 2). It also confirms what was previously mentioned: the repetition of tales constitutes an essential artifice of Koén-Sarano's work.

When an informant tells the same story on different occasions the text and even the plot of the story may undergo changes. So although the same tale may have been told twice or even more times by the same informant, each time it is different, and the scope of the changes between versions might vary. This is owing to the nature of the storytelling process, which Koén-Sarano explains from her experience as a storyteller and collector:

> Oral folktales are formed in the very act of narration, passing from one person to another, from country to country, from generation to generation. Each narrator adapts and alters the elements of a tale around a more or less fixed nucleus frequently by means of mimicry and according to his or her memory [...]. And so every time a tale is told, it emerges differently. (2003: 2)

However, after examining the texts of the same tale-type that Koén-Sarano recorded from the same informant on different occasions, such as the above-cited tale told by Miriam Raymond on two different occasions (1984 and 1994), minor or no variations to the texts have been found. Two possible deductions can be made as to why there are barely any textual changes: either it is the same text that Koén-Sarano published on two or more occasions in spite of the fact that she indicates different dates when she recorded the tales; or, the lack of variation in the texts corroborates the conclusion that this is not a genuine oral transmission but rather an exchange of the same stories by one group of people, who keep repeating them over and over again. The fact that *Folktales of Joha* is in English, whereas her previous collections are in Judeo-Spanish, makes it difficult to detect difference in the language used and thus come to a solid conclusion.

In *Folktales of Joha*, there are four women informants whose purportedly different versions of the same tale were published in previous collections by Koén-Sarano: Jeannette Ben-Nae, Vittoria (Sarano) Eskenazi, Miriam Raymond and Sol Maymaran.[45] They had all settled in Israel when Koén-Sarano interviewed them, but only Maymaran was originally from Israel (Koén-Sarano 2003: 282–90). Each of them told the same story on two or more occasions, and Koén-Sarano published these different versions in her work, as illustrated in the table below.

TABLE 3.6. Tales told by the same informant on two or more occasions and thus bearing minor textual changes

Kuentos de la famiya... (1986)	*Djohá ke dize?...* (1991)	*Folktales of Joha...* (2003)	*Informant and years when the tales were told*
'El shamar de Djohá' (p. 147)		'A Preventative Slap' (p. 130)	Jeannette Ben-Nae (1980; 1982)
'Djohá i el gato' (p. 133)	'Djohá lava el gato' (p. 191)	'If You Wash a Cat' (p. 71)	Vittoria (Sarano) Eskenazi (1984; 1992)
'La fuersa de Djohá' (p. 169)	'La fuersa de Djohá' (p. 309)	'The Strength of Age' (pp. 186–87)	Miriam Raymond (1984; 1994)
	'Ken metió Djohá en mi suká' (p. 229)	'The Conditional Sukkah' (pp. 253–54)	Miriam Raymond (1987; 1999)
	'Espanto djustifikado' (p. 345)	'Something To Be Afraid Of' (p. 271)	Miriam Raymond (1984; 1994)
	'A la letra' (p. 47)	'To the Letter' (p. 36)	Sol Maymaran (1989; 1987)

Alexander-Frizer qualifies the tales in *Folktales of Joha* as purely Sephardic because 'they express a "group self", an ethnic identity along with a particular physical and geographical environment, worldview and way of life' (2003: 10). The proverb 'Ken metió Djohá en mi suká' ('Who put Joha in my *sukkah*?') illustrates Alexander-Frizer's point. The proverb is used as the title of a tale in which the meaning of the proverb is explained. Two versions of this tale were told by Miriam Raymond: the first in 1987 and published in *Djohá ke dize?* (Koén-Sarano 1991: 229) and the second in 1999 and published in *Folktales of Joha* (Koén-Sarano 2003: 254).

In the tale, Djohá is building a *sukkah*, a small booth covered with branches where the Sephardic family lives, eats and sleeps during the Jewish holiday of *Sukkot*. This holiday, which is celebrated on the fifteenth day of the month of Tishri, lasts for nine days (Landman 1969: 94–97). As payment for building the booth, Djohá asks that he be invited to eat in it during the nine days. He abuses the invitation by eating gluttonously, which makes the family regret having accepted his offer and return his *sukkah*. This becomes the origin of the expression which is widely used up to the present day, 'Who put Joha in my *sukkah*?'. The meaning of the proverb is explained at the end of the tale: '[the proverb] is said by one who does not wish to enter a business deal, who does not want under any circumstances to know about something, and does not wish even to hear about it' (Koén-Sarano 2003: 254).

Although the tale is linked to a Jewish holiday such as *Sukkot* and therefore is not exclusively Sephardic, the protagonist of the tale, Djohá, is a Sephardic hero. The proverb within the context of the tale is comprehensible, especially as an explanation of it is usually given at the end. However, once shorn from the context, its meaning is difficult to decipher, as it is rooted in the Sephardic tradition and one needs to be familiar with the tale and the character in order to be able to comprehend the proverb. This makes both the tale and the proverb uniquely Sephardic, since they illustrate what Alexander-Frizer points out about the group identity.

Folktales of Joha comprises not only traditional Djohá tales but also modern ones — that is, stories of the traditional hero in contemporary situations, which make this collection unique compared to the other two: 'I chose both types of tales for this volume because his figure is still alive among the people. His characteristics are well known, and new tales are to this day created around him, adapted to his personality' (Koén-Sarano 2003: 3). This shows that the oral tradition regarding Djohá is still very productive, which undoubtedly contributes to his endurance in Sephardic folklore. Not only do well-known tales about him continue to circulate among the Sepharadim, but new stories have been created, thus enriching the corpus of this popular character.[46]

With regard to Koén-Sarano's editorial work, some changes can be perceived in her style. In the early stages, she stylised the tales in Judeo-Spanish by making her voice strongly present. Later, by her own account, she started to intervene less in terms of stylising so as 'not to deprive the stories of their particular characteristics and flavour' (2003: 4). This change in her editorial method is, as she herself claims, palpable in *Folktales of Joha*. However, it is difficult for us to appreciate these changes once the tales have been translated to English by David Herman. Unlike *Kuentos* or *Djohá ke dize?*, which were bilingual Judeo-Spanish/Hebrew editions, *Folktales of Joha* offers the tales only in their English translation from Judeo-Spanish.

Herman employs a mode of exoticising (or foreignising) translation. This term indicates a type of translation whose aim is to retain features of the source text and the source-language culture within the target text (Venuti 1995: 20; Haywood, Hervey and Thompson 2009: 270). A number of cultural borrowings, which usually appear unaltered, illustrate how a source-language expression was taken verbatim from the source text and introduced into the target text. For example, the tale 'The Nudnik' (2003: 50–51) contains references to common Sephardic dishes, which have no cultural equivalents in English, such as *kubbe* (Iraqi rice pastries with minced meat filling), *borekas* (savoury pastries with cheese or spinach filling) or *mejadara* (rice with lentils). Herman maintains them in Ladino and provides an explanation for them in footnotes. This is the procedure Herman occasionally deploys to provide clarification for the cultural-specific references, which cannot be rendered into English. But he does so only with terms having no cultural equivalents in English, unlike Reginetta Haboucha, who preserves a high number of Judeo-Spanish cultural borrowings in her translation of *King Solomon*, a point which will be discussed later.

Koén-Sarano's choice to publish these tales in English rather than in their original language is related to her aim to propagate the Judeo-Spanish culture outside Israel. In the USA, several important Sephardic communities exist, the largest in New York, Los Angeles and Seattle. However, most of their members, as Harris has shown (1994), have little or no knowledge of Judeo-Spanish. Hence by publishing the collection in English, it became more easily accessible to a wider Jewish readership in the USA, both Sephardic and non-Sephardic.

The choice of the publisher, the Jewish Publication Society (hereafter JPS), suggests that the book was primarily targeting a Jewish audience in the USA. The JPS, based in Philadelphia, is the oldest publisher of Jewish books in the country. From its foundation, the JPS has been the preeminent publisher of books at the heart of Jewish culture:

> Our mission has always been to enhance Jewish literacy through the publication of great books of Judaism. [...] Our authors, donors and readers represent the entire spectrum of the Jewish community. One of the missions is insuring that the legacy of Jewish culture's great books is carried forward to our children.[47]

At the same time, by translating the tales to English, this part of the Sephardic tradition became available to non-Jews as well, which is also in keeping with one of the aims of the JPS: 'educating the English reading community here and abroad about the classics of Jewish culture'.[48] It is safe to assume that Koén-Sarano had a similar goal in mind when she decided to render the Djohá tales in English rather than publishing them in Ladino: to reach a wider readership in order to disseminate and propagate aspects of the Sephardic culture as widely as possible in different cultures and different languages.

Only one year after the appearance of *Folktales of Joha* (2003), Koén-Sarano published another collection of Judeo-Spanish folk narratives in English in the USA, *King Solomon* (2004a). Like *Kuentos*, this collection encompasses a wide repertoire of folk narrative rather than focusing exclusively on Djohá tales. The selection of tales, made by Koén-Sarano and Yoel Shalom Perez (Haboucha 2004: xix), stems from the three goals of the collection, highlighted by Perez himself:

— to take the broader view and have as many narrative genres represented in the book as possible;

— to bring to readers tales reflecting the Judeo-Spanish culture in its characteristic colours; and,

— to choose tales that a general reader would find interesting and amusing and not only those that might be of interest to academics and researchers (2004: xv)

One of the tales from the collection, 'King Solomon and the Golden Fish', lent its name to the entire volume. This tale is offered both in its original Judeo-Spanish ('El rey Shelomó i el pishkado de oro') and in English. The rest of the collection appears only in its English translation done by Reginetta Haboucha.

The collection comprises fifty-four narratives compiled by Koén-Sarano in the 1980s and 1990s. This number of tales is considerably smaller than previous collections by Koén-Sarano, each of which comprised over two hundred stories. This is partly due to the fact that it is an annotated scholarly edition, containing analytical commentaries. As a result of its size, the collection only includes the participation of thirty narrators, twenty-two women and eight men, compared to more than seventy narrators in *Djohá ke dize?* and *Folktales of Djohá*. Koén-Sarano persists in her method of working primarily with women. The majority of the informants are either from Turkey (fourteen) or Israel (eleven), although there is also one informant from each of the following countries: Italy, Spain, Morocco, the USA and Argentina. A short biography of each narrator's life is given as well as the year and circumstances of each recording session. The last chapter of the collection, 'Jokes and Anecdotes', contains a section with fifteen Djohá tales, twelve of which had already been published in *Folktales of Joha* (see the table below).

TABLE 3.7. Tales from *Folktales of Joha* in David Herman's translation which are reprinted in *King Solomon* in Reginetta Haboucha's translation

Folktales of Joha (2003)	King Solomon (2004)	INFORMANT
'The Unmixed Salad' (p. 234)	'Djohá's Salata' (no. 30, p. 238)	Maria de Benedetti (1987)
'Dinner at the King's Table' (pp. 245–47)	'Djohá Eats at the King's Table' (no. 32, pp. 243–45)	Lea Benabu (1993)
'Knowing How to Ask' (pp. 36–37)	'It's All in the Asking' (no. 33, pp. 247–48)	Alex Korfiatis (1993)

'Better to Be Struck by a Sane Person than Saved by a Madman' (pp. 262–63)	'Better a Wise Man Should Strike You Than a Fool Help You' (no. 35, pp. 251–52)	Shmuel Barki (1992)
'The Patient Teacher' (pp. 40–41)	'Djohá's Question' (no. 37, pp. 255–56)	Ester Ventura (1992)
'How to Bring Food Home' (pp. 210–11)	'Djohá Retorts' (no. 38, pp. 259–60)	Sara Yohay (1992)
'Invitation to a Feast' (pp. 237–38)	'Djohá's Invitation to Pranso' (no. 39, pp. 261–62)	Lea Benabu (1993)
'Miracle à la Joha' (pp. 154–55)	'Djohá's Mirákolo' (no. 40, pp. 264–65)	Sara Kent (1992)
'What a Watermelon' (pp. 218–19)	'Djohá and the Karpúz' (no. 41, pp. 267–68)	Alex Korfiatis (1993)
'The Case of the Hard–Boiled Eggs' (pp. 229–31)	'The Eggs and the Grain' (no. 42, pp. 271–72)	Sara Yohay (1991)
'Born Unlucky' (pp. 219–21)	'Djoha's Merás' (no. 43, pp. 276–78)	Ester Ventura (1993)
'Stamp of Servitude' (pp. 215–17)	'Djohá and the Forty Thieves' (no. 44, pp. 280–81)	Rebeka Cohen-Ariel (1989)

Based on the table above, it is safe to assume that both Herman and Haboucha were given the same original texts to translate into English. Only three Djohá tales in *King Solomon* had not been published previously. The first, 'Djohá in the King's House' (2004a: 240), is a combination of two tale-types: ATU1691B, 'The Suitor Who Does Not Know How to Behave at Table', and ATU1696, 'What Should I Have Said (Done)?'.[49] The second hitherto unpublished tale, 'Djohá and the Oil' (2004a: 249–50), belongs to ATU1349*, 'Miscellaneous Numbskull Tales' and it is not the only example of this tale-type in Sephardic tradition (see, for example, Koén-Sarano 1991: 45). No equivalent type is known to exist for the third tale, 'What a Sweet Death!' (2004a: 254).

Why would Koén-Sarano and Perez have selected these particular tales when most of them had already been published a year before, also in English and in the USA? The idea of recycling tales forms part of Koén-Sarano's working method. The repetition of tales from one collection to another is not an unprecedented phenomenon in Koén-Sarano's work. Tables 3.2, 3.3, 3.4, 3.6 and 3.7 all indicate the frequency with which she resorted to this practice of repeating the tales in identical or similar form.

Perez emphasises that the tales included in this volume did not undergo any kind of literary adaptation or significant editing, a trait that he feels makes this collection unique compared to previous works by Koén-Sarano: 'The tales preserve, almost intact, the original text used by the traditional storytellers who narrated them. The anthology thus fills a void that has existed for far too long in this area. This is one of its major values' (2004: xv–xvi). Perez's words corroborate what has been highlighted before: Koén-Sarano adulterated the texts in the initial stages of her work, a practice that she mostly (but not entirely) abandoned in her later publications. However, it is impossible to claim that the tales published in *King Solomon* are completely intact, as they are not presented in the language in which they were told but rather in English translation, and that itself entails a certain degree of adaptation.

However, Haboucha's translation from Judeo-Spanish to English contains a series of strategic decisions as to what source text properties should have priority in both the translation and the overall style and register of the target text.[50] For example, in order to convey the affective attitudes of speakers, Haboucha deploys a specific tonal register, as seen in such expressions as, *Ah, Dió Santo!* ('Oh, Holy God!'), *Amán* ('Have mercy') or *Bay, pezevéng! Bay, kieratá!* ('You, cuckold! You, pander!'), which she offers both in Judeo-Spanish and English. Furthermore, unlike Herman, who only maintains Judeo-Spanish terms lacking cultural equivalents in English, Haboucha preserves a significant number of cultural borrowings that do have an equivalent in English in order to show that Judeo-Spanish is a mixture of different cultural influences. For example, in the tale 'Djohá's Question' (Koén-Sarano 2004a: 255–56 n. 37), Haboucha maintains certain Judeo-Spanish cultural-specific references or sociocultural phenomena: 'What a good teacher, a good *moré*, we have!', *moré* being the Hebrew word for teacher; or, 'What is it you want, *bey*!', the latter a Turkish word meaning 'my dear', both words in use in Judeo-Spanish. She either explains them in the main text by offering their rendering into English as with the word *moré*, or she provides their meaning in the glossary at the end of the volume (Haboucha 2004: xxi). This is also a type of exoticising translation which aims to familiarise the readers of the translation with the source language's culture, offering them some sense of how that culture sounds and feels.

The second feature that makes this collection unique is the fact that it is the first work by Koén-Sarano to be published as an annotated scholarly edition. Haboucha not only translated the tales into English but wrote the analytical commentaries which accompany each narrative, as well. She also described the peculiarities of particular versions and symbols of the acculturation process. A case in point is the previously mentioned tale, 'Djohá's Question', which is followed by a commentary clarifying that this particular tale is a secular adaptation of the Hillel story from the Talmud. Haboucha then provides details of that story and clarifies some cultural references (Koén-Sarano 2004a: 256–57).

Who, then, was the intended audience for this collection? Haboucha herself specifies at whom the book is aimed: 'This work was designed for readers familiar with Jewish culture and its folk beliefs as well as for those who come to it with little prior knowledge of the lore' (2004: xix). Her words indicate an English readership in general. However, the fact that the edition includes analytic commentaries with each narrative and clarifying information on any sociocultural phenomena might suggest that the collection was targeting the academic audience interested in Sephardic folklore. Djohá tales are being presented as part of an academic study, which entails a shift in approach and hence a different type of audience, and makes a claim for the collection's cultural status that is associated with the types of press used. *King Solomon* was published by Wayne State University Press in Detroit, the USA, which specialises in Judaica and African American studies and focuses on disseminating research and improving education.[51]

Whatever the case, the importance of these two collections of Djohá tales lies in several aspects. First, they reveal the fruitfulness of Koén-Sarano's fieldwork regarding Djohá who continues to endure remarkably well in the Sephardic world. *Folktales of Joha* is Koén-Sarano's second volume entirely dedicated to this character, with a significant number of tales included (267) which are a representative sample of Sephardic oral literature and ethnic culture. Most of these tales are new or renewed stories about Djohá that still circulate among members of the Sephardic community.

Second, the fact that the tales became known in English and the USA has helped disseminate one of the aspects of the Sephardic culture outside of the borders of Israel, thus fulfilling one of Koén-Sarano's main goals. Furthermore, a different country of publication and a different language entails a different reading public: the collections in English are now within the reach of the entire Jewish community in the USA, both Sephardic and non-Sephardic, but are also accessible to others, non-Ladino speakers and non-Jews, who might be interested in Sephardic folklore. The scholarly edition of *King Solomon* is aimed precisely at those who want to immerse themselves in this field of study, as it offers commentaries which accompany each tale and a number of cultural and literary explanations. In the case of both collections, particularly *King Solomon*, the use of an exoticising mode of translation, which maintains any specific Judeo-Spanish cultural references and sociocultural phenomena, 'sends readers abroad' and thereby broadens their horizons (see Haywood, Hervey and Thompson 2009: 75).

Finally, with regard to Koén-Sarano's working methods, changes can be observed in her editorial practice. According to her account (2003: 4), in the case of *Folktales of Joha* and *King Solomon*, she has intervened less in the censoring and stylising of vocabulary, with the aim of preserving the orginal tone and language of the tales as they were told to her, as corroborated by Alexander-Frizer (2008: 35) and Perez (2004: xv–xvi). However, since both collections were published in English, it is difficult to quantify these changes in her editorial method.

4. Conclusion to Part III

Part III analysed the presence among the Sepharadim of Djohá, whose origins are to be found in the Arabic-speaking world. We have seen the popularity of this character in the Middle East among Muslims from at least the ninth century. More importantly, the hitherto-unknown presence of this character in al-Andalus from at least the tenth century in the work of Ibn al-Faradī from Cordoba has been established. Later, in the thirteenth century, Djohá also appears in the work of Ibn al-Šayj from Málaga. It can therefore be claimed with great certainty that Muslims from al-Andalus transmitted this character to the Jews prior to their expulsion from Spain in 1492. Upon arriving in the Ottoman Empire, the Sepharadim encountered a similar figure to 'their' Djohá in the Turkish character of Nasr al-Dīn Khodja. The Sephardic tradition was thus enlarged upon with tales from the Turkish tradition, albeit with Djohá as a protagonist.

The endurance of the character in the former Yugoslavia and the Sephardic world as a whole from the end of the nineteenth century to the present day has been discussed in detail. The examples from the former Yugoslavia show that before WWII, Djohá tales were collected in Serbian with the aim of recording evidence of a legacy that was dying out. Thus the aim was merely to preserve the memory of the Sephardic tradition rather than to revitalise it, and consequently the language the tales were written in was not a vital issue — hence their appearance in Serbian rather than in Judeo-Spanish. Examples from after WWII, by contrast, show a change in approach: the tales were now collected in Judeo-Spanish with the intention of revitalising the language and the tradition post-Holocaust. In spite of the assimilation process undergone by the Sepharadim and the annihilation of the majority of them in the Holocaust, this character managed to survive in the region long into the twentieth century.

The testimonies of those who collected the tales as well as those who told them enlighten us as to the role of Djohá among the Sepharadim: although he was similar to other characters in the region, namely the Turkish character Nasr al-Dīn Khodja, he was perceived both by the storytellers and the collectors as an authentically Sephardic character that was used as a means to teach as well as to entertain. Furthermore, he was perceived as a simpleton who appears in both the proverb and the narrative tradition.

Koén-Sarano's fieldwork on Djohá tales from the 1970s to the present day has shown the remarkable presence of the character among the Sepharadim wherever they settled. Koén-Sarano not only interviewed members of the community in Israel and countries of the former Ottoman Empire and North Africa, she included narrators from other countries of the Sephardic diaspora such as the USA and South America, as well. Koén-Sarano's work forms part of a larger movement in Israel for the recovery of the Sephardic language and tradition. She published Djohá tales in Judeo-Spanish, although not all the tales were told to her in that language. She translated some of these tales into Hebrew in order to disseminate them among the wider Jewish population in Israel, and into English, as well, in order to disseminate them outside Israel.

Koén-Sarano's fieldwork consists of interviewing mostly women informants, as she believes that a single-sex group feels free to speak openly without censoring the tales. This decision is a conscious expression of her cultural identity: folk literature is presented as belonging to the realm of women. Her group of women, known as the Ladies of Ladino, meets periodically and exchanges tales they recall. However, this method places limitations on the corpus and leads Koén-Sarano to repeat the same tales from one collection to another. To present them as different, she either gives them another title or publishes them in different languages. This recycling of the material is one of the main traits of Koén-Sarano's editorial practice. Likewise, in the initial stage of her work, she intervened to a great extent in the editorial process by stylising the language.

Finally, Djohá still survives well in the Sephardic world in spite of all the adversities, and he continues to capture the imagination of the Sepharadim who not only continue to foster the old tales about him but also to create new ones. Djohá continues to make the Sepharadim laugh while teaching them at the same time, either as the protagonist of a narrative or as a proverbial character. Furthermore, Djohá embodies aspects of Sephardic culture and identity, because he transmits the Sephardic experience both past and present, which is why the Sepharadim often see their own reflection in the stories about him and in the proverbs which derive from these stories and which can only be understood by members of the Sephardic community. Thus Djoha truly symbolises Sephardic history, mentality and identity.

Notes to Part III

1. When referring to the Sephardic culture, I use the most common Judeo-Spanish spelling of the character's name, Djohá, as applied by Koén-Sarano (1986; 1991). With regard to this character in other cultures, I shall adopt: Juhā for Arabic sources (Marzolph 1998: 417–18), Juhī for Persian culture (Christensen 1922) and Nasr al-Dīn Khodja for Turkish sources (Marzolph 1993: 1018–20).
2. On the phenomenon of literary acculturation, see Kushner and Dimić 1994.
3. For more information on al-Andalus, see Fletcher 1992 and Damián Cano 2004.
4. Also, see Drory 2000: 190–210.
5. For some early examples of Djohá tales among the Sepharadim, see Luria 1930: 29 and Crews 1935: 66. Also, Marie-Christine Bornes-Varol cites a collection of Djohá tales in Judeo-Spanish Rashi script that was published by an anonymous author in 1911 in Thessaloniki, Greece (1995: 62–63).
6. On this, also see Marzolph 1998: 417, Thomas de Antonio 1993: 194 and Charles Pellat 1965: 590. For writers and works in Arabic, I follow the transcription given in the *Encyclopedia of Arabic Literature* (Scott Meisami and Starkey 1998). When a title of a work appears here without its English translation, it is because it is not provided by my source.
7. For more information on early examples of Juhā in the Middle East, see Freytag 1838: 403, Pellat 1965: 590, Walther 1988: 520 and Thomas de Antonio 1993: 191.
8. I would like to express my gratitude to Maribel Fierro (CSIC, Madrid) and Clara María Thomas de Antonio (Universidad de Sevilla) for their help and advice concerning Juhā in al-Andalus; and to François Clément de Blois (University College London) for translating these Juhā tales from Arabic.
9. The information regarding the life of Ibn al-Faradī was taken from Lirola Delgado 2004: 95–111.
10. The book was published for the first time in Cairo in 1870. See Peña Martín 2007: 280.
11. Asín Palacios does not provide the text of the tales.
12. I use García Gómez's edition of these tales.
13. For more information on Luria and his work in Macedonia, see Liebl 2007; 2009; 2010.
14. For a historical overview of the Holocaust as it affected the Sepharadim, see I. J. Lévy 1989.
15. Yalia, as explained before, was a name for a Jewish neighbourhood in Belgrade in the nineteenth century.
16. On this, see García Moreno 2010; 2013; 2014.
17. For more information on the Serbian Nasr al-Dīn Khodja, see Isaković 1984 and Samardžija 2005.
18. On cultural transposition, see Haywood, Hervey and Thompson 2009: 270.
19. For a more detailed account of Djordjević's life and work, see Antonijević 1968; 1969; 1994; Popović 2010.
20. For Djordjević's own testimonies regarding his work among Romani people, see the Prologue and the Introduction to his edition of *Ciganske narodne pripovetke* 1933: iii–vi and vii–xv.
21. For a more detailed description of the nature of these questionnaires and how Djordjević applied them in his fieldwork, see Antonijević 1968: 228.
22. For an issue of elderly individuals recovering earlier experiences, see Hufford, Hunt and Zeitlin 1987.

23. Koén-Sarano's tale collection *Djohá ke dize?* also attests to the great popularity that this character has in the proverbial world as it contains an entire chapter dedicated exclusively to the Djohá proverbs and sayings: 'Reflanes de Djohá' (1991: 355–79).

24. For more information on the storyteller, see Koén-Sarano 1991: xxxvii.

25. On smoking prohibitions in Jewish culture, see Rosner 1982.

26. The following titles from Koén-Sarano's collection (1991) illustrate the above: 'Deuda de Ramadán' ('Debt of Ramadan'; p. 105), 'Simiente de minaré' ('Minaret's Seed'; p.105), 'Oté, Hodjá' ('Move over, Khodja'; p. 307), or 'Los días de Ramadán' ('Days of Ramadan'; p. 325).

27. Kolonomos discusses her participation in the War in her *Monastir without Jews* (2008: 57–63).

28. For a general overview of Kolonomos's life and work, see Vidaković-Petrov 2016.

29. For the names of her informants and a brief outline of their lives, see Kolonomos 1978: 37.

30. For other Sephardic examples, see Haboucha's catalogue under these reference numbers.

31. I have not been able to consult the texts in Judeo-Spanish.

32. An example of a Sephardic proverb from Bosnia with Djohá as a protagonist appears in an unpublished collection of proverbs by Binjo Samokovlija (JIM MS Binjo Samokovlija n. 109), thus confirming its existence in oral tradition there.

33. In Sephardic periodicals, where Konfino published some of his work, his name is spelled as Jacques or Jak Confino. As he wrote most of his work in Serbian, I use here the Serbian spelling of the name, Žak Konfino.

34. The sneezing motif, for instance, appears in the tale of the 'Two Lazy Suitors' in *Libro de buen amor*. On this, see Vasvári 1989: 181–205 and Haywood 2008: 50–52.

35. For more examples of the tale, see Koén-Sarano 1991: 59.

36. As stated earlier, the first-ever collection of Djohá tales appears to be the one by an anonymous author published in Judeo-Spanish Rashi script in Thessalonika in 1911 that has not been studied thus far.

37. Although Djohá is also mentioned in Chapter 1 in the tale, 'Los buenos consejos de Djohá' ('Djohá's Good Advice'), he does not appear as the protagonist of this tale. This undoubtedly explains why Koén-Sarano did not include this particular tale with the other Djohá tales. See Koén-Sarano 1986: 55.

38. For a complete list of her works, see <https://es.wikipedia.org/wiki/Matilda_Koen-Sarano#Obra> [accessed 30 April 2019].

39. See <http://www.akiyerushalayim.com/ay/075/075_05_grafya.htm> [accessed 30 April 2019].

40. See <https://es.wikipedia.org/wiki/Autoridad_Nacional_del_Ladino> [accessed 30 April 2019].

41. For the differences between these mentioned systems, see Koén-Sarano 1999: xxix–xxxii.

42. For a short outline of the informants' biographies, see Koén-Sarano 1986: xxiv–xxix; 1991: xxx–xl; 2003: 282–90.

43. On this, also see Lévy Zumwalt and Lévy 2001: 42.

44. For more information on this issue of Sephardic women being the main guardians of oral tradition, see Romeu 2000: 9–12; Díaz-Mas 2009: 81–101; Weich-Shahak 2009: 273–91; Filipović and Vučina Simović 2010: 259–69.

45. At times, Koén-Sarano herself places part of the name of an informant in bracket as she does here with Sarano, which most likely is the informant's maiden name.

46. The tale 'Foreign Work', told by Eliezer Papo and published in *Folktales of Joha*, is an example of this. See *Part II*.

47. See <http://www.jewishpub.org/about/vision.php> [accessed 3 May 2019].

48. See <http://www.jewishpub.org/about/vision.php> [accessed 3 May 2019].

49. For more Sephardic examples of this tale-type, see Koén-Sarano 1986: 129 and 1991: 43.

50. On strategic decisions in translation, see Haywood, Hervey and Thompson 2009: 274.

51. See <http://wsupress.wayne.edu/> [accessed 3 May 2019].

CONCLUSION

The present study has focused on the Sepharadim of the former Yugoslavia, their efforts to preserve the Judeo-Spanish language and folk tradition as well as the analysis of various practices involved in this endeavour: collection, re-creation, imitation, adaptation, dissemination and even misrepresentation of the Sephardic heritage. The examination of these actions has detailed the people behind them as well as the events which influenced them to undertake these activities.

The period under consideration spans one hundred years: from the late nineteenth to the end of the twentieth century. This was the time when the Yugoslav Sepharadim were confronted with various factors impacting the decline of the Judeo-Spanish language and oral tradition. I have divided the period under study into two parts separated by the Holocaust as a landmark event.

In the pre-Holocaust period, two major factors influenced the stability of the Sephardic communities in the Ottoman Empire. The first was the disintegration of the Empire, which led to the creation of new Balkan states and an imminent assimilation of the Sepharadim into the new societies, which meant more influence from a Western European lifestyle and less from the Eastern Ottoman one they had known. The second major factor was an important change in the educational system. The Sepharadim abandoned their traditional religious education in Judeo-Spanish reserved for boys only and exchanged it for a mixed-sex secular education conducted in either the national languages of the countries where they now lived, or in French, Italian or English, the languages used in foreign schools. These changes in the traditional lifestyle of the Sepharadim prompted the efforts of Yugoslav Sephardic authors to initiate work on the preservation of various aspects of Sephardic culture with particular emphasis on the oral tradition as its most authentic emblem.

The post-Holocaust period is marked by the events of WWII, which made this conservation task even more imperative due to the fact that most Sephardic communities around Europe were practically obliterated or dispersed. This new situation introduced an additional urgency to the idea of safeguarding the Sephardic heritage. As a result, folk literature received a particular place and emphasis in the works of Sephardic authors as an important part of that same heritage.

I have structured the discussion in three parts. In *Part I*, I examined two leading authors from this first time period, i.e., prior to WWII: Haim S. Davičo and Laura Papo, a man and a woman belonging to two generations, the former from Serbia and the latter from Bosnia, both collectors of Sephardic folklore and authors in their own rights. *Part II* is dedicated to the analysis of the work of Gina Camhy and Isak

Papo, a man and a woman, pertaining to the same generation, both from Bosnia, whose work evolved in post-Holocaust Yugoslavia. Finally, *Part III* is structured around the folk tale tradition whose protagonist is an internationally-known character called Djohá (Sephardic), Juhā (Arabic), Nasr al-Din Khodja (Turkish), while the authors highlighted in this part (informants, collectors, translators, publishers) have been selected due to their connection with Djohá tales. This part spans the whole period under study beginning with Davičo and ending with the ongoing work of the Israeli collector Matilda Koén-Sarano, who was born in Milan into a Sephardic family originally from Turkey. Each part is followed by a conclusion where I detail my findings in relation to each time period/author. Thus, I offer here the key points and conclusions of my research as a whole.

The study has emphasised that the techniques implemented by Davičo and Laura Papo in the pre-Holocaust period —— namely, re-creation of the lore, the creation of new elements through translations or adaptations, the introduction of folk literature as an integral part of their own literary works, or simply collection of the material *in situ* —— contrast with the techniques used by Camhy or Isak Papo in the post-Holocaust period. The aim of the latter was to preserve the remnants of the Sephardic heritage and Judeo-Spanish language, which they accomplished by means of one technique: the collection, conservation and dissemination of the legacy. *Part III* has highlighted through the examination of hitherto unknown sources that Juhā/Djohá was known in al-Andalus prior to the expulsion of the Jews and, thus, forms part of their Iberian heritage, in addition to stressing the later interaction of the Sephardic Djohá with the Turkish Nasr al-Din Khodja in the Balkans. Regarding the Sephardic versions of Djohá tales collected in the former Yugoslavia, the issue of the language of this material has been underscored (original Judeo-Spanish versus Serbian translation) and the presence of this character in Sephardic proverbs. Koén-Sarano's fieldwork was included in the study with the aim of showing that tales about Djohá survive well among the Sephardic community as a whole rather than being limited to the former Yugoslavia, and also to pinpoint how methods of collecting and editing (including translations) affect the preservation of Sephardic language and folklore post-Holocaust within organised efforts to revitalise the endangered heritage.

This study has moved to the forefront of the scholars' and readers' attention little known and neglected Yugoslav Sephardic authors, highlighting at the same time a number of folkloric sources hitherto unknown to or missed by the existing scholarship. Although the study underlines the predominant role of women in the preservation and transmission of the oral tradition and the language, a nuance has been added to this standpoint by demonstrating that men as well had an unquestionable role in preserving, transmitting, reworking and collecting examples of folk literature. This was achieved by examining the work of both male and female Sephardic authors/collectors and pointing out similarities and differences in their working methods and results.

Across both time frames three main practices can be discerned: collection, conservation and dissemination of the folk material which, due to the social and political changes mentioned, became an endangered aspect of Sephardic culture along with its language, Judeo-Spanish. As demonstrated, these changes, which seemed to endanger the Sephardic legacy, in fact served to stimulate its conservation in relation to the first time frame. Further, the events of WWII made this conservation task even more important, which is why in 2002 UNESCO declared Judeo-Spanish one of the world's seriously endangered languages. Therefore, the recovery and the study of its literature, especially that which until now has gone unnoticed, represents a vital contribution to its preservation. The goal of this book is to contribute in a scholarly way to the preservation and revitalisation of this endangered heritage, and it was written in the hopes that it will fulfil this purpose.

BIBLIOGRAPHY

Abravanel, Nicole. 2013. '*Le Judaïsme Sépharadi*: une revue transnationale d'expression française (Paris, 1932–Londres, 1966)', in *Recensement, analyse et traitement numérique des sources écrites pour les études séfarades*, ed. by Soufiane Roussi and Ana Stulic-Etchevers (Bordeaux: Presses universitaires de Bordeaux), pp. 113–68

—— 1996. 'Paris et le séphardisme ou l'affirmation sépharadiste à Paris dans les années trente', in *Hommage à Haïm Vidal Sephiha*, ed. by Winfried Busse and Marie-Christine Varol (Bern and Berlin: Peter Lang), pp. 497–523

Alcalá Galán, Mercedes. 1996. 'Las misceláneas españolas del siglo XVI y su entorno cultural', *Dicenda: cuadernos de filología hispánica*, 14: 11–20

Alcalá Galve, Ángel (ed.). 1995. *Judíos, sefarditas, conversos: la expulsión de 1492 y sus consecuencias. Ponencias del congreso internacional celebrado en Nueva York, en noviembre de 1992* (Valladolid: Ámbito)

Alexander, Tamar. 2003. 'Introduction', in Matilda Koén-Sarano, *Folktales of Joha: Jewish Trickster* (Philadelphia: The Jewish Publication Society), pp. 5–16

—— 2004. '"Do Not Trust X", Inter-Cultural Confrontation and Prejudice: Between Judeo Spanish Proverbs & Hispanic Proverbs', in *Shefa Tal: Studies in Jewish Thought and Culture presented to Bracha Sack*, ed. by Zeev Gries, Howard (Haim) Kreisel and Boaz Huss (Beer-Sheva: Ben-Gurion University Press), pp. 349-79 [in Hebrew]

Alexander-Frizer, Tamar. 2008. *The Heart is a Mirror: The Sephardic Folktale* (Detroit: Wayne State University Press)

Alkalaj, David A. 1925. 'Hajim Davičo, književnik sa Jalije', *Gideon*, 4–5.6: 74–85

Alpert, Michael. 2009. 'Introduction', in Elia R. Karmona, *The Chaste Wife*, trans. by Michael Alpert (Nottingham: Five Leaves), pp. 13–36

Alves, Francisco Manuel. 1938. *Memórias arqueológico-históricas do distrito de Bragança: arqueologia, etnografia e arte* (Bragança: Typogr. Académica)

Anahory Librowicz, Oro. 1980. *Florilegio de romances sefardíes de la diáspora* (Madrid: Cátedra-Seminario Menéndez Pidal)

—— 1988. *Cancionero Séphardi du Québec* (Montreal: Collège du Vieux Montréal)

Anonymous. 1982. 'L'Association "Vidas Largas"', *Le Judaïsme Sephardi*, 1: 26–27

Antić, Čedomir. 2013. *Srpska istorija* (Belgrade: Vukotić Media)

Antonijević, Dragoslav. 1994. 'Tihomir Djordjević kao humanista i intelektualac svog i našeg vremena', *Balkanika: godišnjak Balkanološkog instituta*, 25.2: 11–18

—— 1969. 'Tihomir Djordjević i njegovo naučno delo', in *Zbornik za društvene nauke Matice srpske* 53, pp. 139–50

—— 1968. 'Naučne metode i tehnike Tihomira Djordjevića', *Narodno stvaralaštvo: folklor*, 28.7: 224–29

Arie, Janette. 1990. 'The Jewish Schools in Bulgaria during the Period between 1920–1951', *Annual*, 25: 87–106

Armand, Frédéric. 2008. *Chilpéric Ier: le roi assassiné deux fois*, Biographie (Cahors: Louve)

Armistead, Samuel G., and Joseph H. Silverman. 1982. 'Baladas griegas en el romancero sefardí', in *En torno al romancero sefardí: hispanismo y balcanismo de la tradición judeo-española*, ed. by Samuel G. Armistead and Joseph H. Silverman (Madrid: Seminario Menéndez Pidal), pp. 151–68

—— 1971. *The Judeo-Spanish Ballad Chapbooks of Yacob Abraham Yoná* (Berkeley, Los Angeles and London: University of California Press)

—— 1965. 'Christian Elements and de-Christianization in the Sephardic *Romancero*', in *Collected Studies in Honour of Américo Castro's 80ᵗʰ Year*, ed. by M. P. Hornik (Oxford: Lincombe Research Library), pp. 21–38

—— 1962. *Diez romances hispánicos en un manuscrito sefardí de la Isla de Rodas* (Pisa: [s.n.])

—— 1960. 'Hispanic Balladry among the Sephardic Jews of the West Coast', *Western Folklore*, 19.4: 229–44

ARMISTEAD, SAMUEL G., JOSEPH H. SILVERMAN and ORO ANAHORY LIBROWICZ. 1977. *Romances judeo-españoles de Tánger, recogidos por Zarita Nahón* (Madrid: Cátedra-Seminario Ménendez Pidal)

ARMISTEAD, SAMUEL G., JOSEPH H. SILVERMAN and BILJANA ŠLJIVIĆ-ŠIMŠIĆ (eds). 1971. *Judeo-Spanish Ballads from Bosnia* (Philadelphia: University of Pennsylvania Press)

ARMISTEAD, SAMUEL G. 1996. 'Ballad Hunting in Zamora', in *'Al que buena hora nació': Essays on the Spanish Epic and Ballad in Honour of Colin Smith*, ed. by Brian Powell (Liverpool: Liverpool University Press), pp. 13–26

—— 1978. *El romancero judeo-español en el Archivo Menéndez Pidal: catálogo-índice de romances y canciones*, 3 vols (Madrid: Cátedra-Seminario Menéndez Pidal)

ASÍN PALACIOS, MIGUEL. 1932. '*El Abecedario* de Yúsuf Benaxeij el malagueño', *Boletín de la Real Academia de la Historia*, 100: 195–228

AYALA, FRANCISCO. 1965. 'Fuente árabe de un cuento popular en el *Lazarillo*', *Boletín de la Real Academia Española*, 45: 493–95

BAER, YITZHAK. 1981. *Historia de los judíos en la España cristiana*, trans. by José Luis Lacave, 2 vols (Madrid: Altalena)

BARUH, KALMI. 2007. 'Some Instances of Fiction among Bosnian Sephardim', in Kalmi Baruh, *Selective Works on Sephardic and Other Jewish Topics*, ed. by Krinka Vidaković-Petrov and Alexander Nikolić, trans. by Tatjana Jovićević (Jerusalem: Moshe David Gaon Center for Ladino Culture and Shefer Publishers), pp. 132–37

—— 1933. 'Španske romanse bosanskih Jevreja', in *Godišnjak: 'La Benevolencija'* — *Sarajevo i 'Potpora'* — *Beograd* (Sarajevo: Štamparija Menahem Papo), pp. 272–88

—— 1930. 'El judeo-español de Bosnia', *Revista de filología española*, 17.2: 113–54

BATAKOVIĆ, DUŠAN T., MILAN ST. PROTIĆ, NIKOLA SAMARDŽIĆ and ALEKSANDAR FOTIĆ. 2000. *Nova istorija srpskog naroda* (Belgrade and Lausanne: Naš dom and L'Age d' Homme)

BAUSANI, A. 1965. 'Djalāl al Dīn Rūmī', in *The Encyclopaedia of Islam*, ed. by B. Lewis, Ch. Pellat and J. Schacht, 12 vols (Leiden and London: E. J. Brill and Luzac), II: 393–97

BENAZERAF, REPHAEL. 1978. *Recueil de 'Refranes' (proverbs) judéo-espagnols (haketía) du Maroc* (Paris: Imprimerie Continentale)

BENBASSA, ESTHER. 1991. 'L'education feminine en Orient: l'ecole des filles de l'Alliance Israélite Universelle à Galata, Istanbul (1879–1912)', *Histoire, economie et societé*, 4: 529–60

BÉNICHOU, PAUL. 1968. *Romancero judeo-español de Marruecos* (Madrid: Castalia)

BENMAYOR, RINA. 1979. *Romances judeo-españoles de Oriente: nueva recolección* (Madrid: Cátedra-Seminario Menéndez Pidal and Editorial Gredos)

BERENGUER AMADOR, ÁNGEL. 2017. *El libro sefardí 'La güerta de oro' de David M. Atías (Liorna, 1778)*, Hispanica Helvetica 29 (Lausanne: Sociedad Suiza de Estudios Hispánicos)

BERNET, ANNE. 2012. *Frédégonde: épouse de Chilpéric Ier*, Histoire des reines de France (Paris: Pygmalion)

BNE: Madrid, Biblioteca Nacional de España, MS 1014E

BOGGS, RALPH S. 1930. *Index of Spanish Folktales*, Folklore Fellow Communications, 99 (Helsinki: Academia Scientiarum Fennica)

BORATAV, PERTEV NAILÎ. 1955. *Contes turcs* (Paris: Éditions Erasme)

BORNES-VAROL, MARIE-CHRISTINE. 2013. 'Hayim ben Bejarano: *maskil*, lecteur et collaborateur de presse', in *La presse judéo-espagnole: support et vecteur de la modernité*, ed. by Rosa Sánchez and Marie-Christine Bornes-Varol (Istanbul: Libra), pp. 281–94

——1995. 'Djoha juif dans l'Empire ottoman', *Revue du Mondes Musulman et de la Méditerranée*, 77–78: 61–74

BOROVAYA, OLGA. 2017. *The Beginnings of Ladino Literature: Moses Almosnino and his Readers* (Bloomington and Indianapolis: Indiana University Press)

——2012. *Modern Ladino Culture: Press, Belles Lettres and Theater in the Late Ottoman Empire* (Bloomington and Indianapolis: Indiana University Press)

BOŠKOVIĆ-STULLI, MAJA. 1967. *Narodna predaja o vladarevoj tajni* (Zagreb: Institut za narodnu umjetnost)

BRADBURY, JONATHAN DAVID. 2017. *Miscellany of the Spanish Golden Age. A literature of fragments* (Abingdon and New York: Routledge)

——2010. 'The "Miscelánea" of the Spanish Golden Age: An Unstable Label', *Modern Language Review*, 105: 954–72

BRAGINSKI', I. 1957. 'Predislovie', in *Anekdoty o Khodzhe Nasreddine*, ed. by Velet Izbudak, trans. by V. A. Gordlevski' (Moskva: Vostochno' lit-ry), pp. 3–14

BRANCAFORTE, BENITO (ed.). 1990. *'Las Metamorfosis' y 'Las heroidas' de Ovidio en la 'General Estoria' de Alfonso el Sabio* (Madison: Hispanic Seminary of Medieval Studies)

BURNS, ROBERT I. 2001. *Las siete partidas*, trans. by Samuel Parsons Scott, Middle Ages Series, 5 vols (Philadelphia: University of Pennsylvania Press)

BUXÓ REY, M. JESÚS. 1988. *Antropología de la mujer: cognición, lengua e ideología cultural* (Barcelona: Anthropos)

CACHÍA, PIERRE. 1992. 'Andalusī Belles Lettres', in *The Legacy of Muslim Spain*, ed. by Salma Khadra Jayyusi, 2 vols (Leiden: Brill), 1: 307–16

CAMARENA, JULIO and MAXIME CHEVALIER. 2003. *Catálogo tipológico del cuento folklórico español (cuentos religiosos)* (Madrid: Gredos)

CAMHY, GINA, SEE *Part II* for a complete list of her publications

CARR, Derek C. 2005. 'El lenguaje y el léxico de *Los morales de Ovidio* [BN, MS. 10144]: unas observaciones preliminares', in *Deja hablar a los textos: Homenaje a Francisco Márquez Villanueva*, ed. by Pedro M. Piñero Ramírez (Sevilla: Universidad de Sevilla), pp. 193–202

CATALÁN, DIEGO and OTHERS (eds). 1982–84. *Catálogo General del Romancero pan-Hispánico*, 3 vols (Madrid: Seminario Menéndez Pidal)

CATALÁN, DIEGO. 2001. *El archivo del romancero: patrimonio de la humanidad: historia documentada de un siglo de historia*, 2 vols (Madrid: Fundación Ramón Menéndez Pidal and Universidad Complutense de Madrid)

——1972. 'El romance tradicional un sistema abierto', in *El romancero en la tradición oral moderna*, ed. by Diego Catalán, Samuel G. Armistead and Antonio Sánchez Romeralo (Madrid: Cátedra-Seminario Menéndez Pidal)

CATARELLA, TERESA. 1990. 'Feminine Historicizing in the *Romancero Novelesco*', *Bulletin of Hispanic Studies*, 67.4: 331–43

CHEVALIER, MAXIME. 1983. *Cuentos folklóricos en la España del Siglo de Oro* (Barcelona: Editorial Crítica)

CHRISTENSEN, ARTHUR. 1922. 'Jūhī in the Persian Literature', in *A Volume of Oriental Studies Presented to Edward G. Browne on his 60th Birthday (7 February 1922)*, ed. by T. W. Arnold and Reynold A. Nicholson (Cambridge: University Press), pp. 129–36

CIXOUS, HÉLÈNE. 1989. *L'heure de Clarice Lispector: précédé de Vivre l'orange* (Paris: Des femmes)

——1981. 'Castration or Decapitation?', *Signs: Journal of Women in Culture and Society*, 7.1: 41–55

——1980. *Illa* (Paris: Des femmes)

COBBY, ANNE ELIZABETH. 2009. *The Old French Fabliaux: An Analytical Bibliography* (Woodbridge: Tamesis)

COHEN, MARK. 2003. *Last Century of a Sephardic Community: The Jews of Monastir, 1839–1943* (New York: Foundation for the Advancement of Sephardic Studies and Culture)

COHEN, JUDITH. 1995. 'Women's Roles in Judeo-Spanish Song Traditions', in *Active Voices: Women in Jewish Culture*, ed. by Maurie Sacks (Urbana, Chicago: University of Illinois Press), pp. 182–200

CONFINO, JACQUES. 1957. 'Djuha, pasha de la madre', *Le Judaïsme Sephardi*, 14: 642–43

CORREAS, GONZALO. 1967. *Vocabulario de refranes y frases proverbiales*, ed. by Louis Combet (Bordeaux: Féret et fils)

CORRIENTE, FEDERICO. 1999. 'Arabismos peculiares del judeo-español (de Salónica)', *Estudios de dialectología norteafricana y andalusí*, 4: 65–81

COX, JOHN K. 2002. *The History of Serbia* (Westport, CT and London: Greenwood Press)

CREWS, CYNTIA M. 1979. 'Textos judeo-españoles de Salónica y Sarajevo con comentarios lingüísticos y glosario', *Estudios Sefardíes*, 2: 91–258

—— 1935. *Recherches sur le judéo-espagnol dans les pays balkaniques* (Paris: E. Droz)

CURTIUS, ERNST ROBERT. 1976. *Literatura europea y Edad Media Latina*, trans. by Margit Frenk Alatorre and Antonio Alatorre, 2 vols (Mexico-Madrid-Buenos Aires: Fondo de Cultura Económica)

ČAMPARA, E. 1967. 'Laura Papo Bohoreta', in *Jevrejski almanah 1965–67* (Belgrade: Savez jevrejskih opština Jugoslavije), pp. 136–44

DAGKAS, ALEXANDROS. 2003. *Recherches sur l'histoire sociale de la Grèce du Nord. Le mouvement des ouvriers du tabac 1918–1928* (Paris: Association Pierre Belon)

DAMIÁN CANO, PEDRO. 2004. *Al-Andalus: el Islam y los pueblos ibéricos* (Madrid: Sílex)

DANON, ABRAHAM. 1903. 'Proverbes judéo-espagnols de Turquie', *Zeitschrift für Romanische Philologie*, 27: 72–96

DANON, CADIK. 1996. *Zbrika pojmova iz judiazma* (Belgrade: Savez jevrejskih opština Jugoslavije)

DAVIČO, HAIM S. 2000. *Priče sa Jalije*, ed. by Vasa Pavković (Belgrade: Centar za stvaralaštvo mladih)

—— 1913. 'Buena — priča i slika sa Jalije', *Delo*, 66.2: 161–72; 66.3: 361–70; 67.1: 20–31; 67.2: 181–90

—— 1904. *Iz mrzosti u — pakost!* (Belgrade: Štamparija ' Kod Prosvete')

—— 1898. *Sa Jalije. Naumi — Luna — Perla* (Belgrade: Izdanje knjižare D. M. Đorića)

—— 1895. 'Jedne večeri na Jaliji', in *Vojislavljeva spomenica* (Belgrade: Štamparija Kraljevine Srbije), pp. 36–39

—— 1892. 'Jalijske poslovice', *Otadžbina*, 32.129: 654–65

—— 1891. 'Perla: slika iz beogradske jevrejske male', *Otadžbina*, 29.115: 333–58

—— 1900. 'Jovan Dimović, učitelj u Trstu', *Bosanska Vila*, 15 September, 17: 225–27

—— 1888. 'Jalijske zimske noći: Luna', *Otadžbina*, 20.79: 345–56

—— 1885. 'Ženske šale: španjolska priča tije Bohore la Komerčere sa beogradske Jalije', *Videlo*, 41; 43; 45–50

—— 1883. 'Naumi: jalijska noveleta', *Otadžbina*, 14.55: 321–36

—— 1881. 'Slike iz jevrejskog života na Jaliji beogradskoj', *Otadžbina*, 7.26: 296–301

DAVIS, STUART. 2012. *Writing and Heritage in Contemporary Spain: The Imaginary Museum of Literature* (Woodbridge: Tamesis)

DETWEILER, ROBERT. 1974. 'The Jesus Jokes: Religious Humor in the Age of Excess', *Cross Currents*, 24: 55–74

DÍAZ-MAS, PALOMA and MARÍA SÁNCHEZ-PÉREZ. 2013. *Los sefardíes y la poesía tradicional hispánica del siglo XVIII: el 'Cancionero de Abraham Israel' (Gibraltar, 1761–1770)* (Madrid: Consejo Superior de Investigaciones Científicas)

——2010. 'Los sefardíes ante los retos del mundo contemporáneo', in *Los sefardíes ante los retos del mundo contemporáneo: identidad y mentalidades*, ed. by Paloma Díaz-Mas and María Sánchez-Pérez (Madrid: Consejo Superior de Investigaciones Científicas), pp. 11–29

DÍAZ-MAS, PALOMA and CRISTINA DE LA PUENTE. 2007. *Judaísmo e islam* (Barcelona: Crítica)

DÍAZ-MAS, PALOMA. 2009A. 'Folk Literature among Sephardic Bourgeois Women at the Beginning of the Twentieth Century', *European Journal of Jewish Studies*, 3.1: 81–101

——2009B. 'Gordana Kuić: la memoria de las mujeres sefardíes de Bosnia', *Arbor*, 185.A1: 55–79

——2008. 'Las mujeres sefardíes del Norte de Marruecos y el ocaso de la tradición oral (siglos XIX y XX)', *El Prezente: Studies in Sephardic Culture*, 2: 255–66

——2007. 'Cuadernos de mujeres: el cuaderno de Clara Benoudis y otras colecciones manuscritas de cantares tradicionales sefardíes', in *Romances de Alcácer Quibir*, ed. by Kelly Benoudis Basilio (Lisbon: Edições Colibri-Centro de Estudos Comparatistas), pp. 187–200

——2006. *Los sefardíes: historia, lengua y cultura* (Barcelona: Riopiedras)

——(ed.). 2005. *Romancero* (Barcelona: Crítica)

——1989. 'La mención de Granada en los romances sefardíes de Marruecos', in *Literatura hispánica, Reyes Católicos y descubrimiento: actas del Congreso Internacional sobre literatura hispánica en la época de los Reyes Católicos y el descubrimiento*, ed. by Manuel Criado de Val (Barcelona: Promociones y Publicaciones Universitarias), pp. 191–200

——1982. *Temas y tópicos en la poesía luctuosa sefardí* (Madrid: Universidad Complutense)

——1981. 'Romances sefardíes de endechar', in *Actas de las jornadas de estudios sefardíes: [Cáceres 24–26 marzo 1980]*, ed. by Antonio Viudas Camarasa (Cáceres: Universidad de Extremadura), pp. 99–105

DJORDJEVIĆ, TIHOMIR R. 1939A. 'Džuha u predanju Španskih Jevreja u Beogradu', *Glasnik etnografskog muzeja u Beogradu*, 14: 15–19

——1939B. 'Nasr-edin hodža u Bosni', *Prilozi za književnost, jezik, istoriju i folklor*, 19.1–2: 153

——1937. 'Nasr-edin hodža i Arnauti', *Prilozi za književnost, jezik, istoriju i folklor*, 17.2: 270

——1933. *Ciganske narodne pripovetke* (Belgrade: izdanje knjižarnice Radomira D. Ćukovića)

DODDS, JERRILYNN D., MARÍA ROSA MENOCAL and ABIGAIL KRASNER BALBALE (eds). 2008. *The Arts of Intimacy: Christians, Jews, and Muslims in the Making of Castilian Culture* (New Haven and London: Yale University Press)

DRORY, RINA. 2000. 'The Maqama', in *The Literature of al-Andalus*, ed. by María Rosa Menocal, Raymond P. Scheindlin and Michael Sells (Cambridge: Cambridge University Press), pp. 190–210

——1998. 'Hebrew Literature, Relations with Arabic', in *Encyclopedia of Arabic Literature*, ed. by Julie Scott Meisami and Paul Starkey, 2 vols (London and New York: Routledge), 1: 281–83

DUBLIN, LOIS. 1999. *The Port Jews of Habsburg Trieste: Absolutist Politics and Enlightenment Culture* (Stanford: Stanford University Press)

EAGLETON, TERRY. 2007. *Ideology: An Introduction* (London: Verso)

ELAZAR, SAMUEL M. 1987. *El romancero judeo-español: romances y otras poesías* (Sarajevo: Svjetlost)

ENDELMAN, TODD M. 2007. 'Secularization and the Origins of Jewish Modernity: On the Impact of Urbanization and Social Transformation', in *Early Modern Culture and Haskalah: Reconsidering the Borderlines of Modern Jewish History*, ed. by David B. Ruderman and Shmuel Feiner, Special Issue, *Jahrbuch des Simon-Dubnow-Instituts*, 6: 155–68

ESPINOSA, AURELIO M. 1946. *Cuentos populares españoles*, 3 vols (Madrid: Consejo Superior de Investigaciones Científicas)

FEINER, SHMUEL. 2010. *The Origins of Jewish Secularization in Eighteenth-Century Europe* (Philadelphia and Oxford: University of Pennsylvania Press)

——2002. *Haskalah and History: The Emergence of a Modern Jewish Historical Consciousness* (Oxford and Portland, Oregon: The Littman Library of Jewish Civilization)

FILIPOVIĆ, JELENA and IVANA VUČINA SIMOVIĆ. 2010. 'La lengua como recurso social: el caso de las mujeres sefardíes de los Balcanes', in *Los sefardíes ante los retos del mundo contemporáneo: identidad y mentalidades*, ed. by Paloma Díaz-Mas and María Sánchez-Pérez (Madrid: Consejo Superior de Investigaciones Científicas), pp. 259–69

FLETCHER, R. A. 1992. *Moorish Spain* (London: Weidenfeld and Nicolson)

FONTES, MANUEL DA COSTA. 1997. *O romanceiro português e brasileiro: índice temático e bibliográfico (com uma bibliografia pan-hispânica e resumos de cada romance en inglês)*, 2 vols (Madison: Hispanic Seminary of Medieval Studies)

FOULCHÉ-DELBOSC R. (ed). 1924. 'Les cancionerillos de Prague', *Revue Hispanique*, 61: 463–64

——1895. 'Proverbes judéo-espagnols', *Revue Hispanique*, 2: 312–52

FREIDENREICH PASS, HARRIET. 1979. *The Jews of Yugoslavia* (Philadelphia: The Jewish Publication Society of America)

FREYTAG, G. W. (ed.). 1838–43. *Arabum proverbia*, 3 vols (Bonnae ad Rhenum: A. Marcum), I: 403

GAON, MOSHE DAVID. 1965. *A Bibliography of the Judeo-Spanish (Ladino) Press* [in Hebrew] (Tel Aviv: Monoline Press)

GARCÍA GÓMEZ, EMILIO. 1969. *Antología árabe para principiantes: textos árabes sin vocalizar, seleccionados y reeditados con un glosario* (Madrid: Espasa-Calpe)

GARCÍA MORENO, AITOR. 2014. 'Glosas de andar por casa en los cuentos sefardíes tradicionales recogidos por Cynthia Crews en Salónica a principios del siglo XX', *Ladinar: estudios sobre la literatura, la música y la historia de los sefardíes*, 7–8: 95–112

——2013. 'Les gloses comme sources pour l'étude du lexique judéo-espagnol: l'exemple de *Luzero de la Pasensia* (Roumanie)', in *Recensement, analyse et traitement numérique des sources écrites pour les études séfarades*, ed. by Soufiane Roussi and Ana Stulic-Etchevers (Bordeaux: Presses universitaires de Bordeaux), pp. 249–71

——2010. 'Glosas frescas en *La hermośa Hulda de España* (Jerusalén, 1910)', in *Los sefardíes ante los retos del mundo contemporáneo: identidad y mentalidades*, ed. by Paloma Díaz-Mas and María Sánchez-Pérez (Madrid: Consejo Superior de Investigaciones Científicas), pp. 75–85

GARCÍA-RIPOLL, MARTÍ. 1993. 'Els sefardites a Bòsnia-Hercegovina. Història d'un retorn', in *Actes del Simposi Internacional sobre Cultura Sefardita*, ed. by Josep Ribera (Barcelona: PPU), pp. 69–72

GEDALJA, NAFTALI BATA. 1931. 'Veliki uspjeh Matatje u Beogradu', *Jevrejski glas*, 20 March, 12: 2

GIL, JOSÉ S. 1985. *La escuela de traductores de Toledo y los colaboradores judíos* (Toledo: Instituto Provincial de Investigaciones y Estudios Toledanos)

GITLITZ, DAVID M., and LINDA KAY DAVIDSON. 1999. *A Drizzle of Honey: The Lives and Recipes of Spain's Secret Jews* (New York: St. Martin's Press)

GOLDBERG, HARRIET. 1993. 'The Judeo-Spanish Proverb and its Narrative Context', *PMLA*, 108.1: 106–20

GOLDSTEIN, KENNETH. 1964. *A Guide for Field Workers in Folklore* (Hatboro: Folklore Associates)

GÓMEZ ACUÑA, BEATRIZ. 2002. 'The Feminine Voice in the *Romancero*'s Modern Oral Tradition: Gender Differences in the Recitation of the Ballad *La bastarda y el segador*', *Folklore*, 113.2: 183–96

GORDLEVSKI', V. A. 1957. 'Khodzhe Nasreddin', in *Anekdoty o Khodzhe Nasreddine*, ed. by Velet Izbudak, trans. by V. A. Gordlevski' (Moskva: Vostochno' lit-ry), pp. 242–58

GRANDAKOVSKA, SOFIJA (ed.). 2011. *The Jews form Macedonia and the Holocaust: History, Theory, Culture* (Skopje: Euro Balkan Press)

GRANJA, FERNANDO DE LA. 1971. 'Nuevas notas a un episodio del *Lazarillo de Tormes*', *Al-Andalus: revista de las escuelas de estudios árabes de Madrid y Granada*, 36: 223–37

GUASTAVINO GALLENT, GUILLERMO. 1959. 'Notas tirsianas', *Revista de Archivos, Bibliotecas y Museos*, 67: 688–96

GUERRA CASTELLANOS, EDUARDO. 1971. 'La mujer, motivo central en el "Romancero popular galego de tradizón oral"', *Humanitas*, 12: 97–110

GUŠIĆ, SEJDALIJA, EDINA SPAHIĆ and CECILIA PRENZ KOPUŠAR (eds). 2015. *Laura Papo Bohoreta, rukopisi*, vol. 1 (Sarajevo: Historijski arhiv-Filozofski fakultet)

—— 2016. *Laura Papo Bohoreta, rukopisi*, vol. 2 (Sarajevo: Historijski arhiv-Filozofski fakultet)

GUTIÉRREZ ESTÉVEZ, MANUEL. 1981. *El incesto en el romancero popular hispánico: un ensayo de análisis estructural*, 3 vols (Madrid: Universidad Complutense), I: 69–352; III: 5–508

HABOUCHA, REGINETTA. 2004. 'Preface', in Matilda Koén-Sarano, *King Solomon and the Golden Fish* (Detroit: Wayne State University Press), pp. 19–22

—— 1995. 'The Midas Legend in Sephardic Context', in *Oral Tradition and Hispanic Literature: Essays in Honor of Samuel G. Armistead*, ed. by Mishael M. Caspi (New York and London: Garland Publishing), pp. 323–40

—— 1992. *Types and Motifs of the Judeo-Spanish Folktales* (New York and London: Garland Publishing)

HADAR, GILA. 2006. 'Space and Time in Salonika on the Eve of World War II and the Expulsion and Extermination of Salonika Jewry', *Yalkut Moreshet*, 4: 42–80

HARDING, SUZEN. 2003. 'Žene i reči u jednom španskom selu', in *Antropologija žene*, ed. by Žarana Papić and Lydia Sklevicky, trans. by Branko Vučićević (Belgrade: Čigoja štampa), pp. 268–91

HARRIS, TRACY K. 2006. '*Death of a Language* Revisited: Reactions, Results and Maintenance Efforts on Behalf of Judeo-Spanish since 1994', in *Proceedings of the Thirteenth British Conference on Judeo-Spanish Studies: 7–9 September, 2003*, ed. by Hilary Pomeroy (London: Queen Mary, University of London), pp. 63–74

—— 1994. *Death of a Language: The History of Judeo-Spanish* (Newark and London: University of Delaware Press and Associated University Presses)

HASSÁN, IACOB M. 2010. *Las coplas de Purim* (Madrid: Casa Sefarad-Israel and Hebraica Ediciones)

HAYWOOD, LOUISE M., SÁNDOR HERVEY and MICHAEL THOMPSON. 2009. *Thinking Spanish Translation: A Course in Translation Method, Spanish to English* (London: Routledge)

HAYWOOD, LOUISE. 2008. *Sex, Scandal and Sermon in Fourteenth-Century Spain: Juan Ruiz's Libro de Buen Amor* (Basingstoke: Palgrave Macmillan)

HEATH, PETER. 2000. 'Knowledge', in *The Literature of al-Andalus*, ed. by María Rosa Menocal, Raymond P. Scheindlin and Michael Sells (Cambridge: Cambridge University Press), pp. 96–125

HIKMET, MURAT. 1959. *One Day the Hodja* (Ankara: Tarhan)

HOARE, MARKO ATTILA. 2007. *The History of Bosnia: From the Middle Ages to the Present Day* (London: Saqi)

HUFFORD, MARY, MARJORIE HUNT and STEVEN ZEITLIN (eds). 1987. *The Grand Generation: Memory, Mastery, Legacy* (Seattle: University of Washington Press)

IBN ʿĀṢIM. 2019. *El libro de los huertos en flor (Ḥadāʾiq al-azāhir). Cuentos, refranes y anécdotas de la Granada nazarí*, translation, preliminary study and notes by Desirée López Bernal (Granada: Universidad de Granada)

IBN AL-FARADĪ. 1992. *Kitāb al-alqāb*, ed. by Muhammad Zaynahum Muhammad ʿAzab (Beirut: Dār al-Ŷīl)

ISAKOVIĆ, ALIJA (ed.). 1984. *Nasrudin Hodža* (Sarajevo: Svjetlost)

JALĀL AL-DĪN RŪMĪ, MAULANA. 1963. *More Tales from Masnavi*, trans. by A. J. Arberry (London: George Allen and Unwin)

——1961. *Tales from the Masnavi*, trans. by A. J. Arberry (London: George Allen and Unwin)

JIM MS BINJO SAMOKOVLIJA (1956): Belgrade, Jevrejski istorijski muzej, Binjo Samokovlija, '*Refranim*: Poslovice Sefardskih Jevreja na Balkanu prikupio od 1940 god. Samokovlija Binjo, Sarajevo'

JOVANOVIĆ, NEBOJŠA. 1992. 'Pregled istorije beogradskih Jevreja do sticanja građanske ravnopravnosti', in *Zbornik 6: Studije, arhivska i memoarska građa o istoriji beogradskih Jevreja*, ed. by Radovan Samardžić (Belgrade: Savez jevrejskih opština Jugoslavije and Jevrejski istorijski muzej), pp. 115–67

JOVANOVIĆ, ŽELJKO. 2018A. 'Judaisation of a Hispanic Ballad: *Landarico* in the Works of Haim S. Davico and Laura Papo Bohoreta from the Former Yugoslavia', *Abenámar: Cuadernos de la Fundación Ramón Menéndez Pidal*, 2: 43–66

——2018B. 'Two Stories of King Midas in the Judeo-Spanish Speaking World: Isak Papo and Matilda Koén-Sarano's Versions of the ATU782 "Midas and the Donkey's Ears", and ATU775 "Midas' Short-sighted Wish"', *Boletín de literatura oral*, 8: 9–20

——2016. 'Gina Camhy: una primera aproximación a la vida y obra de la autora sefardí de Bosnia', in *Mujeres sefardíes lectoras y escritoras*, ed. by Paloma Díaz-Mas and Elisa Martín Ortega, Collection Tiempo Emulado, no. 49 (Madrid and Fankfurt: Iberoamericana-Vervuert), pp. 221–40

——2014A. 'El cuento de las orejas de Midas entre los sefardíes de Bosnia: contactos culturales', *Ladinar: estudios sobre la literatura, la música y la historia de los sefardíes*, 7–8: 135–48

——2014B. 'Haim Davičo's Text *Ženske Šale* (*Women's Jokes*): A Sephardic Folktale Or a Serbian Translation of Tirso de Molina's *Los tres maridos burlados?*, *Bulletin of Spanish Studies*, 91.7: 981–1002

——2013. 'Le thème de l'inceste dans le romancero séfarade: une approche comparative', in *Recensement, analyse et traitement numérique des sources écrites pour les études séfarades*, ed. by Soufiane Rouissi and Ana Stulic (Bordeaux: Presses Universitaires de Bordeaux), pp. 287–312

JOVIČIĆ, VLADIMIR. 1979. *Časopis Otadžbina: 1875–1892* (Belgrade: Vuk Karadžić and Institut za književnost i umetnost)

KARPAT, KEMAL H. (ed.) 2000. *Ottoman Past and Today's Turkey* (Leiden, Boston and Kölon: Brill)

——(ed.) 1974. *The Ottoman State and its Place in World History* (Leiden: Brill)

KASPI, ANDRÉ (ed.). 2010. *Histoire de l'Alliance Israélite Universelle de 1860 à nos jours* (Paris: Armand Collin)

KAYSERLING, M. 1897. 'Quelques proverbes judéo-espagnols', *Revue Hispanique*, 4: 82

——1890. *Biblioteca española-portugueza-judaica: Dictionnaire bibliographique des auteurs juifs, de leurs ouvrages espagnols et portugais et des oeuvres sur et contre les juifs et le judaïsme: avec une aperçu sur la littérature des juifs espagnols et une collection des proverbes espagnols* (Strasbourg: Charles J. Trubner)

——1889. *Refranes ó proverbios españoles de los judíos españoles* (Budapest: Sr. C. L. Posner y hijo)

KIMBER, R. A. 1998. 'Ibn al-Nadīm', in *Encyclopedia of Arabic Literature*, ed. by Julie Scott Meisami and Paul Starkey, 2 vols (London and New York: Routledge), I: 355–56

KIVISTÖ, SARI. 2014. *The Vices of Learning: Morality and Knowledge at Early Modern Universities* (Leiden: Brill)

KOÉN-SARANO, MATILDA. 2013A. 'Soledad', *Aki Yerushalayim*, 94.34: 55

——2013B. 'Tanye, tanye, mandalino', *Aki Yerushalayim*, 93.34: 56

——2004A. *King Solomon and the Golden Fish: Tales from the Sephardic Tradition*, trans. by Reginetta Haboucha (Detroit: Wayne State University Press)

——2004B. *Kuentos del bel para abasho* (Istanbul: Gözlem Gazetecilik Basin ve Yayin A.S.)

——2003. *Folktales of Joha: Jewish Trickster*, trans. by David Herman (Philadelphia: Jewish Publication Society)

——2000. *Kuentos salados djudeo-espanyoles* (Valencia: Capitelum)

——1999. *Kurso de djudeo-espanyol (ladino) para prinsipiantes* (Jerusalem: Merkaz Eliachar and Universidad Ben-Gurion en el Negev)

——1996. 'Rodeos del mito del rey Midas en el kuento popular djudeo-espanyol', in *Hommage à Haïm Vidal Sephiha*, ed. by Winfried Busse and Marie-Christine Varol-Bornes (Berne: Peter Lang), pp. 115–23

——1991. *Djoha, ke dize?: kuentos populares djudeo-espanyoles* (Jerusalem: Kana)

——1986. *Kuentos del folklore de la famiya djudeo-espanyola* (Jerusalem: Kana)

KOHLER, KAUFMANN. 1902. 'Beelzebub or Beelzebul', in Cyrus Adler and Isidore Signer (eds.). 1901–06. *The Jewish Encyclopaedia: A Descriptive Record of the History, Religion, Literature, and Customs of the Jewish People from the Earliest Times to the Present Day*, 12 vols (New York and London: Funk and Wagnalls Company), II: 629–30

KOLONOMOS, JAMILA-ANDJELA and JASMINKA NAMICEVA. 2006. *Sinteyas de los sefardes de la Makedonia* (Skoplje: La komunita djudiya de la Makedonia)

KOLONOMOS, JAMILA-ANDJELA. 2008. *Monastir without Jews: Recollection of a Jewish Partisan in Macedonia*, trans. by Isaac Nehama and Brian Berman (New York: Foundation for the Advancement of Sephardic Studies and Culture)

——1978. *Poslovice, izreke i priče sefardskih Jevreja Makedonije/Proverbs, Sayings and Tales of the Sephardi Jews of Macedonia* (Belgrade: Savez jevrejskih opština Jugoslavije)

KONFINO, ŽAK. 1994. 'I Djoha onde esta?', *Aki Yerushalayim*, 50: 96–97

——1934. 'Džuha', *Politika*, 9 June, p. 14

KOSTIĆ, STANKA. 1971. 'Videlo', *Enciklopedija Jugoslavije*, 8 vols (Zagreb: Leksikografski zavod FNRJ), VIII: 491

KOVAČEVIĆ, NELA. 2018A. 'Introducción', in her *La mujer sefardí: cuentos, textos y poemas (Laura Papo Bohoreta)* (Granada: Universidad de Granada), pp. 19–42

——(ed.) 2018b. *La mujer sefardí: cuentos, textos y poemas (Laura Papo Bohoreta)* (Granada: Universidad de Granada)

——2014. 'El mundo sefardí en la obra de Laura Papo y el lugar de la mujer en él' (doctoral thesis, Universidad de Granada, 2014), <http://digibug.ugr.es/bitstream/10481/35123/1/24328698.pdf>

——2010. 'Laura Papo: la evolución de la mujer sefardí de Bosnia a partir de 1878', in *Los sefardíes ante los retos del mundo contemporáneo: identidad y mentalidades*, ed. by Paloma Díaz-Mas and María Sánchez-Pérez (Madrid: Consejo Superior de Investigaciones Científicas), pp. 283–91

KRAEMER, DAVID CHARLES. 2007. *Jewish Eating and Identity Throughout the Ages* (New York and London: Routledge)

KUIĆ, GORDANA. 2010. *Balada o Bohoreti* (Belgrade: Alnari)

——2004. *The Scent of Rain in the Balkans*, trans. by Richard Williams (Belgrade: Narodna knjiga)

KUSHNER, EVA and MILAN V. DIMIĆ (eds.). 1994. *Acculturation: Actes du XIe Congrès de l'Association Internationale de Littérature Comparée (Paris, 20–24 août 1985)*, (Bern: Peter Lang)

LANDMAN, ISAAK (ed.). 1969. 'Sukkot', in *The Universal Jewish Encyclopaedia in Ten Volumes: An Authoritative and Popular Presentation of Jews and Judaism since the Earliest Times*, ed. by Isaak Landman, 10 vols (New York: Ktav Publishing House), X: 94–97

LASKIER, MICHAEL M. 1982. 'The Alliance Israélite Universelle and the Struggle for Recognition within Moroccan Jewish Society: 1862–1912', in *The Sephardi and Oriental Jewish Heritage: Studies*, ed. by Issachar Ben-Ami (Jerusalem: The Magness Press), pp. 191–212

LEBEL, JENNIE. 2008. *Tide and Wreck: History of the Jews of Vardar Macedonia*, trans. by Paul Münch (Bergenfield: Avotaynu)

LEBL, ŽENI. 2001. *Do 'konačnog rešenja': Jevreji u Beogradu 1521–1942* (Belgrade: Čigoja)

LEITE DE VASCONCELLOS, JOSÉ (ed.). 1958. *Romanceiro Português*, I (Coimbra: Por Ordem da Universidade)

LEVI, MORIC. 1919. 'Sefardi u Bosni', *Židovska svijest*, 18: 2

LEVY, AVIGDOR. 1992. *The Sephardim in the Ottoman Empire* (Princeton, New Jersey: Darwin Press)

LEVY, DENAH. 1944. 'El sefardí de Nueva York: observaciones sobre el judeo-español de Esmirna' (unpublished master's thesis, Colombia University)

LÉVY, ISAAC JACK. 1989. *And the World Stood Silent: Sephardic Poetry of the Holocaust* (Urbana: University of Illinois Press)

LEVY ZUMWALT, ROSEMARY and ISAAC JACK LÉVY. 2001. 'Memories of Time Past: Fieldwork among the Sephardim', *The Journal of American Folklore*, 451.114: 40–55

LIEBL, CHRISTIAN. 2010. '*Avíe úne vez...*: Julius Subak, Max A. Luria and Phonographic Field Research among Sephardic Communities in the Balkans', in *Los sefardíes ante los retos del mundo contemporáneo: identidad y mentalidades*, ed. by Paloma Díaz-Mas and María Sánchez-Pérez (Madrid: Consejo Superior de Investigaciones Científicas), pp. 237–46

——2009. 'An Introduction to the Recordings by Julius Subak (1908) and Max A. Luria (1927)', in his *Judeo-Spanish from the Balkans: The Recordings by Julius Subak (1908) and Max A. Luria (1927)* (Vienna: WÖAW), pp. 13–16

——2007. 'Early Recordings of Judeo-Spanish in the Phonogrammarchiv of the Austrian Academy of Sciences', *Neue Romania*, 37.11: 7–26

LIROLA DELGADO, JORGE. 2004. 'Ibn al-Faradī, Abū l-Walīd', in *Enciclopedia de la cultura andalusí: biblioteca de al-Andalus, de Ibn al-Dabbāg a ibn Kurz*, ed. by Jorge Lirola Delgado and José Miguel Puerta Vílchez, 5 vols (Almería: Fundación Ibn Tufayl de Estudios Árabes), III: 95–111

LOVRENOVIĆ, IVAN. 2001. *Bosnia: A Cultural History*, trans. by Sonja Wild Bičanić (London: Saqi Books in association with the Bosnian Institute, London)

LURIA, MAX A. 1930. *The Study of the Monastir Dialect of Judeo-Spanish Based on Oral Material Collected in Monastir, Yugo-Slavia* (New York: Instituto de las Españas en los Estados Unidos)

MARISCAL DE RHETT, BEATRIZ. 1987. 'The Structure and Changing Functions of Oral Tradition', *Oral Tradition*, 2: 645–66

MARTINS, FIRMINO A. 1938. *Folklore do concelho de Vinhais* (Lisbon: Imprensa Nacional)

MARZOLPH, ULRICH. 1998. 'Juhā', in *Encyclopedia of Arabic Literature*, ed. by Julie Scott Meisami and Paul Starkey, 2 vols (London and New York: Routledge), I: 417–18

——1993. 'Nasr al-Dīn Khodja', in *The Encyclopaedia of Islam*, ed. by C. E. Bosworth, E. van Donzel, W. P. Heinrichs and Ch. Pellat, 12 vols (Leiden and New York: E. J. Brill), VII: 1018–20

MENÉNDEZ Y PELAYO, MARCELINO (ed.). 1916. *Antología de poetas líricos castellanos: tratado de los romances viejos*, 14 vols (Madrid: Librería de Perlado, Páez y C.ª), XII: 488–92

——1912?. *Antología de poetas líricos castellanos: romances viejos castellanos (primavera y flor de romances) publicada con una introducción y notas de D. Fernando José Wolf y D. Conrado Hofmann, 2da edición corregida y adicionada por D. Marcelino Menéndez y Pelayo*, 14 vols (Madrid: Librería de Hernando y Compañía), IX: 219–20

MENÉNDEZ PIDAL, RAMÓN (ed.). 1960. *Pliegos poéticos españoles en la Universidad de Praga*, 2 vols (Madrid: Centro de Estudios de Bibliografía y Bibliofilia), I: 330–31

——1956. 'Supervivencia del *Poema de Kudrun*: "chansons de geste" y baladas nórdicas', in his *Los godos y la epopeya española* (Madrid: Espasa-Calpe), pp. 89–173

——1953. *Romancero hispánico: hispano-portugués, americano y sefardí: teoría e historia*, 2 vols (Madrid: Espasa-Calpe)

—— 1928. *El romancero: teorías e investigaciones*, Biblioteca de ensayos, 3 (Madrid: Paez)

MENÉNDEZ PIDAL, GONZALO. 1951. 'Cómo trabajaron las escuelas alfonsíes', *Nueva revista de filología hispánica*, 4.5: 363–80

MENOCAL, MARÍA ROSA, RAYMOND P. SCHEINDLIN and MICHALE SELLS. 2000. *The Literature of Al-Andalus* (London and New York: Cambridge University Press)

MICHAEL, IAN. 1993. 'Factitious Flowers or Factitious Fossils?', in *'Al que buena hora naçió': Essays on the Spanish Epic and Ballad in Honour of Colin Smith*, ed. by Brian Powell (Liverpool: Liverpool University Press), pp. 91–105

MIHAILOVIĆ, MILICA. 1992. 'Dve stotine godina porodice Hajim-Davičo u Beogradu', in *Zbornik 6: Studije, arhivska i memoarska građa o istoriji beogradskih Jevreja*, ed. by Radovan Samardžić (Belgrade: Savez jevrejskih opština Jugoslavije and Jevrejski istorijski muzej), pp. 249–76

MILOŠEVIĆ, MIHAILO B. 1967. 'Hajim S. Davičo (1854–1918)', in *Jevrejski almanah 1965–1967* (Belgrade: Savez jevrejskih opština Jugoslavije), pp. 129–35

MINERVINI, LAURA. 2006. 'El desarrollo histórico del judeoespañol', *Revista Internacional de Lingüística Iberoamericana-RILI*, 8: 13–34

—— 1999. 'The Formation of the Judeo-Spanish Koiné: Dialect Convergence in the Sixteenth Century', in *Proceedings of the Tenth British Conference on Judeo-Spanish Studies, 29 June–1 July 1997*, ed. by Annette Benaim (London: Department of Hispanic Studies Queen Mary and Westfield College), pp. 41–54

MIRKOVIĆ, MILOSAV. 1953. 'Žak Konfino: 100 godina 90 groša', *Letopis Matice srpske*, 371.3: 238–39

MIRON, DAN. 1973. *A Traveler Disguised: A Study in the Rise of Modern Yiddish Fiction in the Nineteenth Century* (New York: Schocken Books)

MOLHO, MICHAEL. 1960. *Literatura sefardita de Oriente* (Madrid: Consejo Superior de Investigaciones Científicas and Instituto Arias Montano)

—— 1950. *Usos y costumbres de los sefardíes de Salónica*, trans. by F. Pérez Castro (Madrid and Barcelona: Consejo Superior de Investigaciones Científicas and Instituto Arias Montano)

MONTES ROMERO-CAMACHO, ISABEL. 2001. *Los judíos en la Edad Media española* (Madrid: Arco Libros)

MUJEZINOVIĆ, MEHMED. 1987. 'Uvod', in Mula Mustafa Ševki Bašeskija, *Ljetopis (1746–1804)*, trans. by Mehmed Mujezinović (Sarajevo: Veselin Masleša), pp. 5–24

MUNDAY, JEREMY. 2001. *Introducing Translation Studies: Theories and Applications* (London: Routledge)

NAVÓN, ITSHAK. 1986. 'Prezentasión', in Matilda Koén-Sarano, *Kuentos del folklore de la famiya djudeo-espanyola* (Jerusalem: Kana), p. 13

NEHAMA, JOSEPH. 1977. *Dictionnaire du judeo-espagnol* (Madrid: Consejo Superior de Investigaciones Científicas and Instituto Arias Montano)

NENIN, MILIVOJ. 2007. 'Haim S. Davičo', in *Srpski biografski rečnik*, ed. by Čedomir Popov and others, 3 vols (Novi Sad: Matica srpska), I: 59

NEZIROVIĆ, MUHAMED. 1992. *Jevrejsko-španjolska književnost* (Sarajevo: Svjetlost)

—— 1986. 'El cancionero de los romances judeo-españoles de Sarajevo de Laura Papo-Bojoreta', *Lingüística*, 26: 115–30

ODD, FRANK L. 1983. 'Women of the *Romancero*: A Voice of Reconciliation', *Hispania*, 66: 360–68

OHRANOVIĆ, FUAD, SEJDALIJA GUŠIČ, EDINA SPAHIČ and CECILIA PRENZ KOPUŠAR (eds). 2017. *Laura Papo Bohoreta, rukopisi*, vol. 3 (Sarajevo: Historijski arhiv-Filozofski fakultet)

OLSON, GLENDING, 1982. *Literature as Recreation in the Later Middle Ages* (Ithaca, NY and London: Cornell University Press)

OVIDIO. 2005. *Metamorfosis*, ed. by Consuelo Álvarez and Rosa María Iglesias (Madrid: Cátedra)

PAPO, ELIEZER. 2016. 'Avia de ser, escena de la vida de un tiempo, kon romansas, de Laura Papo Bohoreta: Edision sientifika, anotada i komentada', in *Mujeres sefardíes lectoras y escritoras: siglos XIX–XXI*, ed. by Paloma Díaz-Mas and Elisa Martín Ortega, Collection Tiempo Emulado, no. 49 (Madrid and Frankfurt: Iberoamericana-Vervuert), pp. 339–64

——2013A. 'German Influences on Bosnian Spoken Judeo-Spanish', in *Sefarad an der Donau: lengua y literatura de los sefardíes en tierras del Habsburgo*, ed. by M. Studemunt-Halévy and others (Barcelona: Tirocinio), pp. 295–312

——2013B. 'Laura Papo-Bohoreta: Kommentierte Forschungsbibliographie zum literarischen Werk einer bosnischen Sefardin', *Transversal: Zeitschrift für Jüdische Studien*, 13.2: 65–80

——2012. 'Estado de la investigación y bibliografía anotada de la obra literaria de Laura Papo "Bohoreta"', *Sefarad*, 72.1: 123–44

——2011. 'Entre la modernidad y la tradición, el feminismo y la patriarquía: vida y obra de Laura Papo "Bohoreta", primera dramaturga en lengua judeo-española', *Neue Romania*, 40: 89–107

PAPO, ISAK, RIKICA OVADIJA, GINA CAMHY and CLARISSE NIKOÏDSKI. 1994. *Cuentos sobre los sefardíes de Sarajevo / A Collection of Sephardim Stories from Sarajevo*, ed. Isak Papo, trans. by Zjena Ćulić and Myrna Svičarević (Split: Logos)

PAPO, ISAK. 2010. 'Neke karakteristike jezičkog fundusa djudeoespanjola (tuđice i poslovice)', in *Jevrejskošpanski jezik u Bosni i Hercegovini*, ed. by Eli Tauber (Sarajevo: Institut za jezik)

——1995. 'Turcizmi u jevrejsko-španjolskom Sefarada Bosne i Hercegovine', in *Sefarad '92: zbornik radova*, ed. by Muhamed Nezirović, Boris Nilević and Muhsin Rizvić (Sarajevo: Institut za istoriju Sarajevo and Jevrejska zajednica Bosne i Hercegovine), pp. 241–52

——1987A. 'Il dukadu infurkadu', *Aki Yerushalayim*, 34–35: 77

——1987B. 'La vingansa di lus talimidim', *Aki Yerushalayim*, 34–35: 78

PAPO, LAURA. 2012. *Esterka: drama en tres actos en judeoespañol de la comunidad sefardí de Bosnia*, ed. by Ana Cecilia Prenz Kopušar (Sarajevo: Biblioteca Orbis Tertius and Historijski Arhiv Sarajevo)

——2005. *La mužer sefardi de Bosna. Sefardska žena u Bosni*, trans. by M. Nezirović (Sarajevo: Connectum)

——CLASSMARK: 821.163.4.292, BIBLIOTEKA JEVREJSKE OPŠTINE SARAJEVA, SARAJEVO, PHOTOCOPY OF LAURA PAPO, *Avia de ser: escena de la vida de un tiempo kon romansas en un akto*, classmark O-BP-168, Historijski arhiv Sarajevo, Sarajevo

——1929. 'Por esto akea vieža no se kižo murir', *Jevrejski glas*, 4 October, 30: 9–10

PAVKOVIĆ, VASA. 2000. 'Predgovor: pripovedač Hajim S. Davičo', in Hajim S. Davičo, *Priče sa Jalije*, ed. by Vasa Pavković (Belgrade: Centar za stvaralaštvo mladih), pp. 5–17

PEDROSA, JOSÉ MANUEL. 2012. 'El pájaro que entró por la boca y salió por el culo de un hombre: mitos y cuentos africanos e internacionales (de ATU 235C★ a ATU 715A)', *Quaderns*, 28: 127–52

PELLAT, CHARLES. 1965. 'Djuḥā', in *The Encyclopaedia of Islam*, ed. by B. Lewis, Ch. Pellat and J. Schacht, 12 vols (Leiden and London: E. J. Brill and Luzac), II: 590–92

PEÑA MARTÍN, SALVADOR. 2007. 'Ibn al-Šayj al-Balawī, Yusuf', in *Enciclopedia de la cultura andalusí: biblioteca de al-Andalus: de Ibn Sa'āda a ibn Wuhayb*, ed. by Jorge Lirola Delgado, 5 vols (Almería: Fundación Ibn Tufayl de Estudios Árabes), V: 274–90

PEREZ, AVNER and GLADYS PIMIENTA. 2007. *Diksionario amplio djudeo-espanyol-ebreo: Lashon me-Aspamia* (Maale-Adumim: Sefarad and La Autoridad Nasionala del Ladino i su Kultura)

PÉREZ, JOSEPH. 1993. *Historia de una tragedia: la expulsión de los judíos de España* (Barcelona: Crítica Grijalbo Comerc)

PEREZ, YOEL SHALOM. 2004. 'Preamble', in Matilda Koén-Sarano, *King Solomon and the Golden Fish* (Detroit: Wayne State University Press), pp. 15–17

PETERSEN, SUZZANE H. (ed.). 1982. *Voces nuevas del romancero castellano-leonés* (Madrid: Gredos)

PETROVICH, MICHAEL BORO. 1976. *A History of Modern Serbia: 1804–1918*, 2 vols (New York and London: Harcourt Brace Jovanovich)

PINTO, AVRAM. 1987. *Jevreji Sarajeva i Bosne i Hercegovine* (Sarajevo: Veselin Masleša)

PIÑERO RAMÍREZ, PEDRO M. (ed). 2008. *Romancero* (Madrid: Biblioteca Nueva)

——2001. 'La configuración poética de la versión *vulgata* de *Don Bueso*', in *Sevilla y la literatura: homenaje al profesor Francisco López Estrada en su 80 cumpleaños*, ed. by Rogelio Reyes Cano, Mercedes de los Reyes Peña and Klaus Wagner (Sevilla: Universidad de Sevilla), pp. 109–32

PIRES DA CRUZ, JOSÉ. 1988. *Estudos sobre o Romanceiro Tradicional: Tradição Oral das Beiras* (unpublished doctoral thesis, University of California, Davis)

POMEROY, HILARY. 2006. '"Ojos de berenjena": Some Literary Links Between Food and Religious Identity', in *Proceeding of the Thirteenth British Conference on Judeo-Spanish Studies*, ed. by Hilary Pomeroy (London: Department of Hispanic Studies, Queen Mary, University of London), pp. 137–49

——2005. *An Edition and Study of the Secular Ballads in the Sephardic Ballad Notebook of Halia Isaac Cohen* (Newark: Juan de la Cuesta)

POPOVIĆ, DANIJELA M. 2010. 'Narodna književnost u istraživanjima Tihomira R. Djordjevića' (unpublished doctoral thesis, University of Belgrade)

POPOVIĆ, MIROSLAV. 2010. 'Ličnost Hajima S. Daviča', in *Zbornik radova Pravnog fakulteta Novi Sad*, 44.1: 237–42

PRENZ KOPUŠAR, ANA CECILIA. 2012. 'Introducción', in Laura Papo Bohoreta, *Esterka: drama en tres actos en judeoespañol de la comunidad sefardí de Bosnia*, ed. by Ana Cecilia Prenz Kopušar (Sarajevo: Biblioteca Orbis Tertius and Historijski Arhiv Sarajevo), pp. 3–19

PRENZ, JUAN OCTAVIO. 1968. 'Vicisitudes del judeo-español de Bosnia', *Romanica*, 1: 163–73

PULIDO FERNÁNDEZ, ÁNGEL. 1905. *Españoles sin patria y la raza sefardí* (Madrid: Establecimiento tipográfico de E. Teodoro)

QUINTANA RODRÍGUEZ, ALDINA. 2006A. *Geografía lingüística del judeoespañol: estudio sincrónico y diacrónico* (Bern: Peter Lang)

——2006B. 'La evolución del judeoespañol en el siglo XVII', *Neue Romania*, 35: 157–81

——1998. 'Proceso de recastellanización del judezmo', in *Jewish Studies at the Turn of the 20th Century, Proceedings of the Sixth EAJS Congress, Toledo 1998*, ed. by Judith Targarona Borrás and Ángel Sáenz-Badillos, 2 vols (Leiden: Brill), II: 593–602

——1997. 'Diatopische Variation des Judenspanischen in den Balkanländern und der Türkei', *Neue Romania*, 19: 47–65

RAAS, FRANCIS. 1983. *Die Wette der drei Frauen: Beiträge zur Motivgeschichte und zur literarischen Interpretation der Schwankdichtung* (Bern: Francke)

RADENIĆ, ANDRIJA. 1992. 'Jevreji u Srbiji: narodni poslanici Jevreji u Skupštini Srbije 1878–1888', in *Zbornik 6: Studije, arhivska i memoarska građa o istoriji beogradskih Jevreja*, ed. by Radovan Samardžić (Belgrade: Savez jevrejskih opština Jugoslavije and Jevrejski istorijski muzej), pp. 1–114

RADOVANOVIĆ, M. 2011. 'Konfino, Žak', in *Znameniti Jevreji Srbije: biografski leksikon*, ed. by Aleksandar Gaon (Belgrade: Savez jevrejskih opština Srbije), pp. 120–21

RICHARDS, D.C. 1998. 'al-Jāhiz', in *Encyclopedia of Arabic Literature*, ed. by Julie Scott Meisami and Paul Starkey, 2 vols (London and New York: Routledge), I: 408–09

RODEN, CLAUDIA. 1999. 'Culinary Legacies from Spain and Portugal in the Jewish World: Iberian Echoes in Jewish Cooking Today, Jewish Echoes in Spanish Cooking', in *The Proceedings of the Tenth British Conference on Judeo-Spanish Studies (29 June–1 July 1997)*, ed. by Annette Benaim (London: Department of Hispanic Studies, Queen Mary and Westfield College), pp. 258–64

RODRIGUE, ARON. 1990. *French Jews, Turkish Jews: The Alliance Israélite Universelle and the Politics of Jewish Schooling in Turkey, 1860–1925* (Bloomington: Indiana University Press)

RODRÍGUEZ MARÍN, FRANCISCO. 2005. *Cantos populares españoles*, ed. by Enrique Baltanás (Sevilla: Espuela de Plata)

RODRÍGUEZ MOÑINO, ANTONIO. 1997. *Nuevo diccionario bibliográfico de pliegos sueltos poéticos: siglo XVI* (Madrid: Castalia)

ROMANO, DAVID. 1988. 'El papel judío en la transmisión de la cultura', *Hispania Sacra*, 40.82: 955–78

ROMERO, ELENA. 2011. *Los Yantares de Purim, coplas y poemas sefardíes de contenido folclórico: estudio y edición de textos* (Barcelona: Tirocinio)

——1992. *La creación literaria en lengua sefardí* (Madrid: Mapfre)

——1979. *El teatro de los sefardíes orientales*, 3 vols (Madrid: Consejo Superior de Investigaciones Científicas)

ROMEU FERRÉ, PILAR. 2019. *Guía bibliográfica de memorias sefardíes (segunda parte): Sefardíes originarios del Imperio otomano y del norte de África* (Barcelona: Tirocinio)

——2016. 'Aproximación a las memorias de mujeres sefardíes del Norte de África', in *Mujeres sefardíes lectoras y escritoras, siglos XIX–XXI*, ed. by Paloma Díaz-Mas and Elisa Martín Ortega, Collection: Tiempo Emulado, no. 49 (Madrid and Frankfurt: Iberoamericana-Vervuert), pp. 319–35

——2014. 'Mejor es no prometer que dejar de cumplir lo prometido: memorias y novelas autobiográficas sefardíes publicadas en España', *Ladinar* 7–8: 252–63

——2012. *Guía bibliográfica de memorias sefardíes: sefardíes originarios del Imperio Otomano (1950–2011)* (Barcelona: Tirocinio)

——2008. '*Sin memoria no ay avenir*': memorias escritas por mujeres sefardíes en los últimos 20 años', *Revista de dialectología y tradiciones populares*, 63.2: 101–20

——2000. 'La percepción del universo femenino a través del Me'am Lo'ez', *Ínsula*, 647.55: 9–12

ROSNER, FRED. 1982. 'Cigarette Smoking in Jewish Law', *Journal of Halacha and Contemporary Society*, 4: 33–45

ROSENTHAL, FRANZ. 1956. *Humor in Early Islam* (Leiden: E. J. Brill)

RUBIN, GAYLE. 1975. 'The Traffic in Women: Notes on the "Political Economy" of Sex', in *Toward an Anthropology of Women*, ed. by Rayna R. Reiter (New York: Monthly Review Press), pp. 157–210

RUFFINATTO, ALDO (ed.). 2001. *La vida de Lazarillo de Tormes, y de sus fortunas y adversidades*, Clásicos Castalia, 265 (Madrid: Castalia)

SAID, EDWARD W. (1978). *Orientalism* (London: Routledge and Kegan Paul)

SAMARDŽIJA, SNEŽANA. 2005. 'Nasradin hodža Stevana Sremca', *Zbornik Matice srpske za književnost i jezik*, 1–3.53: 415–29

SÁNCHEZ DE VERCIAL, CLEMENTE. 1961. *Libro de los exenplos por a.b.c*, ed. by John Esten Keller (Madrid: Consejo Superior de Investigaciones Científicas)

SAPORTA Y BEJA, ENRIQUE. 1978. *Refranes de los judíos sefardíes y otras locuciones típicas de los judíos sefardíes de Salónica y otros sitios de Oriente* (Barcelona: Ameller)

SCHORSCH, JONATHAN. 2007. 'Disappearing Origins: Sephardic Autobiography Today', *Prooftexts*, 27.1: 82–150

SCOTT MEISAMI, JULIE and PAUL STARKEY (eds). 1998. *Encyclopedia of Arabic Literature*, 2 vols (London and New York: Routledge)

SEPHIHA, HAÏM VIDAL. 1999. 'Le Judéo-espagnol de Sarajevo: Clarisee Nicoïdski, neé Abinum, conteuse et poétesse judéo-espagnol', in *The Proceedings of the Tenth British Conference on Judeo-Spanish Studies (29 June–1 July 1997)*, ed. by Annette Benaim (London: Department of Hispanic Studies, Queen Mary and Westfield College), pp. 53–64

——1983–84. 'Mos desho la vida un grande djudeo-espanyol: Ovadia Camhy', *Aki Yerushalayim*, 5.19–20: 13–15

——1979. *Le ladino: judéo-espagnol calque, structure et évolution d'une langue liturgique* (Paris: Université de la Sorbonne-Nouvelle)

SEROUSSI, EDWIN. 2003. 'Archivists of Memory: Written Folksong Collections of Twentieth-Century Sephardi Women', in *Music and Gender: Perspectives from the Mediterranean*, ed. by Tullia Magrini (Chicago and London: The University of Chicago Press), pp. 195–214

SERVANTES SAAVEDRA, MIGUEL DE. 1905A. 'Opsenarije: međučin Miguela de Servantesa Saavedre', trans. by H. S. Davičo, *Delo*, 36.2: 234–45

——1905B. 'Sudija za bračne parnice: dramski intermeco od M. Servantesa', trans. by H. S. Davičo, *Nova iskra*, 5: 145–49

SOONS, ALAN C. 1976. *Haz y envés del cuento risible en el Siglo de Oro: estudio y antología* (London: Tamesis Books)

SUBAK, JULIUS. 1906. 'Zum Judenspanischen', *Zeitschrift für Romanische Philologie*, 30: 129–85

STEFANO, GIUSEPPE DI. 1993. *Romancero* (Madrid: Taurus)

STOJANOVIĆ, JASNA. 2005. *Servantes u srpskoj književnosti* (Belgrade: Zavod za udžbenike i nastavna sredstva)

STOKES, GALE. 1990. *Politics and Development: The Emergence of Political Parties in Nineteenth-Century Serbia* (Durham and London: Duke University Press)

STUDEMUND-HALÉVY, MICHAEL. 2013. 'From East to West and Back: Baruh Mitrani, a Turkish Sefardic *Maskil*', in *La presse judéo-espagnole: support et vecteur de la modernité*, ed. by Rosa Sánchez and Marie-Christine Bornes Varol (Istanbul: Libra), pp. 255–80

STULIC, ANA. 2018. 'La variación vocálica a través del prisma de los procesos de textualización en judeoespañol moderno', in *Procesos de textualización y gramaticalización en la historia del español*, ed. by José Luis Girón Alconchel, Francisco Javier Herrero Ruiz de Loizaga and Daniel M. Sáez Rivera (Madrid-Frankfurt: Iberoamericana-Vervuert), pp. 23–48

——2014. 'L'emprunt ostensible face à l'emprunt invisible dans la création du style journalistique judéo-espagnol', in *Empreintes/emprunts: entre forces de conformisation et force d'innovation*, ed. by Emmanuel Marigno, Stéphane Oury and Gregoria Palomar, Special Issue, *ReCherches: Culture et Histoire dans l'Espace Roman*, 12: 147–64

ŠEVKI BAŠESKIJA, MULA MUSTAFA. 1987. *Ljetopis (1746–1804)*, trans. by Mehmed Mujezinović (Sarajevo: Veselin Masleša)

ŠTULIĆ, ANA, IVANA VUČINA and GORANA ZEČEVIĆ. 2003. 'Quince canciones judeoespañolas provenientes de Sarajevo y Salónica: análisis fonético y fonológico', *Res Diachronicae*, 2: 380–96

TAGGART, JAMES. 1990. *Enchanted Maidens: Gender Relations in Spanish Folktales of Courtship and Marriage* (Princeton, New Jersey: Princeton University Press)

TAUBER, ELI. 2011. *Jevrejska štampa u BiH: 1900–2011* (Sarajevo: Mediacentar)

THOMAS DE ANTONIO, CLARA MARÍA. 1993. 'Ŷuhā, un personaje popular en el Magreb y en todo el mundo árabe', *Al-Andalus — Magreb*, 1: 187–223

THOMPSON, STITH. 1966. *Motif-Index of Folk Literature: A Classification of Narrative Elements in Folktales, Ballads, Myths, Fables, Medieval Romances, Exempla, Fabliaux, Jest-Books, and Local Legends*, 6 vols (Bloomington and London: Indiana University Press)

TIRSO DE MOLINA. 1996. *Cigarrales de Toledo*, ed. by Luis Vázquez Fernández, 216 (Madrid: Castalia)

UTHER, HANS-JÖRG. 2004. *The Types of International Folkltales: A Classification and Bibliography Based on the System of Antti Aarne and Stith Thompson*, 3 vols (Helsinki: Soumalainen Tiedeakatemia and Academia Scientiarum Fennica)

VALENTÍN, MARÍA DEL CARMEN. 2010. 'La mujer moderna en el teatro costumbrista sefardí: 1900–1930', in *Los sefardíes ante los retos del mundo contemporáneo: identidad y mentalidades,* ed. by Paloma Díaz-Mas and María Sánchez-Pérez (Madrid: Consejo Superior de Investigaciones Científicas), pp. 293–303

VANCE, SHARON. 2011. *The Martyrdom of a Moroccan Jewish Saint* (Boston-Leiden-Köln: Brill)

VAROL, MARIE-CHRISTINE. 2003–04. 'L'autobiographie en judéo-espagnol: la difficile affirmation du sujet entre tradition et modernité', *Yod: Révue des études Hébraïques et Juives*, 9: 231–60

VASVÁRI, LOUISE O. 1989. 'The Two Lazy Suitors in the *Libro de Buen Amor*: Popular Tradition and Literary Game of Love', *Anuario Medieval*, 1: 181–205

VÁZQUEZ FERNÁNDEZ, LUIS. 1996. 'Introducción biográfica y crítica', in Tirso de Molina, *Cigarrales de Toledo*, ed. by Luis Vázquez Fernández, 216 (Madrid: Castalia), pp. 9–90

VEČERINA TOMAIĆ, JAGODA. 2016. *Bohoreta, najstarija kći* (Zagreb: Židovska vjerska zajednica Bet Israel)

VENUTI, LAWRENCE. 1995. *The Translator's Invisibility: A History of Translation* (London and New York: Routledge)

—— 1992. 'Introduction', in *Rethinking Translation: Discourse, Subjectivity, Ideology*, ed. by Lawrence Venuti (London and New York: Routledge), pp. 1–17

VESELINOVIĆ, JOVANKA. 1998. 'Jevrejska žena u Beogradu od druge polovine 19. veka do Drugog svetskog rata', in *Srbija u modernizacijskim procesima 19. i 20. veka*, ed. by Latinka Perović, 2 vols (Belgrade: Institut za noviju istoriju Srbije), II: 485–95

VIDAKOVIĆ-PETROV, KRINKA. 2016. 'Jamila Andjela Kolonomos: de las memorias al libro conmemorativo', in *Mujeres sefardíes lectoras y escritoras, siglos XIX-XXI*, ed. by Paloma Díaz-Mas y Elisa Martín Ortega (Madrid-Frankfurt: Iberoamericana-Vervuert), pp. 243–60

—— 2014. 'The Gender Perspective in Sephardic Ballads from the Balkans', *Ladinar: estudios sobre la literatura, la música y la historia de los sefardíes*, 7–8: 317–28

—— 2013. 'La presse séfarade de Belgrade et Sarajevo de 1888 à 1941', in *Recensement, analyse et traitement numérique des sources écrites pour les études séfarades*, ed. by Soufiane Roussi and Ana Stulic-Etchevers (Bordeaux: Presses universitaires de Bordeaux), pp. 69–96

—— 2012. *Aspects de la culture des Juifs espagnols dans l'espace yougoslave: XVIe–XXe siècles*, trans. by Emmanuel Carlebach (París: Alliance Israélite Universelle-Editions du Nadir)

—— 2010A. 'Identity and Memory in the Works of Haim S. Davicho', in *Los sefardíes ante los retos del mundo contemporáneo: identidad y mentalidades*, ed. by Paloma Díaz-Mas and María Sánchez-Pérez (Madrid: Consejo Superior de Investigaciones Científicas), pp. 307–16

—— 2010B. 'Mesto biranja neveste u usmenoj poeziji hispanskog kruga', in *Folklor, poetika, književna periodika: zbornik radova posvećen Miodragu Matickom*, ed. by Staniša Tutnjević (Belgrade: Institut za književnost i umetnost), pp. 295–315

—— 2009. 'Usmena poezija španskih Jevreja (Sefarda) i balkansko kulturno okruženje', *Književna istorija*, 137–38: 395–408

—— 2008. 'Književnost Jevreja u Bosni i Hercegovini: označavanje identiteta', in *Sto dvadeset pet godina viskog obrazovanja u Bosni i Hercegovini: zbornik radova sa naučnog skupa (Pale, 19–20 maj 2007)*, ed. by Miloš Kovačević, 2 vols (Pale: Filozovski fakultet Univerziteta u Istočnom Sarajevu), I: 287–99

—— 1997. 'The Sephardim in Yugoslavia: Playwrights, Plays, and Performances', in *Hispano-Jewish Civilization after 1492: Proceedings of Misgav Yerushalaim's Fourth International Congress 1992*, ed. by Michel Abitbol, Yom Tov Assis and Galit Hasan-Rokem (Jerusalem: Misgav Yerushalayim), pp. 153–59

—— 1994. 'Sephardic Folklore and the Balkan Cultural Environment' in *History and Creativity in the Sephardi and Oriental Jewish Communities*, ed. by Tamar Alexander, Abraham Haim, Galit Hasan-Rokem and Ephraim Hazan (Jerusalem: Misgav Yerushalayim), pp. 285–300

—— 1990. *Kultura španskih Jevreja na jugoslovenskom tlu: XVI–XX vek* (Sarajevo: Svjetlost)

——1986. 'An Old Rhetorical Formula in the Modern Judeo-Spanish Tradition', in *Proceedings of the Ninth World Congress of Jewish Studies: Jerusalem 4–12 August, 1985*, 8 vols (Jerusalem: World Union of Jewish Studies), II: 143–50

——1985. 'Istorija jedne književne formule', *Književna istorija*, 18. 67–68: 183–206

VIVAS BAILO, JOSÉ LUIS. 1989. 'Introducción', in *Cuentos de Yehá*, ed. by Tomás García Figueras (Sevilla: Padilla Libros), pp. 3–28

VON SYDOW, CARL W. 1965. 'Folktale Studies and Philology: Some Points of View', in *The Study of Folklore*, ed. by Alan Dundes (Englewood Cliffs: Prentice-Hall), pp. 219–42

VUČINA SIMOVIĆ, IVANA and JELENA FILIPOVIĆ. 2011. 'Judeo-Spanish Language in Bitola and Skoplje: Between Tradition and Modernity', in *The Jews from Macedonia and the Holocaust: History, Theory and Culture*, ed. by Sofija Grandakovska (Skoplje: Evro-Balkan Press), pp. 565–87

——2009. *Etnički identitet i zamena jezika u sefardskoj zajednici u Beogradu* (Belgrade: Zavod za udžbenike)

VUČINA SIMOVIĆ, IVANA. 2016. *Jevrejsko-španski jezik na Balkanu: prilozi istorijskoj sociolingvistici* (Kragujevac: Filum)

——2015A. 'La labor política, cultural e ideologías de Haim S. Davicho de Belgrado: entre judaísmo familiar y patriotismo', *Lipar: časopis za književnost, jezik, umetnost i kulturu*, 58: 61–77

——2015B. 'Život i delo Hajima S. Daviča (1854–1918) između slave i zaborava', *Nasleđe: Journal of literature, language, arts and culture*, 12.37: 109–21

——2013. 'The Sephardim and Ashkenazim in Sarajevo: From Social, Cultural and Linguistic Divergence to Convergence', *Transversal*, 13.2: 41–64

WACKS, DAVID A. 2015. *Double Diaspora in Sephardic Literature: Jewish Cultural Production before and after 1942* (Bloomington and Indianapolis: Indiana University Press)

WALTHER, WIEBKE. 1998. 'al-Maydānī, Ahmad ibn Muhammad', in *Encyclopedia of Arabic Literature*, ed. by Julie Scott Meisami and Paul Starkey, 2 vols (London and New York: Routledge), II: 520

WEICH-SHAHAK, SUSANA. 2013. *El ciclo de la vida en el repertorio musical de las comunidades sefardíes de Oriente: antología de tradición oral* (Madrid: Editorial Alpuerto)

——2009. 'El rol de la mujer en el repertorio musical sefardí: intérprete y personaje', *El Prezente: Studies in Sephardic Culture: Gender and Identity*, 3: 273–91

WESSELSKI, A. 1911. *Der Hodscha Nasreddin*, 2 vol (Weimar: Duncker)

WIENNER, LEO. 1903. 'Songs of the Spanish Jews in the Balkan Peninsula', *Modern Philology*, I.1: 205–16; 1.2: 259–74

WISSE, RUTH R. 2000. *The Modern Jewish Canon: A Journey Through Language and Culture* (New York: The Free Press)

YIACOUP, ŞIZEN. 2015. *Frontier Memory: Cultural Conflict and Exchange in the Romancero Fronterizo* (London: Modern Humanities Research Association)

INDEX OF NAMES AND TEXT

When arranging titles of texts starting with an article, the latter is ignored.
With Arabic proper names I keep the Arabic article al- and I arrange them accordingly.

SUBJECT INDEX